Imperial Life in the Emerald City

Imperial Life

IN THE

Emerald City

INSIDE IRAQ'S
GREEN ZONE

Rajiv Chandrasekaran

ALFRED A. KNOPF NEW YORK 2007

THIS IS A BORZOI BOOK
PUBLISHED BY ALFRED A. KNOPF

www.aaknopf.com

Library of Congress Cataloging-in-Publication Data
Chandrasekaran, Rajiv.
Imperial life in the emerald city : inside Iraq's green
zone / Rajiv Chandrasekaran.
p. cm.
Includes bibliographical references and index.
ISBN 1-4000-4487-1 (alk. paper)
1. Postwar reconstruction—Iraq. 2. Coalition Provisional Authority. 3. Iraq War, 2003– 4. United
States—Politics and government—2001– 5. Political
corruption—United States. I. Title: Inside Iraq's green
zone. II. Title.

DS79.769.C53   2006   2006041014
956.7044'31—dc22

Manufactured in the United States of America
Published September 22, 2006
Reprinted Eight Times
Tenth Printing, February 2007

For my parents

Do not try to do too much with your own hands. Better the Arabs do it tolerably than that you do it perfectly. It is their war, and you are to help them, not to win it for them. Actually, also, under the very odd conditions of Arabia, your practical work will not be as good as, perhaps, you think it is.

T. E. LAWRENCE
August 20, 1917

CONTENTS

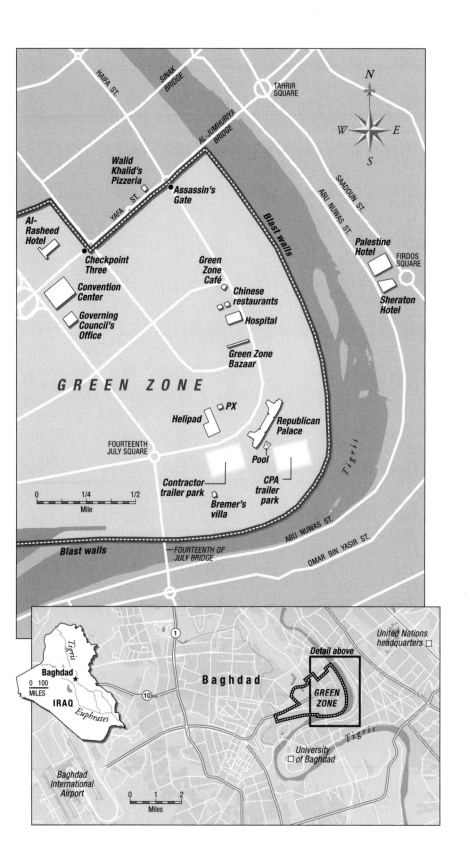

N

W   E

S

HAIFA ST.

SINAK BRIDGE

TAHRIR SQUARE

AL-JUMHURIYA BRIDGE

SAADOUN ST.

ABU NUWAS ST.

Walid Khalid's Pizzeria

YAFA ST.

Assassin's Gate

Blast walls

Al-Rasheed Hotel

Checkpoint Three

Convention Center

Governing Council's Office

Green Zone Café

Chinese restaurants

Hospital

Green Zone Bazaar

Palestine Hotel

FIRDOS SQUARE

Sheraton Hotel

GREEN ZONE

PX

Helipad

Republican Palace

Tigris

FOURTEENTH JULY SQUARE

Pool

Contractor trailer park

CPA trailer park

Bremer's villa

0   1/4   1/2
Mile

ABU NUWAS ST.

OMAR BIN YASIR ST.

Blast walls

FOURTEENTH OF JULY BRIDGE

Tigris

United Nations headquarters

Detail above

1

Baghdad

Tigris

Baghdad

0   100
MILES

IRAQ

Euphrates

GREEN ZONE

10

University of Baghdad

Baghdad International Airport

0   1   2
Miles

Imperial Life in the Emerald City

Prologue

In the back garden of the Republican Palace, deep in the heart of the Green Zone, bronzed young men with rippling muscles and tattooed forearms plunged into a resort-size swimming pool. Others, clad in baggy trunks and wraparound sunglasses, lay sprawled on chaise lounges in the shadows of towering palms, munching Doritos and sipping iced tea. Off to the side, men in khakis and women in sundresses relaxed under a wooden gazebo. Some read pulp novels, some noshed from the all-you-can-eat buffet. A boom box thumped with hip-hop music. Now and then, a dozen lanky Iraqi men in identical blue shirts and trousers walked by on their way to sweep the deck, prune the shrubbery, or water the plants. They moved in single file behind a burly, mustachioed American foreman. From a distance, they looked like a chain gang.

The pool was an oasis of calm in the Green Zone, the seven-square-mile American enclave in central Baghdad. The only disruption was the occasional *whoomp-whoomp* of a low-flying Black Hawk helicopter, a red cross painted on its drab olive underbelly, ferrying casualties to the hospital down the street. A few loungers glanced up at the chopper, but most were unfazed. It was the trilling of a mobile phone that commanded attention. The American firm that had set up the network didn't provide voice mail—answering a call was the only way to find out what the boss wanted or where the party was later that night.

The conversations within earshot focused on plans for vacations at the Dead Sea, the previous night's drinking session, and the sole woman brave enough to sunbathe by the pool amid several dozen sex-starved men. One man proclaimed to his buddies that after a few months in the overwhelmingly male Green Zone, every woman became a "perfect ten."

It was June 2004, and the end of American rule in Iraq was less than a month away. Inside the marble-walled palace, the headquarters of the occupation administration, a few bureaucrats remained cloistered in their air-conditioned offices, toiling for eighteen hours a day to check off one more item on the grand to-do list before they flew home. One woman I knew, a mother of four from Delaware, was scrambling to enlist Iraqis to reopen Baghdad's stock exchange. A lawyer who had once clerked for Supreme Court chief justice William Rehnquist was poring over a draft edict requiring Iraqi political parties to engage in American-style financial disclosure. A blond Californian in his early twenties was creating PowerPoint presentations to send back to Washington showing that the Americans were making progress, that life in Iraq was improving by the day.

These were the exceptions. Most people in the palace had simply given up, seeking instead the solace and fin de siècle merriment of the pool. As the sun set, they repaired to the Sheherazade Bar in the al-Rasheed Hotel, where they drank Turkish beer, Lebanese wine, and third-rate blended Scotch. They shopped for watches, lighters, and old Iraqi banknotes that bore the visage of Saddam Hussein. They bought T-shirts that quipped WHO'S YOUR BAGHDADDY? They ate pizza at the Green Zone Café and Kung Pao chicken at the two Chinese restaurants near the palace. At the gymnasium, they worked out under a poster of the World Trade Center towers. They called friends in America for free on their government-issued mobile phones. They threw raucous farewell parties and had one last fling. They sent e-mails to line up jobs with President George W. Bush's reelection campaign when they returned to America. When they grew tired, they retreated to their rooms to watch pirated DVDs—two for a dollar—hawked by enterprising young Iraqis.

It was in the palace garden where I met with John Agresto for the first time. He had arrived in Baghdad nine months earlier to undertake the daunting task of rehabilitating Iraq's university system—more than 375,000 students enrolled at twenty-two campuses, almost all of which had been decimated in the looting that followed the overthrow of Saddam Hussein's government. Agresto had no background in post-conflict reconstruction and no experience in the Middle East. The institution he ran, St. John's College in Santa Fe, had fewer than five hundred students. But Agresto was connected: Defense Secretary Donald Rumsfeld's wife had been on the St. John's board and Vice President Dick Cheney's wife had worked with him at the National Endowment for the Humanities.

When we met, he was fifty-eight years old. A stocky man with thinning silver hair, a gray-flecked mustache, and a prominent nose, he liked to compare his appearance to that of Groucho Marx.

Puffing on his pipe under the shade of a broad palm—there was no smoking indoors in the Green Zone—Agresto said that he had landed in Iraq with an abundance of optimism. "I saw the images of people cheering as Saddam Hussein's statue was pulled down," he said. "I saw people hitting pictures of him with their shoes."

But the Iraq he encountered was far different from what he had expected. His visits to the universities he was trying to rebuild and with the faculties he wanted to invigorate became more and more dangerous—and infrequent. He told me his Iraqi staff had been threatened by insurgents. His evenings were disrupted by mortar attacks on the Green Zone. His plans to repair hundreds of campus buildings had been scuttled by the White House. He had concluded that Iraq's universities needed more than $1 billion to become viable centers of learning, but he had received only $8 million in reconstruction funds. American colleges and universities had rebuffed his entreaties for assistance. He had asked for 130,000 classroom desks from the U.S. Agency for International Development. He got 8,000.

His agitation grew as he spoke. Then he fell silent, staring at the pool and puffing away. After a moment, he turned to me, his face grave, and said, "I'm a neoconservative who's been mugged by reality."

PART ONE

Building the Bubble

1

Versailles on the Tigris

UNLIKE ALMOST ANYWHERE else in Baghdad, you could dine at the cafeteria in the Republican Palace for six months and never eat hummus, flatbread, or a lamb kebab. The fare was always American, often with a Southern flavor. A buffet featured grits, cornbread, and a bottomless barrel of pork: sausage for breakfast, hot dogs for lunch, pork chops for dinner. There were bacon cheeseburgers, grilled-cheese-and-bacon sandwiches, and bacon omelets. Hundreds of Iraqi secretaries and translators who worked for the occupation authority had to eat in the dining hall. Most of them were Muslims, and many were offended by the presence of pork. But the American contractors running the kitchen kept serving it. The cafeteria was all about meeting American needs for high-calorie, high-fat comfort food.

None of the succulent tomatoes or the crisp cucumbers grown in Iraq made it into the salad bar. U.S. government regulations dictated that everything, even the water in which hot dogs were boiled, be shipped in from approved suppliers in other nations. Milk and bread were trucked in from Kuwait, as were tinned peas and carrots. The breakfast cereal was flown in from the United States—made-in-the-USA Froot Loops and Frosted Flakes at the breakfast table helped boost morale.

When the Americans had arrived, there was no cafeteria in the palace. Saddam Hussein had feasted in an ornate private dining room and his servants had eaten in small kitchenettes. The engineers assigned to transform the palace into the seat of the American occupation chose a marble-floored conference room the size of a gymnasium to serve as the mess hall. Halliburton, the defense contractor hired to run the palace, brought in dozens of tables, hundreds of stacking chairs, and a score of glass-covered buffets. Seven days a week, the Americans ate under Saddam's crystal chandeliers.

Red and white linens covered the tables. Diners sat on chairs with maroon cushions. A pleated skirt decorated the salad bar and the dessert table, which was piled high with cakes and cookies. The floor was polished after every meal.

A mural of the World Trade Center adorned one of the entrances. The Twin Towers were framed within the outstretched wings of a bald eagle. Each branch of the U.S. military—the army, air force, marines, and navy—had its seal on a different corner of the mural. In the middle were the logos of the New York City Police and Fire departments, and atop the towers were the words THANK GOD FOR THE COALITION FORCES & FREEDOM FIGHTERS AT HOME AND ABROAD.

At another of the three entrances was a bulletin board with posted notices, including those that read

BIBLE STUDY—WEDNESDAYS AT 7 P.M.

GO RUNNING WITH THE HASH HOUSE HARRIERS!

FEELING STRESSED? COME VISIT US AT THE COMBAT STRESS CLINIC.

FOR SALE: LIKE-NEW HUNTING KNIFE.

LOST CAMERA. REWARD OFFERED.

The kitchen, which had once prepared gourmet meals for Saddam, had been converted into an institutional food–processing center, with a giant deep fryer and bathtub-size mixing bowls. Halliburton had hired dozens of Pakistanis and Indians to cook and serve and clean, but no Iraqis. Nobody ever explained why, but everyone knew. They could poison the food.

The Pakistanis and the Indians wore white button-down shirts with black vests, black bow ties, and white paper hats. The Kuwaiti subcontractor who kept their passports and exacted a meaty profit margin off each worker also dinned into them American lingo. When I asked one of the Indians for French fries, he snapped: "We have no French fries here, sir. Only freedom fries."

The seating was as tribal as that at a high school cafeteria.

The Iraqi support staffers kept to themselves. They loaded their lunch trays with enough calories for three meals. Between mouthfuls, they mocked their American bosses with impunity. So few Americans in the palace spoke Arabic fluently that those who did could have fit around one table, with room to spare.

Soldiers, private contractors, and mercenaries also segregated themselves. So did the representatives of the "coalition of the willing"—the Brits, the Aussies, the Poles, the Spaniards, and the Italians. The American civilians who worked for the occupation government had their own cliques: the big-shot political appointees, the twentysomethings fresh out of college, the old hands who had arrived in Baghdad in the first weeks of occupation. In conversation at their tables, they observed an unspoken protocol. It was always appropriate to praise "the mission"—the Bush administration's campaign to transform Iraq into a peaceful, modern, secular democracy where everyone, regardless of sect or ethnicity, would get along. Tirades about how Saddam had ruined the country and descriptions of how you were going to resuscitate it were also fine. But unless you knew someone really, really well, you didn't question American policy over a meal.

If you had a complaint about the cafeteria, Michael Cole was the man to see. He was Halliburton's "customer-service liaison," and he could explain why the salad bar didn't have Iraqi produce or why pork kept appearing on the menu. If you wanted to request a different type of breakfast cereal, he'd listen. Cole didn't have the weathered look of a war-zone concierge. He was a rail-thin twenty-two-year-old whose forehead was dotted with pimples.

He had been out of college for less than a year and was working as a junior aide to a Republican congressman from Virginia when a Halliburton vice president overheard him talking to friends in an Arlington bar about his dealings with irate constituents. She was so impressed that she introduced herself. If she needed someone to work as a valet in Baghdad, he joked, he'd be happy to volunteer. Three weeks later, Halliburton offered him a job. Then they asked for his résumé.

Cole never ate pork products in the mess hall. He knew

many of the servers were Pakistani Muslims and he felt terrible that they had to handle food they deemed offensive. He was rewarded for his expression of respect with invitations to the Dickensian trailer park where the kitchen staff lived. *They* didn't have to abide by American rules governing food procurement. Their kitchens were filled with local produce, and they cooked spicy curries that were better than anything Cole found in the cafeteria. He thought of proposing an Indian-Pakistani food night at the mess hall, but then remembered that the palace didn't do ethnic fare. "The cooking had to make people feel like they were back at home," he said. And home, in this case, was presumed to be somewhere south of the Mason-Dixon Line.

Cole's mission was to keep the air in the bubble, to ensure that the Americans who had left home to work for the occupation administration felt comfortable. Food was part of it. But so were movies, mattresses, and laundry service. If he was asked for something, Cole tried to get it, whether he thought it important or not. "Yes, sir. We'll look into that," he'd say. Or, "I'm sorry you're so upset. We'll try to fix it as soon as possible."

The palace was the headquarters of the Coalition Provisional Authority, the American occupation administration in Iraq. From April 2003 to June 2004, the CPA ran Iraq's government—it enacted laws, printed currency, collected taxes, deployed police, and spent oil revenue. At its height, the CPA had more than 1,500 employees in Baghdad, most of them American. They were a motley bunch: businessmen who were active in the Republican Party, retirees who wanted one last taste of adventure, diplomats who had studied Iraq for years, recent college graduates who had never had a full-time job, government employees who wanted the 25 percent salary bonus paid for working in a war zone. The CPA was headed by America's viceroy in Iraq, Lewis Paul Bremer III, who always wore a blue suit and tan combat boots, even on those summer days when Iraqis drooped in the heat. He was surrounded by burly, submachine gun–toting bodyguards everywhere he went, even to the bathroom in the palace.

The palace was Versailles on the Tigris. Constructed of sandstone and marble, it had wide hallways, soaring columns, and spiral staircases. Massive bronze busts of Saddam in an Arab warrior's headdress looked down from the four corners of the roof. The cafeteria was on the south side, next to a chapel with a billboard-size mural of a Scud missile arcing into the sky. In the northern wing was an enormous ballroom with a balcony overlooking the dance floor. The heart of the palace was a giant marble rotunda with a turquoise dome. After the Americans arrived, the entire place took on the slapdash appearance of a start-up company. Dell computers sat atop ornate wooden desks partitioned by fabric-covered cubicle dividers. Data cables snaked along the gilded moldings. Erasable whiteboards hung from the mirrored walls.

A row of portable toilets lined the rear driveway. The palace, designed as a showplace for Saddam to meet visiting dignitaries, lacked enough commodes for hundreds of occupants. Dormitory space was also in short supply. Most new arrivals had to sleep on bunk beds in the chapel, a room that came to resemble a World War II field hospital.

Appearances aside, the same rules applied in the palace as in any government building in Washington. Everyone wore an identification badge. Decorum was enforced in the high-ceilinged halls. I remember hearing a soldier admonish a staffer hustling to a meeting: "Ma'am, you must not run in the corridor."

Whatever could be outsourced was. The job of setting up town and city councils was performed by a North Carolina firm for $236 million. The job of guarding the viceroy was assigned to private guards, each of whom made more than $1,000 a day. For running the palace—cooking the food, changing the lightbulbs, doing the laundry, watering the plants—Halliburton had been handed hundreds of millions of dollars.

Halliburton had been hired to provide "living support" services to the CPA. What that meant kept evolving. When the first Americans arrived in Baghdad in the weeks after Saddam's government was toppled, all anyone wanted was food and water, laundry service, and air-conditioning. By the time Cole arrived, in August 2003, four months into the occupation, the demands had grown. The viceroy's house had to be outfitted with furniture and art suitable for a head of state. The Halliburton-run sports bar at the al-Rasheed Hotel needed a Foosball table. The press conference room required large-screen televisions.

The Green Zone quickly became Baghdad's Little America. Everyone who worked in the palace lived there, either in white metal trailers or in the towering al-Rasheed. Hundreds of private contractors working for firms including Bechtel, General Electric, and Halliburton set up trailer parks there, as did legions of private security guards hired to protect the contractors. The only Iraqis allowed inside the Green Zone were those who worked for the Americans or those who could prove that they had resided there before the war.

It was Saddam who first decided to turn Baghdad's prime riverfront real estate into a gated city within a city, with posh villas, bungalows, government buildings, shops, and even a hospital. He didn't want his aides and bodyguards, who were given homes near his palace, to mingle with the masses. And he didn't want outsiders peering in. The homes were bigger, the trees greener, the streets wider than in the rest of Baghdad. There were more palms and fewer people. There were no street vendors and no beggars. No one other than members of Saddam's inner circle or his trusted cadre of guards and housekeepers had any idea what was inside. Those who loitered near the entrances sometimes landed in jail. Iraqis drove as fast as they could on roads near the compound lest they be accused of gawking.

It was the ideal place for the Americans to pitch their tents. Saddam had surrounded the area with a tall brick wall. There were only three points of entry. All the military had to do was park tanks at the gates.

The Americans expanded Saddam's neighborhood by a few blocks to encompass the gargantuan Convention Center and the al-Rasheed, a once-luxurious establishment made famous by CNN's live broadcasts during the 1991 Persian Gulf War. They fortified the perimeter with seventeen-foot-high blast barriers made of foot-thick concrete topped with coils of razor wire.

Open spaces became trailer parks with grandiose names.

CPA staffers unable to snag a room at the al-Rasheed lived in Poolside Estates. Cole and his fellow Halliburton employees were in Camp Hope. The Brits dubbed their accommodations Ocean Cliffs. At first, the Americans felt sorry for the Brits, whose trailers were in a covered parking garage, which seemed dark and miserable. But when the insurgents began firing mortars into the Green Zone, everyone wished they were in Ocean Cliffs. The envy increased when Americans discovered that the Brits didn't have the same leaky trailers with plastic furniture supplied by Halliburton; theirs had been outfitted by Ikea.

Americans drove around in new GMC Suburbans, dutifully obeying the thirty-five-mile-an-hour speed limit signs posted by the CPA on the flat, wide streets. There were so many identical Suburbans parked in front of the palace that drivers had to use their electronic door openers as homing devices. (One contractor affixed Texas license plates to his vehicle to set it apart.) When they cruised around, they kept the air-conditioning on high and the radio tuned to 107.7 FM, Freedom Radio, an American-run station that played classic rock and rah-rah messages. Every two weeks, the vehicles were cleaned at a Halliburton car wash.

Shuttle buses looped around the Green Zone at twenty-minute intervals, stopping at wooden shelters to transport those who didn't have cars and didn't want to walk. There was daily mail delivery. Generators ensured that the lights were always on. If you didn't like what was being served in the cafeteria—or you were feeling peckish between meals—you could get takeout from one of the Green Zone's Chinese restaurants. Halliburton's dry-cleaning service would get the dust and sweat stains out of your khakis in three days. A sign warned patrons to REMOVE AMMUNITION FROM POCKETS before submitting clothes.

Iraqi laws and customs didn't apply inside the Green Zone. Women jogged on the sidewalk in shorts and T-shirts. A liquor store sold imported beer, wine, and spirits. One of the Chinese restaurants offered massages as well as noodles. The young boys selling DVDs near the palace parking lot had a secret stash. "Mister, you want porno?" they whispered to me.

Most Americans sported suede combat boots, expensive

sunglasses, and nine-millimeter Berettas attached to the thigh with a Velcro holster. They groused about the heat and the mosquitoes and the slothful habits of the natives. A contingent of Gurkhas stood as sentries in front of the palace.

If there was any law in the Green Zone, it was American. Military police pulled drivers over for speeding and drunk driving. When a shipment of office safes arrived, Halliburton prevented its American employees from lifting or delivering them until hand trucks and back braces had been sent to Baghdad. When one CPA staffer complained that she needed her safe—she said she was storing tens of thousands of dollars in her office toilet—Cole explained that Halliburton had to follow American occupational safety regulations.

The Green Zone had no mayor. Bremer was its most important occupant, but he didn't trouble himself with potholes and security fences. The physical area was technically the responsibility of the army commander in charge of Baghdad, but he lived near the airport and didn't delve into minutiae. There was a colonel whose brigade guarded the zone, but he cared more about perimeter security than the operation of the city within a city. If an American staked claim to a villa, there was nobody to stop him.

Veteran diplomats who had lived in the Arab world or worked in post-conflict situations wanted local cuisine in the dining room, a respect for local traditions, and a local workforce. But they were in the minority. Most of the CPA's staff had never worked outside the United States. More than half, according to one estimate, had gotten their first passport in order to travel to Iraq. If they were going to survive in Baghdad, they needed the same sort of bubble that American oil companies had built for their workers in Saudi Arabia, Nigeria, and Indonesia.

Cole, who had been charged, along with his Halliburton colleagues, with creating that bubble, worked in a tiny room in the palace. The sign over his door said CUSTOMER SERVICE. When he wasn't fielding complaints, he posted the cafeteria menu and bus schedules on the CPA's computer network. He refurbished the palace's movie theater and started showing films every night at eight. Shoot-'em-up action movies were the most popular, but they weren't Cole's favorites. He liked *Lawrence of Arabia* and *The Third Man,* the latter based on the eponymous Graham Greene novella about post–World War II Vienna. In his spare time, Cole began writing a novel. It was about two young men who go to a war zone for the first time.

"It feels like a little America," Mark Schroeder said as we sat by the pool on a scorching afternoon, sipping water bottled in the United Arab Emirates.

Schroeder and I had grown up in the same suburb of San Francisco, but we hadn't known each other as children. We connected in Baghdad—first by e-mail, then by phone, and finally in person—because of our mothers, who had struck up a conversation in a grocery store and discovered that they both had sons in Iraq. Schroeder, who was twenty-four at the time, was your typical California kid: he had a tan and wavy blond hair and wore an expensive pair of sunglasses. He had been working for a Republican congressman in Washington when he heard that the CPA needed more staff. He sent his résumé to the Pentagon. A few months later, he was in the Republican Palace.

He was an essential-services analyst. He compiled a weekly report for Bremer with bar graphs and charts that showed the CPA's progress in key sectors. How many megawatts of electricity were being generated? How many police officers had been trained? How many dollars had been spent on reconstruction? The reports were shared only with Bremer and his senior aides. Copies were sent electronically to National Security Advisor Condoleezza Rice and Defense Secretary Donald H. Rumsfeld. After the bigwigs had seen it, analysts at the Pentagon would redact the secret information and distribute the document to hundreds of government employees who worked on Iraq. One of them regularly forwarded the reports to me. Some of those charts and graphs—usually the ones detailing the state of electricity generation and police training—were at odds with the rosy figures released by the CPA public relations office.

Schroeder created his reports in a small office near Bremer's. He spent his days—and many an evening—sitting in front of a computer. He lived in a trailer with three roommates and ate all his meals in the mess hall. On Thursdays, he'd hitch a ride with a friend to the al-Rasheed's disco or another bar. In the two and a half months since he had arrived in Baghdad, he'd left the Green Zone only once—and that was to travel to Camp Victory, the U.S. military headquarters near the airport.

When he needed to buy something, he went to the PX, the military-run convenience store next to the palace. There he could pick up Fritos, Cheetos, Dr Pepper, protein powder, Operation Iraqi Freedom T-shirts, and pop music discs. If the PX didn't have what he wanted, he'd go to the Green Zone Bazaar, a small pedestrian mall with seventy shops operated by Iraqis who lived in the Green Zone. The bazaar had been built so Americans wouldn't have to leave the Green Zone to purchase trinkets and sundries. There was Mo's Computers, run by a savvy young man named Mohammed. Several shops sold mobile phones and bootlegged DVDs. Others hawked only-in-Iraq items: old army uniforms, banknotes with Saddam's face, Iraqi flags with the words GOD IS GREAT in Saddam's handwriting. My favorite was the JJ Store for Arab Photos, the Iraqi version of those Wild West photo booths at Disneyland: you could get a picture of yourself in Arab robes and a headdress.

The Green Zone also provided its own good time. The CPA had a "morale officer" who organized salsa dancing lessons, yoga classes, and movie screenings in the palace theater. There was a gym with the same treadmills and exercise machines you'd find in any high-end health club in America. The devout could attend regular Bible study classes.

Even in the first months after the fall of Saddam's government—when Americans were regarded as liberators, the insurgency was embryonic, and it was safe enough to drive across town without guards and armored vehicles—American civilians working for the CPA and its predecessor, the Office of Reconstruction and Humanitarian Assistance, were dissuaded from venturing beyond the area around the palace. Security officers insisted that Baghdad was insecure. The only safe place was inside the walls. That's why they called it the Green Zone.

If you wanted to leave the Green Zone, you had to travel in two cars, and each car had to have two "long guns"—an M16 rifle or an even more powerful weapon. In the early days, this seemed unreasonable. But then attacks on Americans became more frequent. The rules tightened. More guns were required, then more cars, then a military escort. By the time Schroeder arrived, Iraq was so dangerous that you needed a good reason to get a security detail to leave the zone. If you were a senior staffer who needed to visit a ministry, no problem. But if you were an essential-services analyst who wanted to go shopping, no way.

I couldn't fault Schroeder for not traveling outside. Even if he had wanted to break the rules, as some did, by driving around in a beat-up sedan with Iraqi license plates, he still would have had to leave the Green Zone by one of the three exits. Everyone assumed that the bad guys were watching. Would they notice him? Would they choose to attack? Such an action was perceived as Russian roulette.

Schroeder was incredulous when I told him that I lived in what he and others called the Red Zone, that I drove around without a security detail, that I ate at local restaurants, that I visited Iraqis in their homes.

"What's it like out there?" he asked.

I told him about living in the decrepit Ishtar Sheraton Hotel, just across the Tigris River from the palace. The room service was so abysmal that we had installed our own kitchen—with a four-burner gas stove, a chest freezer, and a meat grinder—in one of the rooms. I described the pleasure of walking through al-Shorja Market, the city's largest bazaar, and of having tea in cafés in the old quarter. I spoke about discussions of Iraqi culture and history that occurred when I went to the homes of my Iraqi friends for lunch. The more I talked, the more I felt like an extraterrestrial describing life on another planet.

From inside the Green Zone, the real Baghdad—the checkpoints, the bombed-out buildings, the paralyzing traffic jams—could have been a world away. The horns, the gunshots, the muezzin's call to prayer, never drifted over the walls. The fear on the faces of American troops was rarely seen by the denizens of the palace. The acrid smoke of a detonated car bomb didn't fill the air. The sub-Saharan privation and Wild West lawlessness that gripped one of the world's most ancient cities swirled around the walls, but on the inside, the calm sterility of an American subdivision prevailed.

To see the real Iraq, all anyone in the Green Zone had to do was peer over the Hesco barriers—the refrigerator-size containers filled with dirt that protected soldiers from shrapnel—at the entrances to the enclave. Checkpoint Three, on the street in front of the Convention Center and the al-Rasheed, resembled a post-apocalyptic wasteland. Concrete slabs blocked off what had been an eight-lane expressway. Dead trees lined the sidewalk. Shell casings, wrappers from military rations, and punctured tires lay scattered on the ground. Coils of razor wire snaked in every direction. Plastic bags and candy wrappers fluttered from the concertina, snagged by the razor blades. Bits of trash filled the air. Garbage had been picked up with Swiss efficiency before the war, but collections had become sporadic after liberation, like every other municipal service.

In the mornings, starting at seven and lasting until eleven, the queue of Iraqis waiting to enter the checkpoint amid the razor wire stretched for hundreds of yards. Each of them had to present two forms of identification and submit to three separate pat-downs. American soldiers, sipping cold water from plastic tubes attached to bladders in their backpacks, barked at the Iraqis. "Stay back!" "One at a time!" "What's your reason for entering?"

"I am here for my salary."

"I want apply for job for translator."

"My son was detained by the coalition forces."

Sometimes the soldiers were gracious. Sometimes they were surly.

"I need help," a middle-aged man in front of me told a soldier one morning. "My son, he was kidnapped five days ago."

"You need to go to the police," the soldier said. "We cannot help you."

"I have gone to the police, but they don't want to help. They wanted a bribe."

"This is an Iraqi-on-Iraqi issue. There's nothing we can do for you."

"I thought you came here to help us. If you won't help us, who will?"

One morning, as a throng of Shiite pilgrims jostled their way inside the Imam Kadhim shrine in northern Baghdad, a suicide bomber detonated his explosives belt. A second bomber waited around the corner and set off his belt when survivors ran away from the first blast. Then a third bomber blew himself up. And a fourth.

The courtyard of the shrine filled with smoke and the screams of the dying. Blood pooled on the concrete floor. Dazed young men staggered about seeking help. Other survivors stacked the maimed onto wooden carts and pushed them toward wailing ambulances.

When I arrived at the scene an hour later, I saw corpses covered with white sheets. Arms and fingers had been blown atop third-story balconies. Piles of shoes belonging to the dead dotted the floor. Later, after visiting the local hospital to talk to survivors, I saw dozens of bodies piled outside the morgue, covered with blue sheets, rotting under the sun. Relatives of the dead and injured sobbed, but the doctors went stoically about their business. "Today is nothing special," one told me. "We see catastrophes like this once a week."

That evening, I met a group of CPA staffers for dinner in the palace. They talked about the interim constitution that had just been drafted, with its expansive bill of rights. "It'll be a model for the Middle East," one said.

Hearing about their work, I stopped thinking about what I had seen earlier that day. In the Green Zone, I could hear stories with happy endings. Nobody mentioned the bombing over dinner. The shrine was just a few miles north of the Green Zone, no more than a ten-minute drive away. Had they heard about what had happened? Did they know that dozens had died? "Yeah, I saw something about it on the office television," said the man to my right. "But I didn't watch the full report. I was too busy working on my democracy project."

Mahmud Ahmed slept through the screeching morning call to prayer. He had been at work until three in the morning. When he woke up at eight, there was no electricity in his neighborhood. Not again, he groaned to himself. The blackouts made no sense to him. Baghdad had had plenty of power before the war.

He turned on a faucet, but nothing came out. This was new. Even during the war, there had always been water. Years ago, the tap water had even been safe enough to drink. He har-rumphed. He could survive without a shower, but not without his morning tea. He had to have tea.

Ahmed was a trim man of medium height with thick black hair and a thin mustache. At the age of twenty-eight, he had the poise of a middle-aged man. He wore a striped Oxford shirt and gray slacks, and carried a leather portfolio.

A 1988 Chevy Caprice was parked in his driveway. The desert sun had weathered the car from royal blue to the hue of a well-worn pair of jeans. He'd bought it used a few years ear-lier from a high-ranking member of Saddam's Baath Party. Ahmed suspected the car had been looted from Kuwait after Iraqi troops invaded in 1990. Every time he got in it, he had the feeling that it didn't really belong to him.

As he entered the Caprice, he noticed that it was almost out of gas. He drove to the nearest service station, where the line of cars waiting for fuel stretched for more than a mile. This never happened under Saddam, Ahmed muttered to himself. But then he bit his tongue. He was happy to be free of the dictator. Liberation meant a satellite dish and a well-paying job. And that meant a chance to save enough for a dowry.

Across from the gas station, greasy kids standing next to jerry cans waved siphon hoses. They charged four dollars a gal-lon. A gallon of regular was less than a dime at the pump.

Ahmed finally decided to leave the car at home and hail a taxi to get to work. It would cost a dollar, but he had no choice. He'd lose his job if he didn't show up.

"If I was working for Iraqis, it is no problem to be late," he said. But in the Green Zone, where he worked, "You have to be on time."

In the taxi, he paused for a moment before telling the driver where to go. "Peace be upon you," he said. "The Convention Center, please."

The Convention Center was the main public entrance into the Green Zone.

"Oh, do you work with the Americans?" the driver asked.

"Of course not," he said. "My brother was taken by the Amer-ican troops. I'm trying to find out where he is."

"May God help you," the driver said.

"*Inshallah,*" Ahmed said. God willing.

In the taxi, a Volkswagen hatchback with worn upholstery and no air-conditioning, he watched the city crawl by. The traffic lights weren't working, the traffic police weren't on duty, the Americans had shut down several main roads, and the CPA had eliminated tariffs on imported vehicles, which had resulted in an influx of cheap used cars from seemingly every European nation. Before the war, the trip from Ahmed's home in eastern Baghdad to the Convention Center took ten minutes. After the Americans arrived, it took more than an hour.

Iraqis who used to stay in their lanes and use turn signals now drove on the shoulders and sidewalks. But the worst offenders were the American soldiers. They drove like they owned the place, sometimes crossing the median and barreling toward oncoming traffic.

The taxi crossed the Tigris River and passed the Assassin's Gate, the northern entrance to the Green Zone, where scores of young men were holding a protest. They were unemployed and wanted jobs from the Americans. A dozen soldiers watched from the gate, ready to block off the road with barbed wire and a tank if the crowd tried to enter.

The taxi passed a chockablock row of shops and stopped at the next intersection. This was as far as the driver could get. From there, Ahmed would have to walk to the Convention Center.

I had first met Ahmed a few days earlier, while we were standing in line to enter the Green Zone. He didn't tell me what he did right away. It wasn't until I shared details of my life that he admitted he worked as an interpreter for the American army.

Ahmed and I talked as we waited to pass through three separate checkpoints. He had to present two forms of photo identification and then submit to a pat-down and a search of his belongings.

"They treat me like everyone else off the street," Ahmed sniffed. He put his life on the line by working with American soldiers six days a week. The least they could do, he believed, was to let him enter in a separate queue, with one pat-down.

After we made it through the third checkpoint, we were

inside the Green Zone. We had been funneled onto a broad sidewalk leading to the Convention Center and the al-Rasheed.

Before the Americans arrived, Ahmed had never been inside the part of the Green Zone that had been walled off by Saddam. When he saw those areas, he had no mental image to compare with the present. But he had driven on the boulevard in front of the Convention Center hundreds of times, and the sight of it now was jarring. Before the war, the eight-lane-wide road was the thoroughfare from central Baghdad to the main highways heading north to Mosul, south to Hilla, and west to the airport, to Fallujah and to the Jordanian border. Then, cars had zipped along at sixty miles an hour. Now it was blocked off with concrete barriers. Three Humvees used the road as a parking lot.

"This doesn't feel like Iraq," he said of the Green Zone. "It feels like America."

I pointed out that in America, we didn't see Humvees parked on the street and that roads were not barricaded.

"Yes, but you have to admit, everything works in here," he said. "The lights. The faucets. The food. It is not like the rest of Baghdad. It's like America."

"Things are really improving," Mark Schroeder declared. He couldn't get into the details. Those were classified. But he wanted me to know that the bar graphs and trend lines were headed in the right direction.

"Do you ever interview Iraqis?" I asked.

"That's handled by someone else," he replied. "I don't do public opinion. I deal with the raw data."

Other CPA staffers did talk to Iraqis at length, but many of those Americans mistakenly assumed that the hundreds of Iraqis who worked for the CPA as translators, secretaries, and janitors represented their twenty-five million countrymen. Those Iraqis on the inside knew they had great jobs—they earned as much as ten times more than the average Iraqi civil servant—and they weren't about to risk their paycheck by complaining about the occupation or informing the Americans that their plans were foolhardy. Instead, they heaped praise on their masters, telling them everything they wanted to hear and minimizing any bad news.

A few thousand other Iraqis lived inside the Green Zone, in bungalows along tree-lined streets between the palace and the al-Rasheed. They were a mix of Sunnis and Shiites who had had jobs in the palace before the war but were too low in the ranks of the Baath Party to flee or wind up in American custody. They traveled outside the walls all the time, to work, to shop, to see relatives. Some of them even spoke English, and had Americans in the palace offered to listen to them, they would have heard an unvarnished description of life in the real Baghdad. But except for the odd, adventurous CPA staffer, most Americans didn't bother seeking out their Iraqi neighbors.

Schroeder and his fellow CPA staffers kept abreast of developments in Iraq by watching Fox News and reading *Stars and Stripes,* which was printed in Germany and flown daily to Baghdad. Some used the Internet to scan their hometown newspapers. But none of those news outlets had much information about the Green Zone.

There was no Green Zone newsletter. Information—and rumor—was shared by word of mouth. When an army officer was stabbed on the way to his trailer one night, everyone assumed a knife-wielding insurgent was on the loose. Investigators quickly determined that the attacker was a fellow American, but that information was never shared with CPA staffers. For weeks, they looked over their shoulders.

Inside the Green Zone, the concern wasn't that too little information was being disseminated; it was that too many secrets were at risk. World War II–era posters urging vigilance were tacked up in the palace. One depicted the hand of Uncle Sam muzzling a fedora-clad man. QUIET! LOOSE TALK CAN COST LIVES, the poster warned. Another showed a cocker spaniel resting his head dejectedly on the chair of a dead soldier. Below it were the words . . . BECAUSE SOMEBODY TALKED!

There were some CPA personnel who damned the torpedoes and traveled outside the bubble to meet and talk to Iraqis, to eat in their homes and shop in the local markets. To those who got outside, the Green Zone came to seem like a fantasyland. They began to call their home the Emerald City.

2

A Deer in the Headlights

I HAD MY FIRST LOOK INSIDE what would become the Emerald City two days after an American tank toppled a garish statue of Saddam in front of the Palestine Hotel. I crossed the al-Jumhuriya Bridge on foot, passing bullet-riddled vehicles and a dead donkey, before turning into the Assassin's Gate. A tank idled under the sandstone arch. It had flattened the imposing iron gate, but its turret pointed outward, an unambiguous message that what lay inside was not open for looting. I flashed my press pass, and the tank commander–turned–bouncer waved me inside. It's a long walk, he warned.

No more than a hundred yards from the tank, I spotted two bedraggled men staggering out of a white stucco villa, their arms full of crystal light fixtures. These were bold looters. They had either sneaked around the tank or had scaled one of the walls nobody had dared to look over a week earlier. When I went up to them, the older one introduced himself as Ahmed Mohsen, a farmer from Kut, a city southeast of Baghdad. I followed him inside the villa, where we found a professional, competition-grade billiards table, gold-inlaid doors, and marble floors.

"We live in mud houses. We don't have water," Mohsen growled. "Our lives are terrible, and he lives like this?"

I didn't break it to him that the villa wasn't Saddam's house, that the dictator had lived in far grander surroundings.

I forged on, passing buildings eviscerated by American munitions, intersections littered with copper shell casings, bunkers reeking with the unmistakable odor of decomposing bodies. A laminated identification card on the sidewalk caught my eye. It belonged to a Republican Guard soldier. There was a small notebook nearby. An Iraqi friend picked it up and flipped through the pages. "This is bullshit," he said as he read. "It's all praise for Saddam."

At the palace, a group of soldiers stood guard to repel even the most determined looters. Seeing my credentials, one of them summoned his lieutenant, an animated young West Point graduate named Joe Peppers. Peppers was in a jovial mood because for the first time in the three-week race to Baghdad, he had relieved himself in a toilet instead of a hole in the desert. "Not just any toilet," he said. "It was one of Saddam's gilded toilets!" He offered to give me a tour of the palace.

I had been in one of Saddam's homes before. Four months before the war, the Information Ministry had invited foreign journalists inside one of his smaller palaces after United Nations weapons inspectors had paid an unannounced visit to the palace and found nothing. The tour was intended to mock the inspectors. I remembered a green plastic fly swatter displayed on a wooden rack atop a table, and I was expecting more of the same kitsch in the Republican Palace.

Peppers heaved open an enormous gilded door and let me inside. As the door creaked shut, he pulled out his flashlight. The power was out inside the palace, as it was across Baghdad. It would be a few more days before American engineers would discover the giant generators Saddam had installed to ensure his palace was not beholden to the country's rickety electrical grid.

I followed the narrow beam of his torch, heeding admonitions to beware of stairs and debris. The marble floor, caked with dirt and broken glass, crunched as we walked. Blast waves from the American shock-and-awe bombing campaign had shattered all the windows early in the war, allowing fine desert sand to blow inside and coat everything. I felt as if we were entering a medieval castle that had been boarded up for a century.

"Guess how many rooms are in here," Peppers said.

"Oh, I don't know," I replied. "Maybe a hundred?"

"Two hundred and fifty-eight," he said. "Can you believe it?"

He had dispatched one of his privates to count. It took him an hour.

Everything seemed gigantic. Our first stop was a ballroom the size of a football field. The walls were adorned with friezes depicting Iraq's eighteen provinces. At the end of the room was a balcony. Peppers hadn't been to Versailles or Buckingham Palace or even to Hearst Castle. His only point of reference was the United States Military Academy.

"Wow," he gasped as he entered the ballroom. "This is even bigger than the dining hall at West Point."

Next on the tour was a meeting room as big as two basketball courts. Peppers's flashlight illuminated one elaborate chandelier after another. Then it was off to the basement movie theater, the spacious swimming pool, and a room that looked like a bordello, with cherry red carpeting and mirrors on the walls. Most of the rooms had been stripped of furniture and files. What remained were tacky knockoffs of French provincial furniture: ornate armchairs with orange upholstery and golden trim. At the end of one hallway hung a plaque that read PALACE OF THE PEOPLE.

We ended up in a giant marble rotunda. Peppers stopped talking and turned off his light. We were in the very center of the palace. Despite the lack of air-conditioning, the darkened room felt almost chilly. All I could hear was Peppers's breathing. Life outside—the looting, the firefights, the chaos in the streets—felt a world away.

On the way out, we passed by the half dozen rooms into which Peppers's battalion was crammed. With so much space, I asked him why they had not spread out. He answered without hesitation.

"We feel the less we occupy, the easier it is to move out when a new government is named," Peppers said. "We're not going to be here long."

President George W. Bush gave the order to begin planning for the invasion of Iraq just a few months after the September 11, 2001, attacks. But the Pentagon's planning for what to do after the war did not commence until the following fall. It was a task delegated to Douglas J. Feith, the undersecretary of defense for policy, who headed a secretive cell called the Office of Special Plans, which mined intelligence reports for data to make the case that Saddam possessed weapons of mass destruction and was in cahoots with al-Qaeda.

Feith was a fan of Ahmad Chalabi, a divisive and mercurial exile who headed a political organization called the Iraqi National Congress. Chalabi, an MIT-trained mathematician who wore bespoke suits, was persona non grata at the State Department and the CIA, where officials regarded him as corrupt and unpopular among Iraqis. But within the neoconservative orbit, which passed through Feith's office, Chalabi's glib talk about creating a secular democracy, one that would embrace the West and recognize Israel, was just what they wanted to hear. He became the neocons' dream candidate to rule after Saddam was toppled.

Feith's office conducted its postwar planning with utmost secrecy. There was little coordination with the State Department or the CIA, or even with post-conflict reconstruction experts within the Pentagon, and there was an aversion to dwelling on worst-case scenarios that might diminish support for the invasion. Feith's team viewed the mission as a war of liberation that would require only modest postwar assistance. They assumed that Iraqis would quickly undertake responsibility for running their country and rebuilding their infrastructure.

On January 17, 2003, two months before the war began, Feith called Jay Garner, a retired lieutenant general, and asked him to take charge of postwar Iraq. It wouldn't be for long, Feith said, perhaps for just ninety days after the war. By then, Feith predicted, an Iraqi government would be formed and an American ambassador would be dispatched to Baghdad.

Garner was an avuncular man, short but solid, with gray hair, metal-frame glasses, and a bourbon-smooth drawl. He exuded Southern hospitality mixed with country-boy informality, greeting people with a firm handshake and bidding them farewell with a back-slapping hug. Feith had called Garner because, for a brief period in 1991, after the Persian Gulf War, Garner had run the American military operation to protect ethnic Kurds in northern Iraq. He knew Iraqis, and he had experience providing humanitarian aid on Iraqi soil. He wasn't eager to return to a war zone—he had a lucrative defense contracting job and a comfortable life in Orlando, Florida—but he was a soldier: when your country asks, you serve.

When Garner arrived at the Pentagon in January, he had no staff and no blueprint for the job ahead. He was assigned to what he called a broom closet in Feith's suite. His first calls were to a few of his buddies—fellow retired generals—whom he beseeched to help him. Over the next few weeks, several military reservists were sent his way, as was a small group from the U.S. Agency for International Development (USAID) and a handful of other civilian government employees. The State Department also insisted on seconding a few of its diplomats. Some of those who joined Garner's team were first-rate; others were the dregs of the federal bureaucracy.

Everything in the Pentagon has an acronym. Garner's group became known as ORHA, the Office of Reconstruction and Humanitarian Assistance. Weeks later, several ORHA staffers joked that the acronym stood for Organization of Really Hapless Americans. Others referred to Garner and his fellow retired generals as the Space Cowboys, a reference to the Clint Eastwood movie in which a bunch of geriatric ex-astronauts blast off to save the world.

Garner claimed he never received any of the plans that were produced by Feith and his deputies. In fact, he said he didn't know that Feith's office was engaged in planning for the postwar administration of Iraq until ten days after he arrived in Baghdad, when his deputy, Ronald Adams, one of the Space Cowboys, returned to Washington because of a lung infection. Adams spent a few days working in the Pentagon and discovered there that Feith's operation was working up policies for how to purge members of Saddam's Baath Party, what to do with Iraq's army, and how to install Chalabi and other trusted exiles as national leaders. An incredulous Adams called Garner and said, "Hey, you know there's a whole damn planning section on postwar Iraq here?"

"No way," Garner replied. "Did they just put it together?"

"I think it's been here for a long time," Adams said.

"What are they doing?"

"I have no idea. They won't let me see the stuff."

What Garner also did not see, but which would have been far more useful, was any of the reams of postwar plans and memoranda produced by the State Department, or any of the analyses generated by the CIA, or even the unclassified report written by the military's own National Defense University based on a two-day workshop involving more than seventy scholars and experts. Garner asked Feith for copies of planning documents that had been drawn up in the Pentagon and elsewhere in the U.S. government. Garner said Feith told him that nothing useful existed and that he should develop his own plans. Feith's hope, as articulated to others in the Pentagon, was that without a clear blueprint for the political transition, Garner would turn to Chalabi and his band of exiles. Feith would get the outcome he wanted without provoking a fight ahead of time with State and the CIA, both of which regarded Chalabi as a fraud.

Flying blind, Garner divided ORHA into what he called "three pillars": humanitarian assistance, reconstruction, and civil administration. He further divided his team into three administrative zones. But his zones bore no resemblance to the boundaries of Iraq's provinces or to the placement of military forces. Given his previous experience in Iraq and a series of dire warnings by the United Nations that disease, hunger, and population displacement could affect millions of Iraqis in the event of war, most of Garner's attention was devoted to planning for a humanitarian crisis. Reconstruction was the domain of a team from the U.S. Agency for International Development. Civil administration—the most important pillar, as it turned out—was handed off to Michael Mobbs, Feith's former law partner. Garner paid little attention to that "pillar."

Garner appeared to be "a deer in the headlights," said Timothy Carney, a retired ambassador who was asked to join ORHA by Paul Wolfowitz, the deputy defense secretary. Garner asked Carney what job he wanted. Carney offered to be ORHA's ombudsman but added that the State Department was seeking to have him named interim minister of industry and minerals. Carney had no background in industry or minerals, but that didn't matter to the upper echelons at State. Carney was their guy, and they wanted as many of their guys as they could get in senior positions at ORHA. Garner agreed that Carney should run the Ministry of Industry and Minerals. Garner's team was heading to Kuwait in two days. Carney, who needed training and equipment before he could deploy, would join them later. "See you in Kuwait," Garner said.

The rest of ORHA was assembled in a similar helter-skelter fashion. The Ministry of Education was assigned to a midlevel bureaucrat from the Treasury Department. Another former ambassador, with no prior trade experience, was told to run the Trade Ministry. Stephen Browning, an engineer from the U.S. Army Corps of Engineers, was asked to head up four separate ministries: transportation and communications, housing and construction, irrigation, and electricity; a week after the fall of Baghdad, he got a fifth—health. ORHA staffers were smart and well intentioned, but they weren't experts in their areas of responsibility, they didn't have much background working in the Middle East, and they were overloaded. Carney had one deputy to help him run the Industry and Minerals Ministry, which had more than one hundred thousand employees.

Back in Feith's office, there was no cause for alarm. According to two people who worked for him, the intention was never to have large teams of American specialists at the ready to run Iraqi ministries. When the war ended, it was anticipated that Iraqi civil servants would return to work and the ministries would run themselves. An interim government, presumably led by Chalabi, would select new ministers. The assumption was that the best-case scenario would prevail.

The ORHA team soon found itself plagued with the same internecine rivalries between the Pentagon and the State Department that had poisoned attempts over the years to formulate a unified plan for dealing with Iraq. Secretary of State Colin L. Powell and his deputy, Richard L. Armitage, wanted as many of their people as possible on Garner's team. They regarded the presence of seasoned diplomats and Arabic-speaking Middle East specialists within ORHA as a bulwark against attempts to hand power over to Chalabi and other exiled politicians. State deemed it essential to involve Iraqis who had been living in Iraq in the creation of a transitional government. Pentagon officials believed that State's old-school Arabists were making excuses to justify their belief that democracy wouldn't work in the Arab world. In the Pentagon, the view was that Chalabi and his colleagues were going to lead the way in creating a secular, stable democracy. The White House let both sides snipe at each other.

It was not until two days before Garner departed for Kuwait that Defense Secretary Donald Rumsfeld took a hard look at the team Feith and Garner had assembled. The next day, Rumsfeld summoned Garner. According to Garner's account of the discussion, Rumsfeld began with an apology.

"Jay, I haven't paid enough attention to you," he said. "I should have given you more of my time."

Then he proceeded to question the credentials of several top ORHA staffers, particularly those from the State Department. "He said, 'I'm just uncomfortable with these people,' " Garner recalled. "I said, 'Uh, it's too late for you to be uncomfortable with them. I'm leaving tomorrow.' "

"He said, 'I'll get you new people.' "

"I said, 'You don't have time to get me new people.' "

After more back-and-forth, Rumsfeld asked Garner to look over his staff list and indicate who "you absolutely have to keep."

"And I said, 'By the way, who would DOD have that's qualified to do agriculture?' And he didn't say anything, so I said, 'How about education?' And I went down [the list] and I said, 'How about banking? Who could do banking?' So he said, 'Look, I don't want to argue with you on this one, but I'm gonna get you better people.' "

As soon as Garner left, Rumsfeld blocked the departure of senior State Department personnel assigned to ORHA on the grounds that they were "too low-profile and bureaucratic." He relented only after Powell called and threatened to pull every State employee from ORHA, which undoubtedly would have been front-page news. The Pentagon wanted as few State people on the team as possible, but not at the price of a public-relations embarrassment.

When Garner's advance team arrived in Kuwait in early March, they were informed that there was no room for ORHA at any of the military bases in the city-state. They would have to find their own accommodations. The only place with enough beds was a Hilton beach resort, which set aside a wing of luxury villas for Garner and 168 other ORHA members, who arrived in Kuwait the day before the war began. The group spent almost six weeks consuming gourmet meals and sipping sparkling water as they worked up plans to deliver food rations and drinking water to Iraqi civilians. The Hilton's two-story, cream-colored villas had down pillows, flat-screen televisions, maids' quarters, and breezy balconies overlooking the Persian Gulf.

Meetings consumed much of the mornings, but most were rambling affairs lacking specificity. Because everyone assumed that Iraq would be in the throes of a humanitarian crisis after the war, several sessions were devoted to planning the distribution of food and water. Garner also convened "rock drills," military-speak for simulation exercises. One drill assumed that corpses would be littering the streets of Baghdad, electricity would be out, and parts of the city would be on fire. Some ORHA members regarded the scenarios as far-fetched, but they nonetheless talked about how they would respond. They knew they didn't have enough staff or equipment, but they figured they would have military units at their disposal to provide transportation, communication, and other much-needed assistance.

It wasn't that Garner didn't have a plan. The one he had was titled "A Unified Mission Plan for Post Hostilities Iraq." It was marked SECRET/REL USA MCFI, meaning it could be shared only among Americans with appropriate security clearances and vetted members of governments who had joined Bush's "coalition of the willing." By the time Garner arrived in Kuwait, the second draft of the document had grown to twenty-five pages. It began with a one-page introduction written by Garner. The first sentence was both prescient and banal: "History will judge the war against Iraq not by the brilliance of its military execution, but by the effectiveness of the post-hostilities activities."

The first section cautioned against staying too long. The document went on to warn of potential civil disorder and noted that the "establishment of a secure environment is the highest priority military task." But key parts of one of the document's most important sections were noticeably blank. Section 8—the civil administration pillar—lacked a mission statement, a concept of operations, key objectives, or time lines. Those parts of the document were unfilled less than a week before American marines felled Saddam's statue in Baghdad.

The responsibility for pulling together a civil administration plan rested with Mobbs, Feith's former law partner and a former arms control official in the Reagan administration. Mobbs had spent months in the Pentagon working up strategies to fight the oil well fires that Iraqi troops were expected to ignite as American troops invaded. He had no prior experience in the Middle East, no history of working with Iraqi exiles, and no exposure to other post-conflict reconstruction operations. He quickly lost the confidence of Carney and the other State Department personnel assigned to his pillar. In Kuwait, Mobbs would convene a morning meeting of the people on his team and then he'd vanish. "He was not a leader. He didn't know what to do," one ex-ambassador said. "He just cowered in his room most of the time." The State people began to joke that Mobbs couldn't organize a two-car funeral. A week after the ORHA team arrived in Baghdad, Garner sent Mobbs back to Washington.

David Dunford, a retired ambassador who was put in charge of the Foreign Ministry, was among the fortunate few to receive a briefing packet before his deployment. In it was a four-page memo about the ministry that seemed to Dunford as though it had been written by a summer intern at the State Department. When his requests for more information from State went unanswered, he posted a plaintive query for advice on an Internet message board frequented by Middle East specialists. The gist of his message, Dunford said, was "Here I am and I don't have a clue as to what to do."

Carney, who was given no guidance or information about the Ministry of Industry and Minerals, also spent his afternoons in Kuwait trolling the Internet. He found a biography of the Iraqi minister, but little more. He had no idea how many workers the ministry had or how many factories and state-run companies there were. He began surfing online for books. He ordered the translated works of al-Mutanabi, Iraq's most famous poet. Miraculously, they arrived before he left for

Baghdad. He quickly settled upon his favorite line: "When a lion shows its teeth, do not assume he's smiling at you."

Although he enjoyed the poetry, there was one set of documents Carney desperately wanted but could not get: the reports of the Future of Iraq Project.

According to people who were privy to what little postwar planning was conducted by the U.S. government, including the classified reports produced by the CIA and the Pentagon's Office of Special Plans, the Future of Iraq Project was Washington's best attempt to prepare for the post-Saddam era. Run by midlevel State Department personnel, the project organized more than two hundred Iraqi exiles into seventeen different working groups to study issues of critical importance in the postwar period, including the reconstruction of shattered infrastructure, the creation of free media, the preservation of antiquities, the administration of justice during the transition, the development of the moribund economy, and, most important, the formation of a democratic government. The working groups produced reports with policy recommendations that totaled about 2,500 pages. Although the finished product was far from exhaustive—it lacked, for instance, a feasible blueprint for how to form a new Iraqi government—it nevertheless was the most ambitious initiative to identify what needed to be done upon liberation.

The task of organizing the project fell to Thomas Warrick, an international lawyer who had left a lucrative private practice five years earlier to work on war crimes at State. The war crimes job had led him to Saddam's villainy and, eventually, to the Iraqi opposition. Warrick spoke in rapid-fire sentences and always seemed to be in the middle of a crisis. He had the pudginess of a man who spent too much time at the office. His fans and detractors—of whom there were many—agreed that he was both whip-smart and overbearing; they disagreed on which trait was more dominant.

The first that Garner heard of the Future of Iraq Project was on February 21—a little more than a month after he was hired—at a predeployment rock drill he convened at the National Defense University in Washington. He knew that others in government had been thinking about postwar Iraq and he wanted to pick their brains. When he entered the conference room, he was amazed that there were more than a hundred people in attendance. As the meeting got under way, Garner noticed that a man in the front row kept asking questions and making comments. At first, Garner was annoyed. But as the session continued, it became clear that the man was asking the right questions and providing insightful comments. At a break, Garner walked up to him.

"You seem to know a hell of a lot about this stuff," Garner said.

"I've been studying it for a year and a half."

"Have you now?" Garner said. "What's your name?"

"Tom Warrick."

"Who do you work for?"

"The State Department."

"Well, you don't need to be sitting here. You need to be working for me."

Warrick joined Garner's team within two days. A week later, Rumsfeld approached Garner.

"Hey, Jay, do you have anyone in your organization named Warrick?" Rumsfeld asked. When Garner said he did, Rumsfeld told him to remove Warrick from ORHA.

"Why?" Garner replied. "Warrick has a difficult personality, but he's probably the smartest guy I've got."

"Look, I got this request from above me," the defense secretary said. "I can't defer it. You're just going to have to do what I ask."

Garner said he was told later that Dick Cheney had objected to Warrick's involvement in ORHA. The reason, like so many foolish decisions before the war, had to do with Ahmad Chalabi. Warrick regarded Chalabi as a smarmy opportunist who believed in democracy only so long as it suited his own interests. The vice president's office, which wanted Chalabi to lead a liberated Iraq, deemed Warrick a threat to its man.

Upon leaving Rumsfeld's office, Garner told one of his aides to inform Warrick that he'd have to return to the State Department. With Warrick gone, Garner never got to see any of the Future of Iraq reports.

THE GREEN ZONE, SCENE I

As I stepped out of the Republican Palace, Lieutenant Peppers called after me. "Hey, you want to see the animals?"

We headed to a neighboring palace in a Humvee, driving along the banks of the Tigris where, just two days earlier, Peppers's battalion had fought against soldiers from Saddam's Special Republican Guard. When we arrived, Peppers led the way through knee-high weeds to a fenced enclosure. "Let's see," he said. "We have seven lions, two cheetahs, and one brown bear." The adorable lions were not quite cubs, but not yet full grown. (Before the war, I heard that Uday, Saddam's elder son, would drive around Baghdad in a Rolls-Royce with lion cubs on his lap.) The bear cowered in the shade. The temperature was already in the nineties—and it was only April. I wondered how he'd survive the summer. And the cheetahs . . . where were they? I called out to Peppers. He couldn't see them, either. Alarmed, he grabbed his radio and summoned his men from the Humvee. "Be ready with your guns," he barked. "We may have two cheetahs on the loose."

A dozen soldiers swooped around Uday's menagerie, switching off the safeties on their M16 rifles. Then we saw the two spotted adolescent cheetahs skulking out of a small shed inside the enclosure. Everyone chuckled. Rifles were clicked back into safe mode and slung over shoulders.

When the soldiers had arrived at the palace, the animals appeared to be dying of hunger and thirst. The groundskeepers who fed them had apparently fled. The soldiers brought the animals water but they didn't know what to do for food. Then one sergeant found a bunch of sheep in a pen, and he tossed one into the enclosure. It was mealtime.

But the supply of sheep was running low. A conversation

about the Geneva Convention ensued. What obligation does an occupying military power have to care for animals? Nobody knew. Peppers didn't want the animals to starve. He figured he could sneak some military rations to them for a few days, until help arrived. He'd heard that hundreds of American civilians were coming to run the country.

"They'll have the answers," he said.

3

You're in Charge!

A FEW HOURS AFTER the American tank toppled the statue of Saddam in front of the Palestine Hotel, the looters arrived at the Ministry of Industry's ten-story headquarters. Seeing no troops there, the first bands of thieves set upon the concrete-and-glass building like wild animals on a carcass. First to go were computers, telephones, and other easy-to-pilfer items. Next came the furniture and file cabinets. Then the hard-core scavengers pulled out wiring and metal ducting from the walls. Over the following hours, Iraqis arrived with pickup trucks and even ten-ton government dump trucks, which themselves had been stolen. After two days, the building was torched, sending a plume of smoke billowing into the sky.

Tim Carney watched the looting of Baghdad on CNN, in his beachfront villa in Kuwait. He couldn't make out which ministry was his—nobody had given him a picture of the Ministry of Industry or even the geographic coordinates—but he felt certain that it was among those being ransacked and burned. The prospect of running his ministry without a building, without inventory records or balance sheets, made him feel ill.

Other ORHA ministers-to-be shared Carney's dread. When the looting began, several of them gathered around a television and played a macabre parlor game: They tried to guess which of the buildings they saw being pillaged might be theirs. "It was like, 'There goes your ministry!' 'There goes mine!'" recalled Robin Raphel, the interim trade minister. They assumed that soldiers were on the way.

Their dismay turned to anger after they realized that no troops had been assigned to protect their ministries, and that there were no immediate plans to commit forces to guard "static sites." At the time, the only government building protected by American troops, other than the Republican Palace, was the Ministry of Oil. Two weeks earlier, the ORHA ministers had worked up a list of sites in Baghdad that needed security. Atop the list was the Central Bank. Then came the National Museum. The Oil Ministry was at the bottom. Weeks later, ORHA personnel discovered that the military had failed to transmit the list to ground commanders in Baghdad.

Even as the impact of the looting was becoming clear, ORHA could not prod the military into action. When Barbara Bodine, a veteran diplomat and Arabic speaker who was to become the interim mayor of Baghdad, got word from an Iraqi contact that looters were perilously close to breaking into a vault under the Central Bank that housed a priceless collection of Assyrian gold, she fired off an e-mail to the U.S. Central Command. The exchange, as she and a State Department official in Washington who was copied on the messages remember it, went something like this:

> BODINE: The Assyrian vault under the Central Bank is in immediate danger of being looted. We need to get on this.
> CENTCOM: What's in the Assyrian vault?
> BODINE (*thinking of the "Who's buried in Grant's Tomb?" line*): Assyrian treasure.
> CENTCOM: What's an Assyrian treasure?
> BODINE: Go read the early chapters of your Bible. It's old stuff. It's really, really valuable. We need to save it.
> CENTCOM: Okay. We'll see what we can do.

There were no apologies from the military. Rumsfeld's war plan did not include enough troops to guard government installations in Baghdad and other major cities. Asked about the looting, he brushed it off with the now-famous phrase "Freedom's untidy."

Because of the looting and bedlam in Baghdad, the military refused to allow Garner and his team to move into the Iraqi capital right away. Eight days after the fall of Baghdad, with the military still unwilling to budge, Garner flew to Qatar to see General Tommy Franks, the top military commander in the region.

"I said, 'Tommy, you have got to get my team to Baghdad,'" Garner recalled. "And he said, 'Jay, I'm not going to do that. Hell, they're still killing people there. I'm not going to send you there.'"

Garner argued that opportunistic Iraqis were claiming leadership of Baghdad's local government and police force. "Power vacuums are going to be filled with stuff you and I aren't going to like, and it's going to take a long time to get rid of that," Garner insisted. Franks finally relented and allowed Garner to be flown into Baghdad on April 21, 2003—twelve days after U.S. troops took over the city.

Carney and his fellow ORHA ministers set out from Kuwait three days later. He and a dozen other senior ORHA personnel waited three hours on the tarmac in Kuwait because the C-130 Hercules transport plane that had been assigned to them was commandeered by a rear-echelon general. Once the ORHA team arrived at Baghdad International Airport, they discovered that the convoy sent to pick them up had left. They had to wait some more.

When they finally arrived at the Republican Palace, it was a marble tent: there were no lights, no windows, no working toilets or sinks. They had been given sleeping bags in Kuwait, but nobody thought to dole out mosquito nets or other camping supplies issued to soldiers. Nor did ORHA receive the satellite phones they had been promised by military communication specialists. Carney grew increasingly alarmed. It was one thing not to have all the documents he wanted in Kuwait. It was quite another to be in Baghdad without basic living quarters.

Moving into the Republican Palace had never been the plan. The civilians wanted ORHA to take over a hotel in Baghdad. If the group squatted in a palace, they worried that Iraqis would see them as occupiers. Military personnel within ORHA opposed a hotel, arguing that it would not have a sufficient perimeter to guard against car bombs and small-arms fire, and instead proposed an Iraqi army base on the outskirts of the city, but the civilians insisted that that would be too far away from the ministry buildings they would have to visit every day. With no other good option, ORHA's leaders agreed to a palace.

The job of picking a palace fell to Major Peter Veale, an army reservist who was also an architect. During the first week of the war, he walked over to the villa at the Kuwait Hilton inhabited by ORHA's intelligence team and asked them for information about all the palaces in Baghdad that had not been bombed by the military. When they told him that it would take a few days to respond to his request, Veale went on the Internet. On a Web site called DigitalGlobe, he pulled up images of a massive edifice with a blue dome—the Republican Palace. It seemed ideal. But when he received a list of standing palaces from the intelligence staff, that one wasn't among the possibilities. He walked back to their villa with the DigitalGlobe printout. "Hey, you didn't show me this one," he said. A day later, they called Veale. "We have good news, Major Veale," one of them said. "Yes, this is a palace and it does exist. But it got hit on the first night of shock-and-awe [bombing] and it's been pretty much destroyed." Veale was skeptical. His image of the palace had been taken within the past week. But the intelligence personnel were certain. "Take our word for it," one analyst said. "These buildings have been pretty well destroyed."

So Veale had planned for ORHA to move into the Sijood Palace, a small structure down the river from the Republican Palace. He spent days diagramming the building, identifying where people would work, where cars would be parked, where helicopters would land. A few days after Baghdad fell, he headed up from Kuwait to begin preparations. But when he got to Sijood, he found it rubbled by an American cruise missile. He thought to himself, *What am I going to do?*

As he sat outside the palace, a few Special Forces soldiers stopped to talk. Veale recounted his plight. One soldier encouraged him to keep looking. "Hey, man, you have to go down the road," he said. "There's a palace that's fully intact." When Veale got there, he discovered that it was the same palace he had seen on the DigitalGlobe Web site.

With Garner due to arrive in less than a week, Veale set about trying to get the lights on and the water running. The

American military had bombed the outbuilding that housed the air-conditioning and power-generating units. Getting the water to flow was difficult because he could not find any schematic drawings indicating where the pipes were buried. Trolling through the labyrinthine basement to look for pipes and wiring was harrowing. "We didn't know if it was booby-trapped," Veale recalled.

As Veale conducted his inspections, he was accompanied by a CIA operative searching for weapons of mass destruction. All they found were a few hard-core looters and two bewildered Republican Guard soldiers who had failed to join their buddies in fleeing home a week earlier. Then Veale heard a rumor that one of Uday's tigers had escaped from its cage and was prowling the palace grounds. Veale soon grew more afraid of running into a feline than a former regime fighter. For the better part of a week, he walked around at night with a flashlight in one hand and a gun in the other.

Tim Carney had hunted elephants, cape buffalo, giraffes, warthogs, and two species of zebra. He owned an elephant gun—a double-barreled, double-triggered weapon whose bullets are almost a half inch in diameter, nearly the size of the largest rifle used by the U.S. Army—and he ate what he shot. The list of exotic animals Carney had bagged was rivaled only by the list of exotic places he had been stationed as a diplomat: Saigon during the Tet Offensive, Phnom Penh as the Khmer Rouge converged, Mogadishu in the throes of civil war, Port-au-Prince when American marines waded ashore.

Carney was tall, soft-spoken, and exceedingly polite. But he also could be blunt and clear-eyed about the failings of American foreign policy. (The chatty American diplomat played by Spalding Gray in the film *The Killing Fields* was based largely on Carney.) By the time he retired in 2000, he had more experience in hostile places than almost anyone else in the State Department.

Nine days before the first bombs and cruise missiles pummeled Baghdad, Paul Wolfowitz called Carney. The two men had known each other since the late 1980s, when Wolfowitz was ambassador to Indonesia and Carney was his top political officer. It was a short phone call, with none of the usual reminiscing. Wolfowitz asked Carney to join the team being assembled to handle postwar reconstruction and governance. Carney, always a sucker for adventure, agreed.

Before he hung up, Wolfowitz expressed unhappiness with the inclusion of State Department personnel on the postwar team. Many of the department's veteran Middle East hands had been openly skeptical of transforming Iraq into a democracy, as Wolfowitz and other neoconservatives had been advocating. Carney was no neocon, but he defined his politics as "center right," instead of the center-left label that applies to many in America's diplomatic corps. Wolfowitz suggested that his old friend call things as he saw them. It was a message that Carney would take to heart—just not as Wolfowitz had intended.

On his first full day in Baghdad, Carney discovered that the military had assigned so few soldiers to ORHA that only two or three staffers could travel out of the palace at one time. He and his fellow ministerial advisers decided that the top priority should go to the American Treasury Department team that wanted to inspect the Central Bank. The bank was atop ORHA's ignored list of places to protect.

As three Treasury specialists headed out the door, wearing their flak vests and helmets, senior ORHA staffers assembled for a morning meeting. Ten minutes later, the Treasury staffers returned, walked up to Carney, and asked to borrow the tourist map of Baghdad he had purchased from a Washington travel store before his departure. "The military doesn't know where it's going, either," one of them said. For the next several days, referring to Carney's map was the only way ORHA staff could identify government buildings in the capital.

When the Treasury officials finally arrived at the site of the Central Bank, they found the building burned to the ground. No one knew the fate of the Assyrian gold in the underground vaults.

The next day it was Carney's turn to visit the Ministry of Industry. He carpooled with Robin Raphel, the adviser to the Trade Ministry. The building was only a half mile across the Tigris River from the palace, but it took them almost half an hour to make the trip. With no policemen at work and no electricity to power the traffic lights, Baghdad's streets had become a free-for-all. Before the day was over, Carney and Raphel had reached two conclusions: the looting had caused far more damage to Iraq's infrastructure than the bombing campaign, and the failure to restore order was creating a climate of near-total impunity. Once government buildings had been stripped bare, miscreants began stealing from fellow Iraqis. When electricity was restored—for no more than a few hours at a time—homeowners began tapping distribution lines so they would not have to pay for service. My driver, an English-speaking law student who had not dared to flout a traffic rule before the war, now coolly drove on the wrong side of the street, into opposing traffic at times, to avoid traffic jams. When I asked him what he was doing, he turned to me, smiled, and said, "Mr. Rajiv, democracy is wonderful. Now we can do whatever we want."

When Carney got to the Ministry of Industry site, he found pretty much what he had expected: a giant, charred honeycomb. He asked the few ministry employees loitering uncertainly in the parking lot to return with their bosses the next day. They did, along with eight senior ministry officials dressed in blazers and ties. Their first order of business was to find someplace other than the parking lot to meet. They quickly determined that most of the ministry's other buildings in Baghdad had also been looted. Finally, someone mentioned the State Company for Batteries, whose factory and adjoining offices on a quiet side street in northern Baghdad had not been ransacked. When Americans inquired why the factory had been spared, ministry officials laughed and said that the batteries were so poorly made, even the looters didn't want them.

In those chaotic weeks after the war, most phones in Baghdad didn't have a dial tone. The Americans had bombed the major telephone exchanges and hit the phone company's headquarters with so many precision-guided bombs that it resembled a giant block of Swiss cheese. Most ORHA members didn't have satellite phones—and none of them had e-mail at the time—which made it almost impossible for them to communicate with fellow ORHA staffers (or with their families in America). Carney resorted to slipping handwritten notes under his colleagues' office doors.

Among Iraqis, the lack of modern technology was no big deal. They had been through this before, in the months after the 1991 Persian Gulf War, when Baghdad had been shattered by weeks of coalition bombardment. They simply passed messages by word of mouth. And it worked. Within three days, most of the ministry's managers had reported for duty at the battery factory. Rank-and-file employees showed up too—with banners calling for a purge of the old guard.

I was on my way to another appointment when I saw the commotion outside the factory. As I walked to the front gate, I met a clean-cut, thirty-year-old laboratory technician named Mohammed Sabah who was holding a cloth banner that read WE DEMAND NEW MANAGEMENT FREE FROM THE PAST REGIME'S THUGS. Sabah, who worked for the al-Sawari Chemical Manufacturing Company, one of forty-eight enterprises owned by the ministry, said that he and seventy fellow employees were protesting the reinstatement of the company's director, a man who Sabah said was corrupt and deeply involved in Saddam's Baath Party. "We want an independent, non-Baathist, honest administrator who will look into the welfare of the employees," Sabah declared to the applause of his obstreperous co-workers.

Inside the factory's gate, the mood was no less tense. Dozens of senior ministry officials milled in front of the director's office. The men said that the office had been taken over by Ahmed Rashid Gailani, the Baathist deputy minister of industry in Saddam's government. He, with the apparent support of several factory directors, had anointed himself as the new minister. At that moment, the men said, Gailani was meeting with his first official visitor: a tall American man with a straw hat named Mister Carney.

Although Carney had introduced himself as the "senior adviser" to the ministry, the men assembled outside the director's office knew he was the new boss. He had arrived with gun-toting soldiers and a leather portfolio. He had the demeanor of a man who had been around and wasn't about to put up with any nonsense.

The men wondered if Carney would let Gailani stay on as minister, and if the protesters would get what they wanted. But more significantly, they wondered how Carney would deal with people who had been affiliated with the Baath Party.

Would it be an automatic disqualification as the protesters wanted, or would it be a nonissue?

A stocky man in an olive safari suit introduced himself to me as Jabbar Kadhim, a twenty-eight-year veteran of the ministry. He was the director of the ministry's technical section. He said his division was responsible for repairing equipment in state-run factories. He also said he was a "sectional" member—one of the top three levels—of the Baath Party.

Surprised by his candor (most Iraqis I had met until then had disavowed any association with the party), I asked if his membership would disqualify him from serving in a senior ministry job. Kadhim launched into a tirade.

"There's no Iraqi who was not in the party," he insisted. He claimed that there were seven million members, which I took to be an outlandish exaggeration. Most reliable estimates put party membership at somewhere between one million and two million.

"Most of them are highly educated and technical," he continued. "In the past, if you weren't a Baathist, you wouldn't be able to rise in the hierarchy."

That was true. While the party did have plenty of thugs, many of Iraq's most capable scientists, engineers, and other professionals also belonged. To gain admission to the best colleges and graduate schools, to get a coveted government job, to get a promotion, you had to be a member. If you excelled at your job, you might be promoted into the party's upper ranks, even if that was not something you sought. Turning down a promotion could get you fired or sent to jail.

Soon I was able to walk inside the director's office, where Gailani announced that he and Carney had made a decision about the chemical company. The protesters would get what they wanted. The director, who was deemed to be a high-ranking party member, would be dismissed. Carney said he would obtain an order to that effect from Jay Garner.

I asked Gailani about his own association with the party. As a former deputy minister, I noted, he certainly had to be a member. He insisted he was only "in a very low rank."

"I went to a meeting once every three months," he said. "I said I was very busy in the ministry."

I couldn't determine just then if he was telling the truth.

When Carney left the room, I followed him and asked how he was addressing the issue of past party involvement. There was no clear directive, he said. He and the other senior advisers were relying on their judgment. "Among the Iraqis, everyone knows who was either too bad or too Baath," he said. "The bottom line is the ultimate triage is going to be with the future Iraqi authority. If we are introduced to someone who was either active in the production or development of weapons of mass destruction or in terrorism or a major human rights violator, we will remove those people as we become aware of them. Others will be subjected more to an Iraqi process than a coalition process."

Kadhim, the senior party member in the safari suit, didn't hear what Carney told me. All he knew was that the chemical company director was getting the boot. As I walked out of the building, he stopped me with a finger-wagging admonition: "If the [Baath] party members are treated in a normal manner and they are given their rights, there will be no more party," he said. "If not, the Baath Party will rise again."

Back at the palace, Carney was becoming increasingly dispirited. ORHA seemed to be a mess.

Part of the problem was that the military did not appear to care about helping ORHA, whose civilian staffers needed more amenities than the average grunt. Carney and other veteran diplomats deemed showers and laundry facilities essential. They had to meet Iraqi government workers who, despite the privation of postwar Baghdad, were showing up at ministries dressed in suits and ties. But water was not always flowing in the palace. Clothes handed over to the military's laundry service, run by Kellogg, Brown & Root, a Halliburton subsidiary, were returned after two weeks, if at all. Instead of finding a laundry in Baghdad or hiring Iraqis to wash items by hand, KBR sent the garments to Kuwait. Cell phone service, which the army had promised to start within weeks of liberation, was nonexistent. So, too, were computers. Getting basic supplies from the military was equally frustrating. Metal-frame canvas cots, which the army brought to Baghdad by the truckload, were not issued to civilians in ORHA. Most galling to Carney was the lack of transportation. There were only about ten military police escort convoys for the more than three dozen ORHA personnel who needed to leave the palace every day.

Unwilling to remain sequestered in the palace, Carney disregarded rules requiring travel in two-vehicle convoys with at least two long-barreled weapons. He tucked a borrowed nine-millimeter Beretta handgun into his waistband, donned his straw hat, and drove his Halliburton-issued GMC Suburban out of the palace grounds by himself. He soon learned his way around Baghdad so well that he stopped consulting his maps. He found Baghdad's best restaurant, a Lebanese place called Nabil's, and became a regular at lunch. In the palace, there was no alcohol in the dining hall. At Nabil's, lunch for Carney included at least one well-chilled, sixteen-ounce can—two if it was a rough day at the ministry—of Efes pilsner from Turkey.

The palace began to resemble a summer camp for adults. Mosquito nets were strung up over sleeping bags. Flashlights and pocket knives became must-carry accessories. Hot food, no matter how greasy or overcooked, was regarded as a luxury after the army's constipating field rations.

Carney was the wise older scout, the guy who knew what to bring that wasn't on the official packing list. He had a box of powdered detergent to wash his own clothes. He had a car charger for his satellite phone so he could make calls when he was driving around the city. A roll of super-strong duct tape and a can of industrial-strength mosquito repellent were always at hand. And he'd brought his own laptop and printer.

Every night before turning out the lights, Carney wrote a few lines in a spiral-bound notebook he had purchased in Kuwait. Some of the entries were prosaic: "Went to ministry for meetings today and then did laundry." When he wanted to note something private or sensitive, he scribbled in Khmer, a language he had learned in Cambodia and was sure nobody else in the palace read or spoke. "Are we in teething problems or fatally flawed in concept?" he wrote soon after arriving.

As the weeks wore on, his assessment became ever more pessimistic. "Military and OSD [Office of the Secretary of Defense] cannot make the transition from military to political-military mission," he wrote.

He kept thinking back to lessons he'd drawn from his experiences in Cambodia: "You had to have a plan. You had to have a lot of money. You had to have really good staff."

ORHA didn't lack just military support. The organization was rudderless. The mission plan still had not been completed. And even if it had been, it would not have guided Carney in dealing with Baathists in his ministry. By then, he had just two people on his staff, both army reservists, to manage a ministry with more than one hundred thousand employees. And he had no budget. ORHA, he realized, was an organization built on a false premise. Had there been no looting, had the police stayed on the streets, had Iraq's infrastructure not been whittled to incapacitation by Saddam's government, then perhaps an outfit such as ORHA, with no plan, no money, and a skeletal staff, would have been appropriate.

While ORHA's overall agenda was still a work in progress, Garner did have a plan to address the most important dilemma he faced: how much power to give the Iraqis and when to hand it over. The problem was that the Pentagon, the State Department, and, most significant, the White House, had not signed off on it.

Exiled Iraqi political leaders wanted to form a transitional government that would take over control of the country from the Americans. The government would be led by a small council comprised of the most prominent exiled politicians: Ahmed Chalabi and Ayad Allawi, Shiite leaders Ibrahim al-Jafari and Abdul Aziz al-Hakim, and Kurdish chieftains Jalal Talabani and Massoud Barzani. To Garner, the group seemed to represent Iraq's diverse society. Chalabi and Allawi, who hated each other, were both secular Shiites. Al-Jafari and al-Hakim were far more religious. The group promised to bring on board at least one Sunni Arab and a few "internals"—Iraqis who had never gone into exile.

Garner thought it was a great idea. The exiled leaders were people the U.S. government had worked with before, all of whom had impeccable anti-Saddam credentials. All of them, except Chalabi, represented large blocs of Iraqis. And they were willing to assume the responsibility of leadership. To Garner, they were the "takeover guys."

Rumsfeld, Wolfowitz, and Doug Feith did not tell Garner

how to manage the political transition. Garner assumed that all three favored a dominant role for the exiled leaders, particularly Chalabi, in a transitional government. But the Pentagon trio worried that an order to Garner to hand over authority to the exiles would have made its way back to the State Department and sparked new debate within the Bush administration. State didn't want the exiles in charge. It believed that authority should rest with the United States, either through a military commander or a civilian governor, until a representative group of Iraqis, internals as well as exiles, formed a government. In State's view, there would have to be elections and perhaps even a new constitution written before the Americans handed over the keys. Although Cheney and his staff were strong backers of Chalabi, the rest of the White House, specifically President Bush and National Security Advisor Condoleezza Rice, had not articulated a clear view of how the transition should unfold. If the issue were forced, Pentagon leaders feared that Bush and Rice might choose elements of the State plan. But if Garner were not given orders, and events on the ground were allowed to run their course, Pentagon officials hoped the exiles would simply form a transitional government. Once that happened, the officials thought, it would obviate the need for State's transition plan.

"I never knew what our plans were," Garner said. "But I did know that what I believed, and what the plans were, were probably two different things."

By the time he left Kuwait for Baghdad, Garner had concluded that elections should be held within ninety days. When he made that view known to reporters, it infuriated his bosses at the Pentagon, who feared that an election would not be in the best interests of the exiles. Once Garner got to Iraq and met with Kurdish leaders Talabani and Barzani, both of whom he had known from running relief operations in northern Iraq after the 1991 Gulf War, his plans evolved. He still wanted elections, but he also threw his support behind the exiles' plan to form a transitional government. That pleased the Pentagon but irritated State. Before long, Colin Powell and Richard Armitage voiced objections to Garner's plan at the White House.

In Baghdad, efforts to get the exiles to broaden their ranks with internals soon ran into trouble. The exile leaders could not agree on whom to invite. As a sign of reconciliation, Allawi wanted to include someone who had been in the Iraqi army or in Saddam's government. Chalabi and the Shiite religious leaders regarded such people as too compromised. Chalabi also expressed concern that anything more than a small expansion of their ranks would dilute the exiles' power. The not-so-subtle message was that he didn't want to loosen his hold on the nascent government.

To make the process appear participatory and to identify promising internals, ORHA convened a conference of about three hundred Iraqis in the Convention Center to discuss the country's future. There were tribal sheiks in gold-fringed robes, men in business suits, and even a few women. They gathered in the cavernous auditorium where, six months earlier, Saddam's deputy had announced that the Iraqi leader had been reelected with 100 percent of the vote and 100 percent turnout. For the first time in more than three decades, Iraqis were now free to speak their minds. Some called for elections to be held within weeks. Some said it was important for religious leaders to weigh in on the formation of a government. Some wanted Iraq's tribes to play a dominant role. Many simply vented about Saddam and the abuses of his henchmen. (The meeting occurred on Saddam's birthday, an irony mentioned by several of the attendees.)

As the meeting wore on, it became clear that most of the internals didn't want the exiles to be in charge. But beyond that, there was little agreement on how to form a government. There was talk of holding another meeting in a month's time to hash out the composition of a transitional government. But the Iraqis were clearly looking for guidance. Garner sat in front of the room with Zalmay Khalilzad, the White House's point man in dealing with Iraqi exiles. Neither man said much beyond his platitude-filled opening remarks. They listened impassively as their interpreters whispered what the Iraqis were saying. Finally, a sheik rose and asked Garner who would be in charge of forming a government.

"You're in charge!" Garner replied.

The crowd gasped. How could it be, they wondered, that the

Americans would cede involvement in such an important question?

What Garner meant, but what he couldn't say at the time, was not that Iraqis were in charge. It was that *he* was no longer in charge.

In Washington, the White House had finally focused on the lack of a political transition plan. Garner's desire to hold elections in ninety days alarmed Rice. The State Department's reservations about putting the exiles in charge also began to resonate inside 1600 Pennsylvania Avenue. The plan all along was to have a "man of stature" take charge in Baghdad. But what would his role be? Would he be an ambassador-like figure supporting an exile-led transitional government? Or would he be more of a viceroy who would administer the country until elections or some other participatory process identified representative leaders?

Bush, Cheney, Rice, and Rumsfeld batted around names. Former New York City mayor Rudolph Giuliani, the hero of September 11, was felt out, but the aftermath of the attacks on his city was grueling enough, and he had just opened a consulting firm. Former Massachusetts governor William Weld and former senator William Cohen were on an informal list, but the Pentagon and the vice president's office expressed concern over whether the two men, both moderate Republicans, were the "right kind of Republican." Would they support the neoconservatives' plans for Iraq's political and economic transformation? Elder statesmen, including former secretary of state James Baker III and former Senate majority leader Bob Dole, were rejected because of their age. The list also contained several people who were not widely known but were regarded as skilled managers and loyal Republicans.

Among them was L. Paul Bremer III, who had been suggested by Cheney's office. Known to friends as Jerry—after his patron saint, Jerome—Bremer was a seasoned diplomat with strong ties to the Republican foreign-policy establishment. He had worked closely in government with two former secretaries of state, Henry Kissinger and Alexander Haig, and been ambassador to the Netherlands and the State Department's counterterrorism czar. After leaving government in the late 1980s, he worked for Kissinger's consulting firm and an insurance company, but he remained in the Washington orbit. In 2000, he headed a congressionally appointed commission on terrorism that issued a series of prescient recommendations. After the September 11 attacks, he was named to a presidential commission on homeland security. He was a sixty-one-year-old workaholic who had a reputation as a can-do, take-charge guy—just the sort of person the White House wanted in Iraq.

The night before the conference in which Garner told the Iraqis that they were in charge, Rumsfeld called Garner with the news that Bremer had been selected by the president to head a new organization, the Coalition Provisional Authority, that would supplant ORHA. Garner kept it to himself for a week, not wanting to be seen as a lame duck. But when word began leaking out in Washington, he had to inform the rest of ORHA that he was on the way out, after less than a month in Iraq. He warned ORHA personnel that some of them also would be replaced by Bremer's new team. In the following days, he told at least three of his subordinates in private meetings that he thought he had failed. Each of them said roughly the same thing: Jay, it's not your fault. You were set up to fail.

THE GREEN ZONE, SCENE II

General Order 1 prohibited military personnel from consuming alcohol in Iraq, but it didn't apply to CPA staffers.

Drinking quickly became the most popular after-work activity. The Green Zone had no fewer than seven watering holes: the Halliburton-run sports bar in the basement of the al-Rasheed Hotel, which had a big-screen television along with its Foosball table; the CIA's rattan-furnished bar—by invitation only—which had a mirrored disco ball and a game room; the pub in the British housing complex where the beer was served warm and graffiti mocked the Americans; the rooftop bar for General Electric contractors; a trailer tavern operated by Bechtel, the engineering firm; the Green Zone Café, where you could smoke a water pipe and listen to a live Arab drummer as you drank; and the al-Rasheed's disco, which was the place to be seen on Thursday nights. A sign at the door requested patrons not to bring firearms inside. Scores of CPA staffers, including women who had had the foresight to pack hot pants and four-inch heels, danced on an illuminated Baath Party star embedded in the floor.

The atmosphere was thick with sexual tension. At the bar, there were usually ten men to every woman. With tours of duty that sometimes stretched to six months without a home leave, some with wedding rings began to refer to themselves as "operationally single."

The guys did whatever they could to gain the attention of the gals. Before heading to the disco, soldiers changed out of their camouflage fatigues, and CPA staffers slipped off their khakis and polo shirts. The Texans wore cowboy hats and jeans. Others put on dress shirts or baggy hip-hop duds with whatever bling-bling they could find in the Green Zone Bazaar.

There were prostitutes in Baghdad, but you couldn't drive into town to get laid like in Saigon. There was a persistent rumor of a whorehouse in the Green Zone, but CPA staffers said it was a military thing. Only the soldiers knew the location, and they weren't talking.

CPA staffers were forced to do the mating dance with one another. The women led. In an e-mail to her friends back home, a staffer wrote,

> *The men, faced with a shortage of women, are eager to find a girlfriend, so that they have a reliable source of, um, companionship. The women, on the other hand, have every incentive to refuse to commit to any one man, given the vast array available to them. Some of the women clearly enjoy the attention. Others think it's skeezy (and aren't too flattered knowing that the attention is more a result of scarcity than anything else). But it is kind of fun to watch if you can keep from getting depressed.*

The men joked about it too. They claimed to know someone who knew someone who was on a British Royal Air Force flight to Kuwait where the pilot announced, "Ladies and gentlemen, we're exiting Iraqi airspace. Ladies, you are no longer beautiful."

The most attractive women received discomfiting attention. When one fetching CPA staffer introduced herself to a man she'd never met, he smiled and said, "I know who you are. Everyone knows who all the pretty women are."

If staffers were lucky enough to find love, or more likely, lust, finding a place to canoodle wasn't easy. Those who lived in a trailer or at the al-Rasheed had at least one roommate. Residents of the palace chapel had two hundred. Would-be lovers drove or walked to secluded parts of the Green Zone and hoped they wouldn't get caught by a military patrol. Some soldiers claimed that the safest, but perhaps least romantic, place to hook up was in the portable toilets.

4

Control Freak

OUR MOTORCADE ROARED AWAY from the Republican Palace while most CPA staffers were still eating breakfast. In front were two tan Humvees, one with a fifty-caliber machine gun mounted on the roof, the other with a Mark-19 grenade launcher. Each had four soldiers armed with M16 rifles and nine-millimeter pistols. Two more Humvees outfitted the same way brought up the rear. In the middle rolled three GMC Suburbans. The first carried five men with arms as thick as a tank's turret, all wearing tight black T-shirts, lightweight khaki trousers, and wraparound sunglasses. They were equipped with Secret Service–style earpieces, M4 automatic rifles, and Kevlar flak vests with ceramic plates strong enough to stop a bullet from an AK-47. They bore no insignia and kept their identification badges tucked into their flak vests. All of them were ex–Navy SEALs working for a private security contractor called Blackwater USA. They had but one job: protect the viceroy.

I rode with Jerry Bremer in the second Suburban, a custom-built, twelve-cylinder version of the popular American sport utility vehicle, with half-inch-thick bulletproof windows and steel-plated doors that could withstand even a rocket-propelled grenade. Bremer sat in the middle row, next to Dorothy Mazaka, the senior adviser for primary and secondary schools. Two Blackwater guards were up front. I was in the rear, with Bremer's press adviser. The third Suburban contained three television cameramen and two still photographers meant to record Bremer's foray out of the Green Zone.

Bremer was pressed and peppy. Every steel gray hair on his

head was in place. He had awoken at five that morning to jog three miles in the palace garden. After showering and donning his uniform—a navy pinstripe suit with a pocket square, a crisp white shirt, a red tie, and tan combat boots—he dropped into the mess hall for a quick breakfast before going to his office to read the overnight cable traffic, the morning news clippings, and the day's agenda. At eight, he met with his staff in one of Saddam's gilded conference rooms. It was a no-nonsense affair. Participants were encouraged to make their points in thirty seconds or less. Decisions were made as swiftly.

Our first stop of the morning was at an elementary school in southwestern Baghdad. It was June 2003. Bremer had arrived less than a month earlier, and he was keen to demonstrate to Iraqis and Americans that he was no Jay Garner. The way to do that, Bremer and his advisers figured, was to be out and about, in front of the cameras, with the air of a head of state. There were daily photo opportunities and weekly press conferences. There were barnstorming visits across the country in his Black Hawk helicopter. A United Nations Security Council resolution had granted the United States broad occupation power, and President Bush had delegated much of that power to Bremer. He was the boss.

The school visit was another photo op, but it was also a chance to show Iraqis that the occupation authority cared about their needs. Iraqis value education more than almost anything else, and Bremer hoped that a pledge to help fix decrepit schools would persuade ambivalent Iraqis to support the CPA.

The school had two adjoining campuses built in a square, one for boys and the other for girls, with a courtyard in the middle. Mazaka had carefully selected the venue. Saddam's government had stored weapons in one of the classrooms during the American shock-and-awe campaign. The headmistress of the girls' campus supported the American invasion. There was no electricity or running water in either campus. Students relieved themselves behind the building.

"*Salaam alaikum,*" Bremer said as he entered the courtyard. Peace be upon you.

"*Alaikum salaam,*" the teachers replied. And upon you be peace.

The headmistress took Bremer on a tour of the girls' campus. Her 635 students had to be taught in two shifts because there were not enough desks. She showed Bremer several rooms with no lights, fans, or chalk for the blackboard. After the camera crews had finished filming, the CPA team churned out the sound bites.

"Engineers will visit in the next few weeks to work with you to rehabilitate the school," Mazaka said.

"We are committed to helping you," Bremer added.

Then we walked to the boys' campus. Bremer strolled into a classroom of fifteen young boys, none of whom spoke English. The cameramen followed behind.

"We are working to be sure the school is completely renovated," Bremer said. Curriculum revision was a "matter for Iraqis to decide," but he promised that paeans to Saddam would be expunged. An interpreter was summoned. "What's your favorite sport?" Bremer asked the kids. Soccer, one boy said. "Well, we'll bring you some soccer balls in a few days," Bremer said with a flourish. He turned to one of his aides. He said nothing, but his look conveyed the message. *Get someone to get some soccer balls down here pronto!*

By the time he walked out of the classroom, word had gotten out in the neighborhood that the viceroy was there. Hundreds of people crowded around the campus.

"Please help us," one woman shouted in broken English as she gripped the arm of her son. "We are very worried about security. There are people kidnapping our children."

"Security is a big problem," another woman said. "We are scared."

Bremer walked up to the women. "We understand your concerns," he said. "We are working very hard to restore security. We're arresting people every day."

The women nodded, but the crowd didn't give up. Several teachers joined in the questioning.

"Can we have security around the school during the exams?" one asked.

"We'll talk to the military about that," he said.

"Please, mister," another teacher yelled. "We want to be paid."

"We're paying salaries as fast as we can," he said.

Bremer's guards hustled him back into the Suburban. "Good luck," he said as the door closed.

"*Inshallah,*" the headmistress replied.

As we sped off, I asked Bremer if, given the continuing looting, he thought there were enough American troops in Baghdad. Bremer would later write in his book *My Year in Iraq* that in May 2003 he sent Rumsfeld a copy of a draft report by the Rand Corporation, a military-affiliated think tank, that estimated that five hundred thousand troops were needed to stabilize Iraq—more than three times the number of foreign forces then in the country. According to Bremer, Rumsfeld did not respond. Bremer also wrote that he raised his concerns with President Bush at a lunch that month, and again in June in a video link with a National Security Council meeting chaired by Bush. But Bremer never acknowledged these efforts when queried by journalists about force levels at the time.

"I think we've got as many soldiers as we need here right now," he told me. The problem, in his view, was getting Iraqi police officers back on the job. Many still had not reported to their stations.

"You know, it's Saddam who's responsible for this problem," he said. "He released tens of thousands of criminals from prison before the war." But Bremer suggested that they alone were not responsible for the looting; it was a communal reaction to the repression. "When you get here and you see the rage and the pain on people's faces, it's very clear how very evil the old regime was."

"What's your top priority?" I asked.

Economic reform, he said. He had a three-step plan. The first was to restore electricity, water, and other basic services. The second was to put "liquidity in the hands of people"— reopening banks, offering loans, paying salaries. The third was to "corporatize and privatize state-owned enterprises," and to "wean people from the idea the state supports everything." Saddam's government owned hundreds of factories. It subsidized the cost of gasoline, electricity, and fertilizer. Every family received monthly food rations. Bremer regarded all of that as unsustainable, as too socialist. "It's going to be a very wrenching, painful process, as it was in Eastern Europe after the fall of the Berlin Wall," he said.

"But won't that be very complicated and controversial?" I asked. "Why not leave it up to the Iraqis?"

Bremer had come to Iraq to build not just a democracy but a free market. He insisted that economic reform and political reform were intertwined. "If we don't get their economy right, no matter how fancy our political transformation, it won't work," he said.

As we talked, I was struck by his zeal to help the people of Iraq. While Washington remained focused on Saddam's alleged weapons of mass destruction and the human rights abuses of his government, Bremer's emphasis on the future was refreshing. I wondered if his aspirations would change once he heard from more Iraqis, or if he would demonstrate a missionary's unshakable commitment to doctrine from the home country, but those thoughts were soon eclipsed by the viceroy's vision of a new Iraq. It sounded like he wanted America to be as ambitious in Iraq as it had been in Germany and Japan after World War II. After fifteen minutes of conversation, I found myself believing in Bremer.

By then, we had arrived at Baghdad University, a sprawling campus of fifty thousand students on the eastern side of the Tigris River. Bremer was there for a meeting with the deans. Like the elementary school teachers, they complained about security. They also griped about a Saddam-era regulation that prevented professors and deans from traveling abroad. Saddam had been afraid they'd never return. Bremer listened intently. This was something he could fix.

The next day, he issued Coalition Provisional Authority Order Number 8.

> Any statute, regulation, instruction or policy of the for-
> mer Iraqi government that imposes restrictions or proce-
> dures on faculty, employees or students of public
> universities, colleges or other institutions of higher
> education who desire to travel abroad for educational
> purposes is hereby rescinded.

As the viceroy, Bremer need only put down his signature to impose a new law, or to abolish an old one. He wasn't required to consult with Iraqis or even seek their consent. "As long as we're here, we are the occupying power," he said as we drove back to the Green Zone. "It's a very ugly word, but it's true."

As we pulled up to the palace, I asked Bremer if he saw himself as another General Douglas MacArthur, the obsessive, all-powerful American ruler of Japan for three years after World War II.

"I'm not MacArthur," he said as he exited the Suburban. "I'm not going to be anybody but myself."

Shortly after Bremer arrived in Baghdad, Henry Kissinger dropped by to see Colin Powell in his vast, wood-paneled office at the State Department. Kissinger, who had been secretary of state in the 1970s, visited Powell occasionally for wide-ranging chats. The conversation that day soon turned to Iraq, and Powell asked Kissinger about Bremer's management style. Bremer had spent fifteen years working for Kissinger, as his special assistant when he was secretary and then as a managing director of Kissinger's consulting firm.

"He's a control freak," Kissinger replied.

Powell snorted grimly. If Kissinger, a legendary micromanager, thought Bremer was one too, then Bremer had to be a control freak without parallel.

Over at the White House, Rice and her deputy, Steven Hadley, had come to a similar conclusion. In his Oval Office interview with President Bush, Bremer had made it clear that he wanted complete control of the reconstruction and governance of Iraq. He didn't want Washington, as he would say later, to micromanage policy "with an eight-thousand-mile screwdriver."

A few weeks after he landed in Iraq, Bremer informed Hadley that he didn't want to subject his decisions to the "interagency process," a bureaucratic safety valve that allowed the State Department, the Pentagon, the CIA, and the NSC to review and comment on policies. Bremer said he couldn't wait around for approval from the home office. Rice and Hadley were reluctant to remove Bremer's very long leash, but he was the man on the ground. And after the Garner debacle, the White House wanted a take-charge guy. All right, Hadley told him, you don't have to go through the interagency process. But make sure you run the big stuff by us first.

Bremer told confidants in Baghdad he didn't want to "deal with the Washington squirrel cage." He was a presidential appointee who reported to the president through the secretary of defense. He had no obligation to answer to anyone else. When Paul Wolfowitz or Doug Feith sent messages to him, Bremer directed his deputies to respond.

If Washington wanted something from Bremer's underlings, the request had to be approved by Bremer himself. The rule even applied to queries from the White House. Bremer's executive assistant, Jessica LeCroy, dispatched an e-mail to every senior adviser titled, "CPA Senior Advisors May Not Accept Taskings Directly from the NSC/Inter-agency Process."

Bremer didn't view the palace as an American embassy that had a responsibility to report developments on the ground to the State Department and the NSC. He gave his updates directly to the president and Rumsfeld in a weekly video teleconference. Although Powell and Rice usually participated in the calls, they and their staffs yearned for more information. Powell's aides quietly encouraged State personnel working for the CPA to write back-channel memos to the State Department. To avoid detection, the authors used personal Hotmail and Yahoo e-mail accounts to send their dispatches. At the NSC, one of Rice's senior deputies began checking the CPA's Web site every day to see what new orders Bremer had issued. It was faster than waiting to receive reports through official channels.

In his first several months in Baghdad, Bremer had no formal deputy. Although he brought along three veteran diplomats to serve as advisers—one of them, retired ambassador Clayton McManaway, was an old friend, and another, Hume Horan, was one of the State Department's foremost Arabists—their roles were soon eclipsed by a coterie of sycophantic young aides who rarely challenged Bremer's decisions. Most of them had never worked in government before, and those who had were too junior to be beholden to anyone back home. They had no preconceived notions other than an unfailing belief in building a democratic Iraq, and their only loyalty was to the viceroy.

Before he even arrived in Iraq, Bremer sidelined Zal Khalilzad, the White House's envoy working on the political transition. The Afghan-born Khalilzad, who would eventually become an American ambassador to post-occupation Iraq, had spent months interacting with Iraq's exiled political leaders. He knew more about them than anyone else in the U.S. government, and he had their trust. When Bush tapped Bremer to be the viceroy, Powell and others in the State Department assumed Khalilzad would become Bremer's top deputy and would remain in charge of assembling an interim government. But Bremer didn't want someone in Baghdad who had pre-existing relationships with Iraqi leaders. Bremer regarded Khalilzad as a potential threat—someone who knew more about the players and the country than he did, and could disagree with the viceroy's agenda.

Bremer insisted on approving every substantive CPA policy. Staffers sent him thousands of one-to-two-page documents titled ACTION MEMO or INFORMATION MEMO, because he required it. He read them over breakfast, in the late hours of the night, and on helicopters. One staffer remarked to me that history was repeating itself: Saddam signed off on even the most insignificant decisions because nobody else wanted to, lest they mistakenly contradict the dictator's whims. "Nothing's changed," the staffer said. "We can't do anything without Bremer's okay."

Bremer tolerated, and even welcomed, differing opinions in policy debates. But once he arrived at a decision, he expected everyone to get on board. Public questioning of his edicts was verboten. And nobody was above reproach. When Sir Jeremy Greenstock, British prime minister Tony Blair's personal representative in Baghdad, dared to suggest at a meeting with Powell and Bremer that one of Bremer's edicts might have been too severe, the viceroy snapped at him. The message was clear: *Don't contradict me.*

In a 2002 article for *Directors & Boards* magazine, Bremer wrote that in a crisis, "quick decisive action is vital, even though decisions have to be taken in 'fog of war' conditions." He practiced what he preached. Paperwork never languished on his desk. The same staffers who complained about having to write endless memos were amazed at the speed with which Bremer sent those memos back, often with comments scrawled in the margins.

Bremer's article should have been required reading for everyone in Washington dealing with Iraq. "Crisis management plans cannot be put in place 'on the fly' after the crisis occurs," he wrote. "At the outset, information is often vague, even contradictory. Events move so quickly that decision makers experience a sense of loss of control. Often denial sets in, and managers unintentionally cut off information flow about the situation."

In his first few weeks, Bremer slept on a twin-size cot on the palace's second floor, in a room with no air-conditioning. He soon moved into a trailer and, eventually, into his own villa, which Halliburton had furnished with plush sofas, a dining table for a dozen, and a study.

After his morning run, a quick shower, and breakfast, he was in his office by six-thirty, sitting behind a large wooden desk on top of which was a telephone, a Dell computer with a flat-panel screen, and a stack of memos. In front of the desk was an octagonal coffee table, around which aides gathered for meetings. Maps of Iraq's power grid and administrative districts were tacked to the walls. Bremer's bookshelves were nearly empty, save for a guide to the management of financial crises, Rudy Giuliani's book *Leadership,* and a box of Raisin Bran. On one shelf was a framed photo of Bremer finishing the 1991 Boston Marathon in three hours and thirty-four seconds. He was fifty then, and the time was good enough to place him in the top ten for his age group, although he often joked that "those thirty-four seconds"—which kept him from finishing in less than three hours—"I will take with me to my grave." On his desk was a wood carving that looked like a large nameplate. It read SUCCESS HAS A THOUSAND FATHERS. When a visitor noted, during his first weeks on the job, the second line of the aphorism—"failure is an orphan"—Bremer tensed. "There won't be any failure," he said.

He ran the CPA like a mini–White House. At seven-fifteen, he received a security and intelligence briefing. At seven-thirty, he huddled with Lieutenant General Ricardo Sanchez, the top military commander in Iraq. At eight, he gathered his senior staff for the cabinet meeting. Then it was time to play the role of front man for the occupation. He met with Iraqi leaders. He visited hospitals, schools, and power plants. He posed for photos. There was usually a working lunch and formal dinner with prominent Iraqis. Sometimes he played host in the al-Rasheed Hotel, where black-jacketed waiters served four-course meals. Or he traveled to the home of an Iraqi politician. The evenings brought more meetings, more paperwork, and the videoconferences with Washington. He rarely crawled into bed before midnight.

It was clear that Bremer was a workaholic, but other appearances could be deceiving. He often wore blue chinos with his navy pinstripe suit jacket. It looked like a matching ensemble from afar, and it was much easier to launder. He wolfed down the dining hall fare, leading many to conclude he saw food only as fuel. In fact, he was a French-trained chef who had taught cooking classes in Vermont and once spent thirty-six hours making a sauce. His antipathy toward French government policy on Iraq didn't diminish his love of French cuisine, the French language, or the French countryside. He owned a house in France, and he was, perhaps, the only Bush appointee to have studied at the Institut d'études politiques (Sciences-Po) in Paris.

He'd grown up in Hartford, Connecticut, gone to high school at Phillips Academy in Andover, Massachusetts, and graduated from Yale University with a bachelor's degree in history in 1963. He went on to earn a master's in business administration from Harvard University before entering the Foreign Service. His initial posting was in Kabul in the 1960s, where he famously set up Afghanistan's first ski run, in the mountains near the capital, jury-rigging a loop of rope to a tractor motor to pull skiers up the hill. After his studies in Paris, he was stationed in Malawi before returning to Washington, where he was tapped to be Kissinger's special assistant.

Even in his early years, Bremer was work-obsessed. He traveled with Kissinger as he engaged in shuttle diplomacy after the 1973 Arab-Israeli War. That year, during which his daughter, Leila, was born, he was away from home for two hundred days. His wife, Frances Winfield Bremer, eventually wrote a book titled *Coping with His Success: A Survival Guide for Wives at the Top.* "One day he came home and said he had had lunch with Kissinger and David Rockefeller," she told a *Washington Post* reporter in 1982. She'd had peanut butter sandwiches with Leila and their son, Paul. As Jerry described the lunch, Francie, who studied at Harvard, sat there thinking, "I'm as smart as he. Why am I sitting here with peanut butter?" She took a qualifying test for Mensa as well as the Foreign Service entrance exam, passing both, and it "defused the whole question of competition" with her husband. A year after the *Post* article appeared, the family moved to the Netherlands, where the Dutch named a tulip variety after Francie.

In 1994, the couple converted to Roman Catholicism. Jerry, who was born an Episcopalian, had been visibly moved watching television coverage of Pope John Paul II at World Youth Day celebrations in 1993. "Yet another influence was our exposure, while living in Europe, to the historical beauty of a Church of saints, shrines and simple people at prayer, a Church that was truly the bedrock of western civilization," the Bremers wrote in their parish newsletter.

When the White House approached Jerry about going to Iraq, Francie said that the couple "held hands and prayed about it."

In Baghdad, Bremer attended Mass every Sunday in the palace chapel, the vast room adorned with a mural of a Scud missile.

Before departing for Baghdad, Bremer told an associate that he planned to "make some bold decisions." He was coming to bail water from the foundering ship and set it on a new course.

After accepting the job as CPA administrator, he spent a week in briefings and meetings at the Pentagon. He asked for proposals that could be put into action right away. He heard about plans to repair schools and power plants, but he knew Iraqis wouldn't see the results immediately. Shooting looters on sight would be bold, and he even proposed this at his first staff meeting in Baghdad, but he eventually concluded that such an action would be too politically risky. Forming an interim government at once, as Garner was trying to do, would be significant, but Bremer feared that Iraqi political leaders weren't ready. Then he heard about de-Baathification.

Bremer had concluded on his own that senior members of Saddam's Baath Party would have to be purged, and that lower-ranking members would have to renounce their affiliation. He compared it to the de-Nazification undertaken by the Allies after World War II. But he didn't know much about the Baath Party's structure and operations.

Doug Feith's office was armed with answers. In the months leading up to the war, there had been a vigorous debate between the Pentagon and the State Department over the scope of de-Baathification. State advocated a policy of "de-Saddamification," which entailed purging two classes of Baathists: those who had committed crimes and those at the very top of the command structure. Defense had a more expansive view. Influenced by a paper on de-Nazification written by Ahmed Chalabi's Iraqi National Congress, Feith's office advocated a broader purge, as well as a prohibition on rank-and-file members holding senior government posts. The CIA agreed with State, while the vice president's office weighed in with the Pentagon. The dispute eventually made its way to the White House, where the National Security Council tried to strike a compromise: Those in the highest ranks of the Baath Party—about 1 percent of the membership—would be fired from government jobs. Others would be subjected to a South Africa–style "truth and reconciliation process." The plan was included in a PowerPoint presentation for President Bush and other members of his war cabinet—Cheney, Rumsfeld, Powell, and Rice—on March 10. Frank Miller, who chaired the NSC steering group on Iraq, was the presenter. According to two people present in the room, Bush gave the nod.

The decision lacked specificity. The NSC staff didn't know how the top ranks were structured or how many people were at those levels, even though this information was available on the Internet and in academic papers. But "the thrust was clear: treat these people leniently and try to work with them," one of the people at the meeting said.

At the Pentagon, the mechanics of de-Baathification were

handled by Feith's Office of Special Plans, which took its cues from the Iraqi National Congress. Chalabi and other INC officials argued passionately that a wholesale purge of the Baath Party was necessary to demonstrate America's commitment to a new political order in Iraq. If the old guard were allowed to stick around, they maintained, there would be no way a democracy would bloom. The INC advocated extending the ban on government employment to the top four levels of the party to include the rank of *udu firka,* or group member. Below that rank were only regular members and cadets. To people in Feith's office, including *firkas* in the ban comported with the president's decision to fire top-ranking members.

When Bremer held his first substantive discussions with Feith and his staff, de-Baathification was on the agenda. As soon as they outlined the policy as they saw it, Bremer seized on it. It was just the sort of bold decision he wanted to implement. He wrote a memo to Pentagon officials noting that he wanted his arrival in Iraq to be "marked by clear, public and decisive steps to reassure Iraqis that we are determined to eradicate Saddamism."

Feith's office drafted a one-and-a-half-page executive order titled "De-Baathification of Iraqi Society." Not only did it include a prohibition on employing *firkas* and above, but it also banned regular members from "holding positions in the top three layers of management in every national government ministry, affiliated corporations and other government institutions." The document was shown to Pentagon lawyers and to Wolfowitz and Rumsfeld but not to Rice or Powell, who believed the policy drafted in Feith's office did not represent the compromise forged at the March 10 war cabinet meeting. The final draft was printed in the Pentagon and carried to Baghdad by one of Bremer's aides.

Three days after he arrived in Iraq, Bremer dispatched an aide to Jay Garner's office with a copy of the de-Baathification policy. It was going to be the viceroy's first executive order. He planned to issue it the next day.

Garner read it. *Holy Christ,* he thought to himself. *We can't do this.*

He contacted the CIA station chief and asked him to meet him in front of Bremer's office right away. As Garner walked down the hall to the viceroy's suite, he ran into one of the State Department ambassadors and explained what was happening.

"We've got to put a stop to this one," Garner said. "It's too hard, too harsh."

Garner and the station chief barged into Bremer's office.

"Jerry, this is too harsh," Garner said. "Let's get Rumsfeld on the phone and see if we can't soften it."

"Absolutely not," Bremer said. "I'm going to issue this today."

Garner asked the station chief what would happen if the order were issued.

"You're going to drive fifty thousand Baathists underground before nightfall," he said. "Don't do this."

Bremer politely ended the discussion. That night, he summoned all of the CPA's senior advisers to a meeting to outline the order. Several senior CPA staffers knew about the proposed de-Baathification policy and they held out hope of softening it. One of them, Meghan O'Sullivan, who would later become a top political adviser to Bremer, wrote a memo recommending a narrower purge.

After Bremer summarized the order, Steve Browning, the army engineer who by this time was running five ministries, said that Baathists were "the brains of the government . . . the ones with a lot of information and knowledge and understanding." If you sent them home, he said, the CPA would have "a major problem" running most ministries.

Bremer responded tersely that the subject was not open for discussion.

Another CPA staffer, who had been seconded from USAID, asked Bremer if he understood the impact of the policy, her face growing redder as she spoke. Browning thought she was going to burst.

Bremer cut her off. The subject was not open for discussion. Then he walked out.

Browning didn't have to fire anyone. The day after the order was announced, senior Baathists in the Health Ministry stopped coming to work. Eight of the ministry's dozen top posts were now empty. A third of the staff was gone. *This is crazy,* Browning thought as he walked through the ministry's offices. *This is a huge mistake.*

David Nummy, a Treasury Department specialist who was

an adviser to the Finance Ministry, told one of Bremer's aides, "If you want me to enforce this, I'm leaving on the next plane out of the country, because it's ill-advised, and you have no idea how far you're gonna set us back. If those people disappear, we don't have the tools to find the next generation."

Nummy held on for a month, until he left. Then his successors handed out the pink slips.

Tim Carney, the senior adviser to the Ministry of Industry, played the role of dutiful bureaucrat. A few weeks earlier, he had told ministry employees that de-Baathification would be an Iraqi-led process. Now he had to tell them the rules had changed.

From that moment on, most of his work with the ministry was devoted to de-Baathification. He held interminable meetings with the ministry's management, first to explain the policy and then to comb through employment records to identify *firka*s and those above. He eventually removed twelve of forty-eight directors of state-owned companies. The interim minister also had to go. He had been a regular Baath Party member.

"It was a terrible waste of time," Carney said later. "There were so many more important things we should have been doing, like starting factories and paying salaries."

A few weeks into the purge, two travel-weary men in their late thirties came to see him. They introduced themselves as shop floor workers at a fertilizer plant in Bayji. They said they were former soldiers who had been captured by Iranian forces in 1981, the second year of the Iran-Iraq War, and held as prisoners of war for seventeen years. Upon their release, Saddam promoted both men, who had been Baath cadets, to *firka*. They said they didn't care about the rank, but you couldn't turn down a promotion in Saddam's Iraq, not unless you were willing to do another seventeen years in an Iraqi prison. Besides, they said, the promotion had resulted in a monthly bonus of about twenty-five dollars.

"We are poor and the money is important to us," one of the men said.

"Take the *firka* bonus away," the other said. "But just let us keep our jobs. We are not important people. We are just ordinary men."

Carney was so moved by their story that he sent a request to Bremer for a humanitarian exemption for the men. Bremer granted it—six months later.

Around the time Carney submitted his petition, the CPA began to receive reports that ten thousand to fifteen thousand teachers had been fired. They were *firkas* who had joined the party because they were told to do so by the Ministry of Education. The CPA's education advisers were worried. As a result of de-Baathification, entire schools were left with just one or two teachers in some Sunni-dominated areas.

Bremer said that an Iraqi-led de-Baathification commission would handle appeals from the teachers. Then he allowed Ahmed Chalabi to take charge of that commission.

"It was like putting the fox in charge of the henhouse," one CPA official told me. Chalabi sat on the appeals. If the Ministry of Education needed more teachers, they should hire new ones, he said. When CPA officials complained to Bremer, he downplayed the problem and trumpeted the overall importance of de-Baathification.

"It's the single most important thing we've done here," he said. "And it's the most popular thing too."

A few days before the war began, Doug Feith called his predecessor, Walter Slocombe, a centrist Democrat who'd had the job for six years under President Clinton and was well known in the Pentagon. "We'd like you to be the civilian in charge of the Iraqi military," Feith said. "Are you interested?"

Slocombe, who was practicing law in Washington, said yes. During his years at the Pentagon, he had spent countless hours on Iraq policy. Now he had the chance to get in on the action.

He went to the Pentagon for a briefing. The U.S. military hoped that the Iraqi military would sit out the fight but expected a mixed bag. The Republican Guard and the Special Republican Guard, along with the Fedayeen Saddam paramilitary forces, would probably fight, the Pentagon officials said, but the regular army could be persuaded to stand aside. That assessment was shared by the CIA, which had made contact with several Iraqi commanders.

The plan, as Slocombe and Feith envisioned it, was to disband the Republican Guard and the Fedayeen. The four-hundred-thousand-strong regular army would be vetted. Top commanders, who were assumed to be high-ranking Baathists, would be sent home, but midlevel officers and below would be allowed to stay. At the outset, they would be used to clear debris, rebuild infrastructure, and perform basic security functions, such as guarding buildings. Reconstituting them as an army was debated. Some in the Pentagon argued, based on reports from Chalabi and other exiles, that the army was too corrupt and bloated. They proposed forming a new corps.

The plan to disband the Republican Guard but retain the regular army was approved by President Bush and his war cabinet on March 12, two days after de-Baathification was discussed. One of the PowerPoint slides shown to Bush, which he endorsed, stipulated "maintain current status" of the army as one component of the postwar plan. The United States "cannot immediately demobilize 250K–300K personnel and put them on the street," the same slide said. Feith told the president that the army would be used as "a national reconstruction force during the transitional phase."

Everyone seemed to be on board. Feith's office hired two consulting firms with experience in military demobilization to draw up plans to vet and redeploy Iraqi forces. The Central Command dispatched planes over Iraq to drop leaflets imploring soldiers not to fight. One depicted a couple and their five children sitting at a meal. "Stay home in safety with your families," the leaflet stated. "Please do not attempt to interfere with coalition operations or you will become a target."

The Iraqis, by and large, complied. Although several Republican Guard units did put up a fight, many members of the regular army changed into civilian clothes and went home. That's where they were when American tanks rolled into Baghdad, and that's where they were when Bremer landed.

"We're waiting for our orders," Mustafa Duleimi, a rangy lieutenant colonel, told me a few days before Bremer's arrival. "We are ready to help our country."

To Slocombe and Feith, the Iraqi army appeared to have vanished. The bases were empty. Many had been looted by fleeing soldiers or by civilians. A month after the liberation of

Baghdad, General John Abizaid, who would become the overall American military commander in the Middle East, reported in a videoconference that not a single Iraqi military unit remained intact.

Despite the leaflets instructing them to go home, Slocombe had expected Iraqi soldiers to stay in their garrisons. Now he figured that calling them back would cause even more problems. The bases had been looted, so there was no place for them to live. And he assumed that most of the army's rank and file, who were Shiite conscripts, wouldn't want to come back anyway. If there had been proper barracks, only corrupt Sunni officers keen to regain their positions of authority would have returned. As far as Slocombe and Feith were concerned, the Iraqi army had dissolved itself; formalizing the dissolution wouldn't contradict Bush's directive.

Many in the American military and the State Department would later disagree with that assessment, saying that a voluntary callback would have provided a chance to identify and vet promising leaders. And it would have mollified the soldiers, providing them with money and military training. The soldiers could have lived in tent camps while they rebuilt their barracks. Perhaps there would have been a disproportionate number of Sunnis, particularly in the ranks of general officers, but thousands of Shiites, eager for a paycheck, likely would have returned as well.

By the time Bremer was briefed at the Pentagon prior to his departure for Baghdad, Slocombe was receiving reports that Iraqi army officers were trying to claim control of government institutions. Perhaps, Slocombe said to Bremer, you should issue an order formally dissolving the whole structure of the security system, including Saddam's dreaded intelligence agencies. It was a chance for Bremer to make another bold decision.

He told Slocombe to work up a draft order dismantling the security forces. Before he left the United States, Bremer sent a copy of that draft to Rumsfeld with a message saying that this was what he was thinking of doing.

Bremer didn't ask State what it thought, or the CIA, and he didn't consult with Rice or Hadley at the NSC. Most CPA staffers were in the dark too. He did mention it to Iraqi politicians who had returned from exile—Shiites and Kurds who had been victimized by the army. Dissolving the security forces sounded like a great idea to them. If he had queried more Americans and Iraqis, however, perhaps he would have heard the sentiments of people such as Lieutenant Colonel Duleimi, who was ready to return to work in the service of his nation. The army, Duleimi said to me repeatedly, did not exist to serve Saddam. "The army was formed long before Saddam became president. We are loyal not to one man, but to our country."

Eleven days after he arrived in Iraq, Bremer issued CPA Order Number 2, which dissolved not just the army but the air force, the navy, the Ministry of Defense, and the Iraqi Intelligence Service. With the scrawl of his signature, he created legions of new enemies. Many were conscripts, eager for their freedom, but they would be forced to find jobs in a country where 40 percent of the adult population was already unemployed. Tens of thousands of those affected by the order were career soldiers like Mustafa, who knew nothing but military life. They'd get a onetime severance payment, but then they, too, would have to look for work in a land bereft of jobs.

If Bremer had asked the American military for its opinion, he would have heard what Lieutenant General David McKiernan, the first commander of ground forces in Iraq, said the day the order was issued: "There are a large number of Iraqi soldiers now unemployed. That is a huge concern."

Within a week, thousands of angry soldiers converged on the Assassin's Gate to protest Bremer's decision. "We want our jobs back," many of them shouted. Some of the demonstrators carried signs that read WHERE ARE YOUR PROMISES, COALITION FORCES? or RESTUDY THE DECISION OF THE IRAQI ARMY. American troops pushed the crowd back.

"We don't want to be treated this way," Major Saad Omri, the sole breadwinner for a family of six, told me. "If the Americans don't change this policy, there will be trouble. The Iraqis will not tolerate this."

Bremer eventually announced that army officers who were not senior Baathists would receive monthly stipends. He also unveiled plans for a new army. It would consist initially of forty thousand soldiers, all of them infantrymen. There would be no tanks or artillery, and the army would be limited to guarding Iraq's borders. Former soldiers were not guaranteed positions. They'd have to go to boot camp.

By then, however, it was too late. In a land of honor and tradition, the viceroy had disrespected the old soldiers. I never ran into Omri again, but months later, I did see another former soldier who had been at the protest.

"What happened to everyone there?" I asked. "Did they join the new army?"

He laughed.

"They're all insurgents now," he said. "Bremer lost his chance."

A few days before he issued the order dissolving the army, Bremer summoned the exiles for a meeting in the palace. The six whom Garner had met with were there: Ahmed Chalabi and Ayad Allawi, Shiite politicians Ibrahim al-Jafari and Abdul Aziz al-Hakim, and Kurdish chiefs Jalal Talabani and Massoud Barzani. They were joined by a seventh, Adnan Pachachi, a stately Sunni octogenarian who had been foreign minister before the Baathists took power in the late 1960s. The Iraqis were expecting Bremer to talk about plans to hold another national conference, one that would select an interim government. They also expected to be asked to play a lead role.

Since the fall of Saddam, the seven men had acted with the swagger of a government in waiting. Chalabi had returned from London and ensconced himself, with the help of his own militia, in a private club in Baghdad's poshest neighborhood, where he received a procession of visitors who treated him with the deference due an incoming president. Talabani and Barzani, surrounded by dozens of heavily armed guards, came down from Kurdish-controlled northern Iraq to hold court in large hotels. Allawi set himself up in a large Baath Party office near the Green Zone.

After an opening round of pleasantries, Bremer got right to the point. There would be no interim government. The United States was not going to be ending its occupation anytime soon. He was the viceroy, and he was in charge. When one of the exiles interrupted him to say that Iraqis wanted Iraqis in charge, not Americans, he bristled. "You don't represent the country," he said.

It was a breathtaking volte-face in American policy. Bremer and his aides tried to fob the responsibility off on the White House, but it was the viceroy's decision. Before he left Washington, everyone had sought to influence his political plan. Doug Feith had urged him to form an exile-led interim government. Paul Wolfowitz had urged him to hold elections as soon as possible. State had urged him to convene caucuses aimed at promising internal candidates. Bush, however, had urged Bremer to take stock of the situation and make his own judgments. The president told Bremer to slow it down if he needed to. The goal, Bush said, was to create an interim administration that represented the Iraqi people.

Bremer quickly realized that the exiles were too disorganized and too unpopular—signs denouncing Chalabi appeared on walls near the club where he was living—to get the keys to the country. The exiles had promised Garner they would broaden the ranks of their leadership council with women, internals, and Sunni Arabs, but they had failed to do so.

"The idea that some in Washington had—that we would come in there, set up the ministries, turn it all over to the seven, and get out of Dodge in a few months—was unrealistic," one of Bremer's advisers told me. "We gave them a chance. We bankrolled some of them. But they just couldn't get their act together. It was amateur hour."

Bremer's plan, which he outlined to the exiles, was to form a council of twenty-five Iraqis strictly to advise him on policy matters. The members would be a combination of exiles and internals, Arabs and Kurds, Shiites and Sunnis, men and women, and they would be handpicked by the viceroy. He'd have the final say on all matters.

A council made sense—if it was to be a stopgap measure until elections could be held to select a legitimate government. But ambition got the better of Bremer. He told the exiles that he planned to stay in Iraq until a new constitution was authored, national elections were held, and a new government was installed. Although he never articulated a time line, his aides suggested that it could take two years or more.

The exiles huffed and puffed and threatened to boycott the council. In the end, they all participated. On July 13, two months after Bremer arrived, the twenty-five-member Governing Council was unveiled. There were thirteen Shiites, eleven Sunnis, and one Christian, a carefully calibrated acknowledgment that Shiites in the country outnumbered Sunnis. Among the Sunnis, five were ethnic Kurds, five were Arab, and one was an ethnic Turkmen. Three of the members were women, and only nine were former exiles.

While Bremer had been busy choosing council members, Iraq's most influential Shiite leader was looking ahead. Grand Ayatollah Ali al-Sistani was concerned that Americans would seek to influence the drafting of the constitution. His worry may have been piqued by a *New York Times* article about Noah Feldman, a New York University Law School professor who had been hired by the CPA to advise Iraqi constitution writers. Arab satellite television stations picked up the story and added one more detail: *Feldman is a Jew.*

Al-Sistani was a frail man with a black turban and a snowy beard. Born in Iran but schooled in Iraq, he lived in the holy city of Najaf, about ninety miles south of Baghdad. Although he worked out of a modest office on a decrepit alley, he had enormous authority in Iraq to interpret Islamic law in everyday life.

It took months for Bremer and his aides to grasp al-Sistani's clout. Because the ayatollah didn't want to meet with Americans, the CPA was forced to rely on Iraqi interlocutors. The viceroy's first emissary was an Iraqi American from Florida who had been part of the team of Iraqi exiles recruited by Wolfowitz to assist in reconstruction. He was neither a diplomat nor a politician, but a wealthy urologist who had developed and patented a penile implant for impotent men. After receiving reports that the urologist was exaggerating his ties to the White House, the CPA replaced him with a pharmaceutical executive from Michigan. Neither man, Shiite politicians told me later, projected the requisite gravitas.

"If you were occupying Italy, would you send a doctor to visit the Pope?" one of the politicians asked.

Two weeks before Bremer announced the formation of the

Governing Council, al-Sistani made an announcement of his own. He issued a fatwa, a religious decree, stating that Iraq's constitution had to be written by elected representatives. An American-selected drafting committee was "unacceptable," he said, because there was "no guarantee that such a committee will draft a constitution upholding the Iraqi people's interests and expressing their national identity and lofty social values."

Al-Sistani's fatwa was all but ignored by the CPA. "It didn't register," one of Bremer's senior aides said later. "The view was, 'We'll just get someone to write another fatwa.'"

THE GREEN ZONE, SCENE III

Bumper stickers and mouse pads praising President Bush were standard desk decorations in the Republican Palace. Other than military uniforms, "Bush-Cheney 2004" T-shirts were the most common piece of clothing. (Dan Senor, Bremer's spokesman, wore one for a Thanksgiving Day "Turkey Trot" road race in the Green Zone.) CPA staffers weren't worried about employment prospects after Baghdad. "Oh, I'll just work on the campaign"—the Bush-Cheney reelection campaign—several told me.

"I'm not here for the Iraqis," one staffer said. "I'm here for George Bush."

When Gordon Robison, a staffer in the Strategic Communications office, opened a care package from his mother to find a book by Paul Krugman, a liberal New York Times *columnist, people around him stared. "It was like I had just unwrapped a radioactive brick," he recalled.*

The CPA did have a small contingent of Democrats. Most were soldiers and diplomats who, by law, could not be queried about their political leanings. Several of them, led by a young Foreign Service officer, formed a support group called Donkeys in the Desert. They gathered by the pool on Monday evenings to eat pizza and vent about life in the Republican Party Palace. Occasionally, they met in the palace theater to watch movies. Their best-attended screening was of Michael Moore's Fahrenheit 9/11.

The group faced regular harassment from hardcore Republicans, whom the Donkeys dubbed Palace Pachyderms. Their posters were either ripped from the bulletin board or defaced with pro-Republican graffiti. Most Donkeys in the Desert kept their membership a secret, afraid it would turn them into pariahs in the Emerald City. Members of the group received T-shirts emblazoned with the words "A Democratic Iraq," depicting a donkey between two palm trees. But most of them just stuffed the shirts into their duffel bags. One Donkey compared being a Democrat in the Green Zone to being gay in a small town. "If you know what's good for you, you stay in the closet," he said.

They wanted to expand their ranks by reaching out to Rhinos—Republicans in Name Only—in the military, particularly reservists frustrated with Donald Rumsfeld's decision to deploy them for a year or longer. But approaching the Rhinos was risky business. When one Donkey whom I knew poked fun at Bush in mixed company over lunch, his table fell silent. "It was like I had let out a loud fart," he told me later. "They stared for a moment and then looked away."

5

Who Are These People?

BEFORE THE WAR, shops in Baghdad didn't close for the night until ten o'clock. The city's finest restaurants stayed open past midnight. Dinner parties carried on even later. Nobody worried about driving home in the wee hours. If you weren't a dissident, Iraq's capital was one of the world's safest cities.

Few police officers patrolled the streets. Everyone knew that unless you were one of Saddam's relatives or cronies, you could be locked up in Abu Ghraib for even the smallest offense—if you were lucky. Others had their hands chopped off or were sent straight to the gallows.

Most Iraqi police officers, as I would later learn, often spent all day in their stations. They went out on the rare occasion that someone reported a crime. If investigative work or an interrogation was needed, one of Saddam's intelligence services took over.

As the war approached, the National Security Council asked the Justice Department to draw up a plan for the Iraqi police. The job fell to Richard Mayer, then the deputy director of the department's international training program, who had helped rebuild police forces after conflicts in the Balkans and Haiti. He started with a basic assumption: you couldn't be sure if Iraqi police would stay on the job, or if they were any good. Working with international policing specialists at the State Department, Mayer crafted a proposal that called for five thousand international law enforcement advisers who would help to train Iraq's police force. If it became necessary, the advisers would be able to carry out police duties themselves, as international police officers did in Kosovo.

Mayer's plan was presented to the Deputies Committee, an interagency decision-making group chaired by Steve Hadley. The deputies shot it down, based in part on a CIA report that claimed that Iraq's police already had extensive professional training and a Pentagon prediction that the police would keep working after the war. Concern about popular Iraqi perception also played a big role in the plan's downfall. "The view was, 'We can't send this many police officers. It'll look like we're taking over the country,' " one of the participants said. The National Security Council came up with a new plan: the Justice Department would send a small team of law enforcement experts to Iraq immediately after the war to conduct an assessment.

When the experts arrived in mid-May, it was too dangerous for them to drive after sundown. During the day, they traveled in two-vehicle convoys. Everyone was armed. Back then, in the days before the insurgency, the Americans had to be careful, but not as careful as Iraqis. Every Iraqi I knew either had been a victim of a violent crime or knew someone who was. Thugs armed with AK-47s carjacked vehicles at busy intersections. Businessmen were snatched off the street and held hostage until their families paid exorbitant ransoms.

The Iraqi police were almost nonexistent. They had fled their stations as American troops converged on Baghdad. Most were at home. Some had even joined the orgy of looting. The few who had reported back to work were too scared to enforce the law. They had pistols. The criminals had AK-47s.

It didn't take long for the experts to conclude that more than 6,600 foreign police advisers should be sent to Iraq immediately.

The White House dispatched just one: Bernie Kerik.

Bernard Kerik had more star power than Bremer and everyone else in the CPA combined. Soldiers stopped him in the halls of the Republican Palace to ask for his autograph or, if they had a camera, a picture. Reporters were more interested in interviewing him than they were the viceroy.

Kerik had been New York City's police commissioner when

terrorists attacked the World Trade Center. His courage (he shouted evacuation orders from a block away as the South Tower collapsed), his stamina (he worked around the clock and catnapped in his office for weeks), and his charisma (he was a master of the television interview) had turned him into a national hero. When White House officials were casting about for a prominent individual to take charge of Iraq's Interior Ministry and assume the challenge of rebuilding the Iraqi police, Kerik's name came up. President Bush pronounced it an excellent idea.

Kerik wasn't one of those highfalutin criminal-justice theoreticians. His mother, a prostitute, died when he was four. He was a high school dropout. After a stint as a jail warden in New Jersey, he joined the NYPD as a street cop before becoming an undercover narcotics detective and, eventually, the city's corrections chief. He first worked for Rudy Giuliani as his bodyguard. His language was coarse. He shaved the hair on the sides and back of his balding head, and he maintained the thick-necked, don't-mess-with-me physique of a bouncer. Years earlier, when he was appointed to a senior job in the city's Corrections Department, one official told the department's then-commissioner, "Congratulations. You've just hired Rambo."

Kerik had worked in the Middle East before, as the security director for a government hospital in Saudi Arabia, but he was expelled from the country amid a government investigation into his surveillance of the medical staff. He lacked policing experience in post-conflict situations, but the White House viewed that as an asset. Veteran Middle East hands were regarded as insufficiently committed to the goal of democratizing the region. Post-conflict experts, many of whom worked for the State Department, the United Nations, or nongovernmental organizations, were deemed too liberal. Men such as Kerik— committed Republicans with an accomplished career in business or government—were thought to be ideal. They were loyal and they shared the Bush administration's goal of rebuilding Iraq in an American image. With Kerik, there was a bonus: the media loved him, and the American public trusted him.

Robert Gifford, a State Department expert in international law enforcement, was one of the first CPA staffers to meet

Kerik when he arrived in Baghdad. Gifford was the senior adviser to the Iraqi Interior Ministry, which oversaw the police. Kerik was to take over Gifford's job.

"I understand you are going to be the man, and we are here to support you," Gifford told Kerik.

"I'm here to bring more media attention to the good work on police because the situation is probably not as bad as people think it is," Kerik replied.

This is a guy who's just walked in, Gifford thought to himself.

"I'm not here to get into your shit," Kerik told Gifford. He said he didn't plan to stay more than six months. He was a partner in Giuliani's consulting firm, and he told Gifford he made $10,000 a pop from speaking engagements. "I can't afford to be here," he said. But Giuliani and his wife had told him he couldn't say no to the president.

As they entered the Interior Ministry office in the palace, Gifford offered to brief Kerik. " 'I'll sit with you and describe where we are, who the players are, and the process.' And it was during that period I realized he wasn't with me," Gifford recalled. "He didn't listen to anything. He hadn't read anything except his e-mails. I don't think he read a single one of our proposals."

Kerik wasn't a details guy. He was content to let Gifford figure out how to train Iraqi cops to work in a democratic society. Kerik would take care of briefing the viceroy and the media. And he'd be going out on a few missions himself.

Kerik's first order of business, less than a week after he arrived, was to give a slew of interviews saying that the situation was improving. He told the Associated Press that security in Baghdad "is not as bad as I thought. Are bad things going on? Yes. But is it out of control? No. Is it getting better? Yes." He went on NBC's *Today* show to pronounce the situation "better than I expected." To *Time* magazine, he maintained that "people are starting to feel more confident. They're coming back out. Markets and shops that I saw closed one week ago have opened."

When it came to his own safety, Kerik took no chances. He hired a team of South African bodyguards who had worked for Garner, and he packed a nine-millimeter handgun under his safari vest.

The first months after liberation were a critical period for Iraq's police. Officers needed to be called back to work and screened for any Baath Party connections. They'd have to learn about due process, how to interrogate without torture, how to simply walk the beat. They required new weapons. New chiefs had to be selected. Tens of thousands more officers would have to be hired to put the genie of anarchy back in the bottle.

Kerik held only two staff meetings while in Iraq, one when he arrived and the other when he was being shadowed by a *New York Times* reporter, according to Gerald Burke, a former Massachusetts State Police commander who participated in the initial Justice Department assessment mission. Despite his White House connections, Kerik did not secure funding for the desperately needed police advisers. With no help on the way, the task of organizing and training Iraqi officers fell to American military-police soldiers, many of whom had no experience in civilian law enforcement.

"He was the wrong guy at the wrong time," Burke told me later. "Bernie didn't have the skills. What we needed was a chief executive–level person. . . . Bernie came in with a street-cop mentality."

Instead of dwelling on the big picture, Kerik focused on one Iraqi, Ahmed Kadhim Ibrahim. Ibrahim was an Iraqi version of Kerik: a back-slapping man of the people with the instincts of a beat cop who'd attached himself to a powerful patron. Ibrahim's Giuliani was none other than Kerik himself. Ibrahim was only a midlevel officer in Baghdad before the war. (He was jailed in the late 1970s for criticizing Saddam and was subsequently denied promotions because of his refusal to join the Baath Party.) He came to Kerik's attention because he was one of the few police officials who spoke English, albeit badly. But what sealed the relationship was a press conference at which Bremer stood with several Iraqi police officials. At the end, Ibrahim snapped to attention and thanked the viceroy in front of the cameras. Within a few weeks, Kerik named Ibrahim, who had claimed the rank of general, to be chief of investigations and deputy interior minister.

Ibrahim occupied a spacious office in Baghdad's police academy, which served as the police headquarters because the Interior Ministry's building had been torched. His office was decorated with pictures: Ibrahim with Kerik, Ibrahim with Bremer, Ibrahim with Rumsfeld. Like Kerik, he was a master of the sound bite. "We are teaching the police to be new people," he told me once. "They must forget about how they behaved in the past."

With Kerik's assent, Ibrahim assembled a hundred-man paramilitary unit to pursue criminal syndicates that had formed since the war. People working for Kerik had no idea where Ibrahim found his men. Burke, who stayed in Iraq to help with police training after the Justice Department assessment mission ended, suspected that they were part of a military unit or security organization that had been banned by Bremer. But nobody probed. The unit was armed with U.S.-issued M16 rifles and walkie-talkies. While Burke and others on the CPA's Interior Ministry team regarded Kerik's paramilitary unit as a distraction from rebuilding the overall force, Bremer and one of his top aides, a shadowy former army colonel named James Steele, cheered Kerik on.

Steele, who served as Bremer's counselor for Iraqi security forces, couldn't have been more different from Kerik. He was tall and rangy, and he shied away from the spotlight. He rarely spoke to journalists, and when he did, he came off as reserved and disciplined. But he had a taste for adventure in hostile areas. In the 1980s, he led a team of U.S. military advisers to assist the government of El Salvador in its campaign against Marxist guerrillas. A few years later, he was subpoenaed to testify before the Senate about his involvement with Oliver North's program to supply arms to the Nicaraguan Contras from a Salvadoran air force base. He left the army in the 1990s to work for Enron and other private firms. Before the war, Paul Wolfowitz, an old friend, called him up and asked him to serve as the senior adviser to Iraq's Electricity Ministry. But when Steele arrived in Baghdad, Garner put him to work training police officers.

It was never fully clear to people on the Interior Ministry team what Steele did. He traveled outside the Green Zone all the time, often at great personal risk, to visit police stations. But his missions were rarely coordinated with those of other staffers. At times, he seemed to be a lone sheriff trying to pacify Baghdad. One member of the Justice Department assessment team who rode with Steele to a meeting remembers Steele trying to pull over an Iraqi driver.

"Who are you?" the Iraqi shouted.

Steele's sidekick, an Iraqi American police officer from Philadelphia, interpreted for Steele, who brandished his handgun.

"I'm the law," he yelled back. "Pull the fuck over."

Steele and Kerik often joined Ibrahim on nighttime raids, departing the Green Zone at midnight and returning at dawn, in time for Kerik to attend Bremer's senior staff meeting, where he would crack a few jokes, describe the night's adventures, and read off the latest crime statistics prepared by an aide. Ibrahim's Rangers, as Burke called them, did bust a few kidnapping gangs and car theft rings, generating a stream of positive news stories that Kerik basked in, and Bremer applauded. But the all-nighters meant that Kerik wasn't around to supervise the Interior Ministry during the day. He was sleeping.

There were persistent allegations about Ibrahim's Rangers. The military discovered that Ibrahim had been holding on to dozens of rocket-propelled grenades and mortars seized in raids, and a counterfeiting machine that some said was kept in operation. His unit was also accused of torturing nine jailed prostitutes with electrical shocks from a hand-cranked Russian military field telephone.

The raids rankled the U.S. military, which often was not informed when dozens of armed Iraqis, and a few Americans, were driving around the city, knocking down doors. On a few occasions, military units opened fire on Ibrahim's Rangers, mistaking them for insurgents. "There was no coordination," said Colonel Teddy Spain, who commanded a military police brigade in Baghdad. "I wasn't sure what they were trying to achieve other than acting like cowboys out to have a good time."

Several members of the CPA's Interior Ministry team wanted to blow the whistle on Kerik, but they concluded that any complaints would be brushed off. "Bremer's staff thought he was the silver bullet," a member of the Justice Department assessment mission said. "Nobody wanted to question the [man who was] police chief during 9/11."

Nobody, that is, except Jim Otwell, a firefighter from Buffalo who was trying to rebuild Iraq's fire-fighting directorate. Under Saddam, the firefighters had been part of the national police force, and had demanded bribes from those requiring their services. One of Otwell's first priorities was to make the fire directorate an independent entity reporting to the interior minister. Doing so required Kerik's approval, so Otwell tried to set up a meeting to discuss that issue as well as a budget request for new equipment. All but one of the nation's fire stations had been looted. There were no water pumps, axes, masks, or ladders.

Otwell sent Kerik's administrative assistant a note asking for a meeting. He waited two days for a response. On the third day, he went to Kerik's office and confronted the assistant.

"When I tell you I need to see him, and I request to see him, I expect that I be put on his calendar and be made a priority," Otwell said. Kerik, who was standing nearby, turned to Otwell.

"I decide who I want to see, and I make a priority who I want to see, and I'm the only one who directs who I want to see. You understand that? Who do you think you are?" Kerik growled at Otwell, then stomped off.

Otwell eventually went to Bremer, who approved the funding request.

The CPA's Interior Ministry team shared a modest office in the palace with American advisers working with the Justice Ministry. They often brought in Iraqi judges, along with interpreters, for meetings.

"Bob, who are these people?" Kerik asked Gifford one day. "Who the fuck are these people?"

"Oh, those are Iraqis," Gifford replied.

"What the fuck are they doing here?"

"Bernie, that's the reason we're here."

Three months after he arrived, Kerik attended a meeting of local police chiefs at the Convention Center. When it was his turn to address the group, he stood and bid everyone farewell. Although he had informed Bremer of his decision a few days earlier, Kerik hadn't told most of the people who worked for him. He flew out of Baghdad a few hours later.

"I was in my own world," he told me. "I did my own thing."

. . .

The hiring of senior advisers in the Coalition Provisional Authority was settled upon at the highest levels of the White House and the Pentagon. The selection often followed the pattern of Kerik's appointment: a well-connected Republican made a call on behalf of a friend or trusted colleague. Others were personally recruited by President Bush. The White House also wanted a new team to replace Garner's staff, which was viewed as suspect because it had been drawn from the State Department and other federal agencies without any screening for political loyalty.

The rest of the CPA staff was assembled with the same attention to allegiance. The gatekeeper was James O'Beirne, the White House liaison at the Pentagon. He took charge of personnel recruitment, dispatching queries for résumés to the offices of Republican congressmen, conservative think tanks, and GOP activists. "The criterion for sending people over there was that they had to have the right political credentials," said Fredrick Smith, who served as the deputy director of the CPA's Washington office.

Smith said that O'Beirne once pointed to a young man's résumé and pronounced him "an ideal candidate." The young man's chief qualification was that he had worked for the Republican Party in Florida during the presidential election recount in 2000.

O'Beirne's staff asked questions in job interviews that could have gotten an employer in the private sector hauled into court. (The Pentagon was exempted from most employment regulations because they hired people—using an obscure provision in federal law—as temporary political appointees.) Two CPA staffers said that they were asked if they supported *Roe v. Wade* and if they had voted for George W. Bush. One former CPA employee who had an office near the White House liaison staff wrote an e-mail to a friend describing the recruitment process: "I watched résumés of immensely talented individuals who had sought out CPA to help the country thrown in the trash because their adherence to 'the President's vision for Iraq' (a frequently heard phrase at CPA) was 'uncertain.' I saw senior civil servants from agencies like Treasury, Energy, . . . and Commerce denied advisory positions in Baghdad that were instead handed to prominent RNC [Republican National Committee] contributors."

Another CPA staffer told me that when he went to the Pentagon for his predeployment interview, one of O'Beirne's deputies launched into a ten-minute soliloquy about domestic politics that included statements opposing abortion and supporting capital punishment. The staffer didn't agree with what was said, but he nodded. "I felt pressure to agree if I wanted to go to Baghdad," he said.

Mounzer Fatfat, an American citizen of Lebanese descent who applied to be the senior adviser to the Ministry of Youth and Sport, told me he was asked during his interview at the White House liaison's office if he was a Republican or a Democrat. When he replied that he was a registered Democrat, he was asked whom he had voted for in the 2000 presidential election.

"I avoided the question," Fatfat said.

Fatfat, who is a Muslim, was then asked about his religion. "I told them I was a Muslim but that I'm married to a Christian. My children go to Catholic schools. I went to a Catholic school," he said.

Fatfat had a doctorate in youth policy studies. He had worked for the United Nations for four years as the minister of youth and sport in Kosovo. He also had the support of a Republican congressman from Pennsylvania. In the end, he got the job. But he was subjected to five separate interviews at the Pentagon. Most staffers had just one.

When he arrived in Baghdad, his faith once again became an issue. "One of Bremer's top aides asked me what my religion was. When I answered, he was surprised. 'Oh, you're a Muslim?' he said. 'But you're not, like, a terrorist, are you?' "

As the Muslim holiday of Eid al-Fitr approached, a fellow senior adviser asked him exactly when it would begin. Fatfat explained that there was no firm date; it depended on when the first sliver of the moon was seen over Mecca. "He said to me, 'This is stupid. This is in a week and you don't know when you're going to celebrate it?' I was speechless."

As soon as Bremer arrived in Baghdad, he put out the call for more bodies. The CPA needed hundreds more staffers, most of them with special expertise. He and his chief of staff raised the issue in phone calls and video teleconferences. They wrote letters to cabinet secretaries and the White House. On Bremer's first trip back to Washington in late July 2003, he met with Fred Smith and told him that his number one priority was to be sent more people. Smith went around Washington to plead for help. Some agencies, such as the Treasury Department, offered people right away. Others, particularly the Justice Department, blew him off. "What we heard from them constantly was, You know, we've got a war on terrorism at home. We would say, 'This is one of the president's top priorities.' And we just got pushed back, pushed back, pushed back."

Bremer eventually dispatched one of his top aides, Reuben Jeffrey III, to take charge of the CPA's Washington office. His marching orders were to send more people to Baghdad. Jeffrey, a former Goldman Sachs banker, approached the problem like a businessman: he hired two executive headhunters to scour the corporate world for talent. When O'Beirne's staff found out what Jeffrey was up to, they ordered the headhunters to clear out their desks and leave the Pentagon. Jeffrey interceded and managed to keep them in the building, but it was clear he had lost the turf war. The headhunters were told that their roles were restricted to helping interview and process applicants who had already been screened by O'Beirne's staff.

"If you're picking advisers for an administration, I understand perfectly the political connections and all," Smith said. "That's the right of a president in managing a government in peaceful times in the United States. But we were dealing with a crisis situation in Iraq. It's a unique situation and I think you have to throw away all the normal political traditions and ways of doing things and appointing people, and get the best team out there to work the problem."

But that never happened. "I just don't think we sent the A-team," he said. "We didn't tap—and it should have started from the White House on down—just didn't tap the right people to do this job. It was a tough, tough job. Instead we got people who went out there because of their political leanings."

The recruiting process worked fastest when there were no requirements other than political loyalty. When Bremer's budget chief asked for "ten young gofers" to perform administrative tasks, O'Beirne's staff had a list of names at the ready. It included Simone Ledeen, the daughter of neoconservative commentator Michael Ledeen; Casey Wasson, a recent graduate from an evangelical university for home-schooled children; and Todd Baldwin, a legislative aide for Republican senator Rick Santorum. A few days later, all ten received an e-mail from O'Beirne's office. It wasn't until they arrived in Baghdad that they discovered how they had come to the Pentagon's attention: they had all sent their résumés to the Heritage Foundation, a conservative think tank in Washington.

Because of the personnel shortage in Baghdad, six of the gofers were assigned to manage Iraq's $13 billion budget, even though they had no previous financial-management experience. They quickly earned the nickname the "Brat Pack."

Before the war, Baghdad's stock exchange looked nothing like its counterparts elsewhere in the world. There were no computers, electronic displays, or men in colorful coats scurrying around on the trading floor. Trades were scrawled on pieces of paper and noted on large blackboards. If you wanted to buy or sell, you came to the exchange yourself and shouted your order to one of the traders. There was no air-conditioning. The place was loud and boisterous. But private firms were nevertheless able to raise hundreds of thousands of dollars, and ordinary people learned about free enterprise.

After the war, the exchange was gutted by looters. The first wave of American economic reconstruction specialists from the Treasury Department ignored it. They had bigger issues to worry about: paying salaries, reopening the banks, stabilizing the currency. But the brokers wanted to get back to work, and investors wanted their money.

In June 2003, Thomas Briggs, a senior Treasury Department official in Iraq, decided that the CPA's strategy should be pragmatic and modest. He concluded that the Baghdad Stock Exchange, known as the BSE, should be reopened at a new location and allowed to resume operating as it had before the war. The task of making that happen fell to Thomas Wirges, an army reservist who worked on economic issues for the CPA. Although Wirges held the rank of specialist, just a rung above private, he knew what he was doing: he had worked for American Express as a stockbroker. Wirges had been seconded to the CPA at Treasury's request to scout a new location for the BSE.

"Reopening the BSE requires three things: (1) a building, (2) some cell phones, and (3) a blackboard," Briggs wrote in an e-mail to two other Treasury officials. "That is all. BSE management told me that that was all they needed. We do not need to further complicate our lives by insisting on anything else. In my view Treasury does not need to send somebody to Baghdad to accomplish those three things. I thought using Specialist Wirges was a great idea. The accomplishment of those three tasks should be well within his competence."

But when Wirges delved into the BSE's operating procedures, he discovered that the market "was corrupt from head to toe." Basic safeguards to prevent manipulation of the market were nonexistent. Licensing of brokers was spotty. The auditing rules were weak. So Wirges came up with a two-phase plan. He'd reopen the market, but then he'd make structural and regulatory changes to bring the exchange up to international standards of transparency and efficiency. He outlined his plans in a long memo to Thomas C. Foley, the CPA official in charge of Iraq's privatization.

Nobody else had examined the market as Wirges had. When Foley and other senior CPA officials saw his memo, they ordered the market to remain closed while the regulatory issues were addressed. "It became a very, very political hot potato," Wirges said.

Wirges told Foley he needed help drawing up new regulations. Foley promised to have a securities expert sent over. *I'm going to get a high-level person coming in from the New York Stock Exchange or the Securities and Exchange Commission,* Wirges thought. *I'm going to get someone who knows what to do.*

Instead, he got a restless twenty-four-year-old.

Jay Hallen didn't much like his job at a real-estate firm. His passion was the Middle East, and although he had never been there, he was intrigued enough to take Arabic classes and read histories of the region in his spare time.

He had mixed feelings about the war to topple Saddam, but he viewed the American occupation as a ripe opportunity. In the summer of 2003, he sent an e-mail to Reuben Jeffrey, whom he had met when applying for a White House job a year earlier. Hallen had a simple query for Jeffrey: Might there be any job openings in Baghdad?

"Be careful what you wish for," Jeffrey wrote in response. Then he forwarded Hallen's résumé to O'Beirne's office.

Three weeks later, Hallen got a call from the Pentagon. The CPA wanted him in Baghdad. Pronto. Could he be ready in three to four weeks?

"It was really a shock," Hallen recalled. "In my entire life, that was probably the single most life-changing phone call I received."

Despite his eagerness to go, he asked for a few days to consult with his family. After he accepted, he settled in for the monthlong wait. And then he began to have second thoughts. It started with the car bombing of the Jordanian embassy. Then the United Nations headquarters in Baghdad was blown up, killing twenty-two people. "I came within inches of declining [the post]," Hallen said. "I was really on the fence and really tormented about it and had a good week or two of sleepless nights."

His family told him they didn't want him to go. In the end, Hallen decided to take the job. "I knew that this was really one of the few great chances to really crack my life open in a positive way," he said. "I believe strongly that in this life you won't have any rewards unless you take risks."

It wasn't just Hallen who was taking a risk. So was the CPA. Hallen had not followed American stock markets. He hadn't studied economics or finance. But he had had a brief fling as an entrepreneur—onstage. At Yale University, where he majored in political science, he had appeared in a campus adaptation of Dr. Seuss's *The Lorax*. He played the Once-ler, an enterprising scoundrel who chops down trees to produce a polyester-like fabric, transforming a once-beautiful countryside into a barren wasteland. *The Yale Herald* wrote that Hallen's "remarkably pliable, green-painted face creates a sympathetic villain, teaching the audience that the concepts of absolute good and absolute evil are often far too simple for the complexities of the real world."

Upon graduation, Hallen went to work for a private consulting company in Washington. After a year and a half, he sent his
résumé to the White House and was called in for an interview
by Jeffrey—but no job materialized. Hallen held on to Jeffrey's
e-mail address, and when he learned that Jeffrey was working
for Bremer, he tried again.

Before his departure, Hallen was sent to an army base in Virginia for a "training session." He received two immunizations
and a flak vest that lacked the ceramic plates required to stop
AK-47 bullets. He then flew to Kuwait, where he received a gas
mask, a lecture on the four most common types of explosive
devices in Iraq, and a full set of army fatigues (in case of an
attack on the Green Zone, American civilians were told to don
the uniform so they wouldn't be mistaken for "the enemy"). He
visited an amusement park and sampled a "tequila-flavored"
virgin margarita before boarding a C-130 cargo plane bound
for Baghdad.

The day he arrived, he met with his new boss, Thomas Foley.
Hallen was shocked to learn that Foley wanted him to take
charge of reopening the stock exchange.

"Are you sure?" Hallen said to Foley. "I don't have a finance
background."

"It's fine," Foley replied. "Your job is to be the project manager. Your job is to get other people to get things done and contract things out. You will just be the main point of contact."

After the meeting with Foley, Wirges invited Hallen onto
one of the second-floor balconies of the palace. As they gazed
out over the pool, Wirges offered Hallen a Cuban cigar and
told the younger man about himself. He was thirty-nine years
old. He was married and had two children. He had been in
the navy for six years, before he became a private investigator,
and then a sheriff's deputy, and then an insurance agent, and
then a mutual funds salesman, and then a personal financial
adviser.

Hallen told Wirges about his time at Yale and the two jobs
he had had since graduation.

He has no business being here, Wirges thought as Hallen
spoke.

Wirges thought he struck a deal with Hallen. Hallen would

interact with the higher-ups at the CPA. He'd attend the meetings and deliver the briefings to Foley. Wirges would interact with the Iraqis. He'd travel outside the Green Zone and build the exchange.

Five days after Hallen arrived, he sent an e-mail to his family and friends:

> The whole green zone feels like a college campus: roughly the same number of people, everyone does different things during the day, but in the same buildings, and uses the same living, dining and recreational facilities. It's a small world, and there's nothing like a dangerous, uncomfortable, or just plain different environment to create a sense of closeness among people. . . .
>
> The Iraqis I've met are extremely gracious and supportive of us. But then again, any Iraqi that I, as a CPA person, would come in contact with probably would be (unless he's throwing a grenade at me, of course). But seriously, they are a great people, and maybe it's the naïveté of being here less than a week, but I have very high hopes for this country. The reconstruction effort is thriving, so many incredible initiatives going on at once that never get any publicity. The Americans and other coalition people are so dedicated to the cause, and they are very talented and accomplished people, and the Iraqis I've met are very supportive and eager themselves.

Two weeks later, Hallen called Wirges in for a meeting. There'd been a change of plans, he said.

"Jay told me that this was no longer my personal project," Wirges recalled. "I was no longer involved. It's no longer an issue for the army. Have a nice day."

Hallen had a new plan. He didn't just want to reopen the exchange; he wanted to make it the best, most modern stock market in the Arab world. He wanted to promulgate a new securities law that would make the exchange independent of the Finance Ministry, with its own bylaws and board of directors. He wanted to set up a securities and exchange commission to oversee the market. He wanted brokers to be licensed, and listed companies to provide financial disclosures. He wanted to install a computerized trading and settlement system. All in less than four months.

THE GREEN ZONE, SCENE IV

The hand-tossed, wood oven–baked pizzas at Pizzeria Napoli were on a par with anything you'd find in Italy. Napoli was run by Walid Khalid, who had worked at a pizzeria next to the Trevi Fountain in Rome for two years. He returned to Baghdad a month after liberation to introduce real pizza to his homeland. Even if Iraqis didn't warm to pizzas, he figured he'd have more than enough customers among the thousands of Americans who had descended on Baghdad.

He rented space in a strip of shops on Yafa Street, just north of the Green Zone, and set out to create an authentic Italian eatery. He hired bricklayers to build a wood-fired pizza oven. He found a dairy near the Abu Ghraib prison that was willing to make mozzarella according to his specifications. He struck a deal with a farmer who grew the same sort of juicy tomatoes you'd find in Tuscany, and he cultivated basil and oregano in his garden. His brother was recruited to take orders.

Walid looked like a man who spent too much time cooking and eating: He was perpetually covered in flour, and his belly almost popped the buttons on his shirts. He always seemed tired. He woke at dawn to make the dough and the sauce. Then he'd spend the day in front of the oven. He had an air-conditioner, but power wasn't a sure thing. On most days, he'd have three hours of electricity, followed by a three-hour blackout. When there was no power, opening the glass front door didn't cool the place down. It was 130 degrees outside.

I met Walid one day as I was leaving the Green Zone. I was hungry, and his tricolor wooden sign advertising pizza prompted me to stop the car to investigate. He had no tables, just a narrow bar with four seats. He had underesti-

mated the space he'd need; by the time the oven was con-structed, there was no room for anything else.

As he made me a green pepper, mushroom, and onion pizza, he told me about his time in the army, his studies at Baghdad University, his escape to Jordan, his years in Italy. After my first bite, I knew I had found culinary salvation in Baghdad.

Walid sat next to me and nursed a Pepsi. "Where are the Americans?" he asked in halting English. "I build this place that is very good for take-away pizza, but nobody comes."

"They're in the Green Zone," I said. "They have to follow their rules."

"Rules?" he replied. "What do you mean? I am very close to them. They can even walk to me."

Walid had no concept of what life was like on the other side of the walls. He didn't know that the lights were always on, that drivers obeyed the speed limit, that there was an all-you-can-eat buffet in the palace.

6

We Need to Rethink This

IT WAS TWO MONTHS AFTER the fall of Baghdad and I wanted to know why almost all of Iraq's factories were still shut down. When I asked Tim Carney, the senior adviser to the Ministry of Industry, all he would say was, "Go visit the vegetable oil factory."

The State Company for Vegetable Oils was in a blighted industrial park just three miles west of the Green Zone, at the end of a street lined with automobile repair shops. Dirt caked the floor, and a thick layer of oily crud coated the rusted machinery. The windows were shattered, and the lights were out. A genial man in a navy blue boiler suit informed visitors that the factory manufactured cleaning products as well as tins of cooking grease. But nobody, it seemed, used any of the factory-made soap on the factory itself.

The elevator wasn't running, so I walked up three flights of stairs to meet with Faez Ghani Aziz, the company's director general. Aziz, an animated man with thick black hair and a broad grin, shook my hand and immediately apologized for the out-of-order elevator. "There's no power," he said. "Nothing is working now."

We sat in a glass-walled office that overlooked what appeared to be a large laboratory. The lights were out in the entire building. The machines were idle. Carney had said the company employed four thousand people. I couldn't see more than a dozen milling about.

Aziz, a fifty-three-year-old soil chemist, explained that the office in which we were sitting wasn't really his. It belonged to the manager of the product-testing lab. Aziz was there because the company's administration building had been looted. Everything had been taken—computers, furniture, files, pallets of soap, even the light switches in the walls.

He summoned tea. (An office boy had set up a gas burner in the stairwell to boil water. The office could make do without power, but not without tea.) As we waited for it, Aziz pulled a glossy, tri-fold product brochure from his desk. There were photos of a tin of al-Raie cooking oil, a bottle of Yasmeen shampoo, a can of Anbar shaving cream, and a bar of al-Jamal soap. All the pictures were yellowed and faded. It was clear that the brochure had been printed years ago, in the days when the company exported products to Syria and India.

"We are a good investment opportunity," Aziz told me.

I had introduced myself as a journalist, but he obviously thought I was an investor. When I repeated that I was there to write about his company, not pour money into it, he sighed and said, "We are facing a very difficult future."

The dormant production line below his office constituted one of six factories owned by the vegetable oil company, he explained. The others produced packaging materials, detergents, and sunflower oil. The company itself was one of forty-eight businesses owned by the Ministry of Industry. Aziz claimed that the company had cleared a $3.3 million profit in 2002, but when he described how the government subsidized state-run factories, it became evident that his woes were worse than a dirty building. In fact, the company was grossly unprofitable. The books looked good only because the company had received its raw materials for next to nothing: due to a government edict valuing the Iraqi currency for official imports at the rate before the 1991 Gulf War—when one dinar was worth more than $3, instead of the prevailing rate of 2,000 dinars to the dollar—the vegetable oil company had to pay just $1 for each $6,000 worth of imported products. The Finance Ministry made up the difference. Electricity was free. The company didn't have to pay pensions either; the government took care of that as well.

All that financial assistance didn't result in decent products. The fifty-year-old production line, built by Russian engineers, churned out goods that appeared to have been made in the communist, you-can-have-any-car-so-long-as-it's-black factories of the former Soviet Union. When I asked Iraqi friends why they bought al-Jamal soap and Yasmeen shampoo, the answer was the same: "What choice did we have?" For years, Iraqi-made consumer goods enjoyed a virtual monopoly in the local market. Even when the government began allowing more imports, the vegetable oil company's products were far cheaper than those of foreign competitors.

Aziz wanted to modernize the company, but under Saddam, the Ministry of Industry refused to allow him to solicit foreign investment or enter into a joint-venture partnership. He was told from which suppliers to purchase raw materials. Price didn't matter. Nor did quality. The operative question was whether the country that was selling the goods supported Saddam. "If somebody from Syria wanted to sell us something, even if he didn't have a competitive price, they made a deal with him," Aziz said.

Even if Saddam's government approved, that didn't mean Aziz got what he wanted. The purchase of modern soap-making equipment from Germany, to replace half-century-old machines Aziz called "primitive," was held up by a United Nations sanctions committee because of concerns that the technology could be used in the manufacture of biological or chemical weapons.

Aziz also didn't need four thousand employees. But he couldn't fire any of them. Every year, the ministry would send over a few dozen more. Some were college graduates promised lifetime government employment. Others had Baath Party connections. Because only about a thousand workers were actually required to run the factories, the rest sat around and drank tea. Some didn't even bother to show up for work.

But those rules no longer applied. Nor could Aziz count on the same fat subsidies. He knew the score. "We were not very efficient," he said. "If we do not change, we will not survive."

He paused for a moment, then continued in a near whisper. The company, he said, should be privatized. Perhaps it should be sold to the employees, or to a private investor. Having the government own a vegetable oil company makes no sense.

As I got up to leave, he admonished me not to utter a word about privatization to the workers. "It's a very sensitive subject," he said. Iraqis lucky enough to get a job with a state-run company assumed they were guaranteed employment until retirement. Any suggestion that the safety net had disappeared along with Saddam had the potential to inflame the workforce. "You can't solve one problem by creating a new problem," he said. "You have to prepare the people for the decision."

The next time I saw Tim Carney, over a lunch of grilled lamb and cold beer at Nabil's, I asked him about the vegetable oil company and privatization. He said it made no sense over the long run for the Iraqi government to own factories that made cooking oil, carpets, paper, batteries, and leather shoes. The companies had to be sold off. Iraq didn't even need a Ministry of Industry. But Carney figured the decision of what to sell, when to sell, and for how much rested with the Iraqis. The ministry's management agreed. So did the political leaders angling for a role on the Governing Council.

Because Iraqis were in no position to make those decisions right away, Carney's first priority was to get the ministry—and all of its companies—working again. So what if the factories were inefficient? He assumed it would do the economy good to get people back to work. And he thought it would also help with privatization: a factory that was actually producing something, even if it was third-rate shampoo, would fetch a higher price than a shuttered one.

Carney knew he wasn't the right guy to tinker with the nuts and bolts of restarting factories. He was an ambassador. Foreign policy was his thing, not economic policy. At the time, he had only one person working for him, a lieutenant colonel in the army reserves named Brad Jackson, who was no expert in balance sheets and cash-flow statements. Jackson did, however, have valuable real-world experience. Back home, in upstate New York, he had run the industrial development agency for Franklin County.

As Carney was beginning to despair, Jackson announced that help was on the way: a high-powered consultant named Glenn Corliss would be joining their team. Jackson said that Corliss had worked on Wall Street and was an expert in rescuing distressed companies. And he understood corporate accounting.

"Great," Carney said. "Sounds like just the guy we need."

.   .   .

Corliss arrived in the Republican Palace wearing an Armani suit and black loafers. He told people he worked for JPMorgan and Fidelity Investments. He had the self-confidence of a general.

It was months before anyone other than Jackson knew the real story.

Corliss was everything he claimed: he had worked for Fidelity, as an analyst, and at JPMorgan's private equity division, where he had invested in industrial companies; he had experience in venture capital and had specialized in restructuring failing businesses.

His secret was that he was an army reservist. He was not a big-shot lieutenant colonel like Jackson, or even an officer. He was a specialist—just one rank above private.

In early 2001, Corliss had begun to feel restless on Wall Street. He had a lucrative venture-capital job, but trying to further enrich already wealthy investors was losing its appeal. International development sounded intriguing. He began to think about joining the World Bank or the International Monetary Fund or the U.S. Agency for International Development. One friend said that Corliss could sign up for a part-time job to be on a "sort of SWAT team that runs into a disaster area and helps rebuild the economy."

"Well, geez, that sounds perfect," Corliss responded. "Who runs those teams?"

The army, his friend said, explaining that the military had civil-affairs teams comprised of reservists who performed post-conflict reconstruction.

"Do you wear a uniform and carry a gun?" Corliss asked.

"Yeah, you do," the friend replied. "But you're not kicking down doors. You're helping to rebuild."

Maybe I could do this, Corliss thought. But he wanted to contemplate it. He didn't rush out to an army recruiting center.

Then came September 11. Corliss was in New York City. He enlisted within a few weeks. He didn't want to spend months training to be an officer. He just wanted to work on development projects in support of the new war on terrorism.

Before his formal enlistment and boot camp, he was allowed

to spend a few weekends observing civil-affairs soldiers from New York as they drilled. It was there he met Brad Jackson.

Jackson was the deputy director of the economics and commerce team at the civil-affairs command where Corliss was sent. When Jackson went through the files of new recruits, Corliss's stood out—not because of his professional experience but because of his place of birth: Pittsfield, Massachusetts. Jackson was from the same city. He called Corliss into his office.

"What the hell are you doing?" Jackson said to Corliss. "You haven't taken a dime from Uncle Sam. Get the hell out of this contract while you can."

A junior enlisted person, Jackson said, "will never get to do the kind of work you're talking about. You have far too much experience to be an enlisted person."

"It's just the ticket to the show," Corliss replied. "Once you get in there, I think anyone that's creative, a go-getter, will be able to do the kind of work I want to do."

"No, Glenn," Jackson responded. "You don't understand the army system."

"Well, that's okay," Corliss said. "I'll take my chances."

Two weeks after the fall of Baghdad, Corliss found himself on the grounds of a dusty, sprawling Iraqi army base fifty miles north of the capital. His orders were to coordinate with nongovernmental organizations. But the few NGOs operating in Iraq at the time were in Baghdad. With nothing to do, he was close to being relegated to kitchen patrol or, even worse, guard duty. When you're one rank above private, no matter if you were earning six figures on Wall Street two months earlier, you don't have any say in what you do.

At the time, Jackson was in Baghdad, as part of an advance party of civil-affairs soldiers working with Jay Garner's ORHA. When he was assigned to work with Carney in resuscitating the Ministry of Industry, he knew he could use Corliss's help. A search of deployment rosters revealed that Corliss was elsewhere in Iraq. So using all the political capital he could muster, Jackson set about to get Corliss reassigned to ORHA. It took more than a week of paperwork and cajoling before Corliss got the orders to ship out for the palace.

Once he arrived in the Green Zone, Jackson issued one of the very few official orders he would give Corliss: "Get the hell out of your uniform. Put on your civilian clothes, and let's pretend you're some high-powered consultant."

"What's the big deal?" Corliss asked.

"If you wear your uniform," Jackson said, "you won't get a lot of respect. You'll have to get people coffee."

Corliss's youth and stature didn't help matters. Thirty years old and five foot seven, he looked like a fresh-faced private sent over from Central Casting. In uniform, nobody would have believed he had worked on Wall Street.

Maintaining the pretense required vigilance. Corliss's e-mail account initially identified him to recipients as "Corliss, Glenn (E-4)," the code for specialist. When Jackson saw this, he ran over to the computer guys and ordered them to remove the E-4. Another time, a personnel roster listed Corliss as the driver for the CPA Ministry of Industry team. Most E-4s in the palace were drivers, so someone had assumed that Corliss was one, too. Again, Jackson got it changed.

Months later, when the top U.S. commander in Iraq ordered that all military personnel had to wear their uniforms, Corliss still bent the rules. He'd wear his desert camouflage—on the collar was an upside-down triangle with a curved top to identify him as an E-4 specialist—when eating or walking to his sleeping quarters. But when he had meetings in the palace, he would rush into the bathroom and change into a suit.

After an initial round of introductions in the palace, he got his first assignment. Peter McPherson, Jerry Bremer's economics czar, wanted an analysis of all 150 factories owned by the Ministry of Industry's forty-eight companies, in order to determine which were the most viable, and thus most deserving of financial assistance. The task fell to Corliss, the one guy with the skills to chew through lots of numbers and work up a big spreadsheet.

"This was the very first evidence that I knew that these guys had no idea what they were talking about or what they were in for," he told me. "They said, okay, you have a hundred fifty factories. We want you to evaluate all of them."

"I said, 'Okay. Well, where's my staff?' "

"Well, it's you," Jackson told Corliss.

"Okay. Where's the management of these companies?"

"Well, we fired most of the management because of de-Baathification."

"Okay. Where are the financial statements?"

"There are no financials."

"Okay. What do you know about the companies?"

"Nothing. We have a list of the names. Here are the names."

"How much time do I have?"

"You have two weeks."

Corliss was stunned. Jackson was sympathetic. "This is kind of silly," he told Corliss. But he said it was useless to protest. "If you go and try to explain it to them, they won't care," Jackson said. "They'll say, 'You have what you have.' "

For the next two weeks, Corliss slept no more than a few hours a night. He begged ministry officials and factory directors for whatever records had not been looted. The documents he received, which had to be translated from Arabic to English, were so shoddy that he concluded that nobody at the ministry had ever taken an accounting class. Among other outlandish claims, the ministry's financial statements asserted that every one of the 150 factories was profitable. When Corliss learned about the Finance Ministry's policy of subsidizing imports for state-run businesses at the old exchange rate, he raised the issue with officials at the Ministry of Industry.

"I tried to explain to them that it was an apparition, that it was simply a faulty exchange rate that was funded by oil dollars," Corliss recounted. "They didn't understand that, because these guys don't exactly have a background in understanding international currencies. They would constantly say to me, 'I'm profitable. It's not my fault that you guys aren't valuing our dinar appropriately. Our dinar is worth three U.S. dollars. I am profitable.' When you say it now takes two thousand dinars to buy a dollar, they say, 'No, it doesn't. A dinar is worth three dollars. You guys are just screwing up our currency. Adjust the currency back.' But you can't just adjust the currency back. And then you get into a back-and-forth, and you're trying to explain macroeconomics to someone who has never even heard anything about that. They were convinced, truly convinced, that they were all profitable. The only problem was the stupid currency, 'which you Americans screwed up.' "

The exchange provided Corliss with an insight into the way ordinary Iraqis and even senior ministry officials viewed their economy. Bremer and McPherson had just begun to convene meetings on Monday evenings with a select group of Iraqis, many of them former exiles, to talk about economic reform. But what Bremer, McPherson, and much of the rest of the CPA's economic team failed to grasp was that the mostly Western-educated participants were by no means representative of Iraqi society. Their desire for a fundamental economic restructuring—abandoning Saddam's centrally planned, socialist welfare state for a globalized, free-market system—had little resonance on Iraqi streets. To most Iraqis, even those who would later become ardent critics of the American occupation, the political side of the equation was a no-brainer: Saddam was a brutal tyrant who had to go. When it came to economics, however, there was no such consensus.

Under Saddam's Baathist government, state-owned factories produced a plethora of goods including school notebooks (which were so substandard that the pages fell out), car batteries (which weren't much better), and leather coats (which were favored by members of the secret police). Government jobs, either in a factory or a ministry or in the security services, were plentiful and guaranteed you a salary for the rest of your life. Paychecks were low, but the cost of most goods and services was subsidized by the government. Gasoline was sold for less than a nickel a gallon. Nobody paid for electricity, not even the state-owned factories that guzzled hundreds of megawatts. Every family received monthly food rations from the state. Education, even college, was free. So was health care. The price of fertilizer was so heavily subsidized that Iraqi farmers would often sell their annual allotment in Jordan and Syria instead of using it to grow crops; doing so took a truck and a few days, and it netted more money than spending months toiling in the fields.

Iraqis experienced an unparalleled degree of affluence because of the country's plentiful oil revenue. Before the 1991

Gulf War bankrupted and isolated the country, government-run department stores managed by the Ministry of Trade sold Italian loafers, Pierre Cardin ties, and Breitling watches at a fraction of their retail price anywhere else in the world. International tickets on Iraqi Airways were subsidized, as were imported Volkswagens, Volvos, Mercedes-Benzes, and Chevrolets. In the 1970s and even into the early 1980s, before the apex of Iraq's eight-year war with neighboring Iran, Iraq's health-care and university systems were regarded as the best in the Arab world. Tens of thousands of Egyptians, Somalis, Pakistanis, and Indians moved to Iraq to work on massive infrastructure projects: the construction of a six-lane highway to Jordan, luxury hotels in Baghdad, bridges across the Tigris and Euphrates rivers. "We had a very, very good life," Faez Ghani Aziz, the director of the vegetable oil factory, told me. "We were the richest country in the Middle East."

Iraqis blamed their financial meltdown on Saddam and the West. Their leader drained the national coffers—and put the country tens of billions of dollars into debt—by waging war with Iran. Then he had the lunacy to invade Kuwait, which resulted in debilitating United Nations sanctions that cut off Iraq from the world. In the eyes of the Iraqis, America was also at fault because it refused to support lifting the sanctions, despite widespread reports that the sanctions were strengthening Saddam while impoverishing his people. But all along, there was little, if any, recognition among ordinary Iraqis that their economic system was rotten to the core. After all, it was the same system that had given them a good life a generation earlier. The thinking among those Iraqis was that if Saddam and the sanctions were gone, they'd be wealthy again.

"When I told them, 'No, it's not just Saddam but your entire economic system that's screwed up,' they looked at me like I was from Mars," Corliss said. "They must have been thinking to themselves, *Who is this crazy American?*"

Like Carney, Corliss believed that the Iraqi government should get out of the business of running factories. He, too, thought that Iraq didn't need a Ministry of Industry. But Iraq was still a volatile country. The three-week war to topple Saddam and its immediate aftermath had just ended, but the country was far from calm. American soldiers were being shot at. Thousands of former Iraqi soldiers had recently conducted their march across the Tigris to the Assassin's Gate to protest Bremer's decision to disband the Iraqi army. Corliss knew that privatization would have to wait. The sale of factories to private investors would certainly result in layoffs. Who would keep four thousand workers at the vegetable oil company when the director himself had admitted that it only needed a thousand? The last thing Corliss wanted to do was add to the ranks of the unemployed.

Corliss also worried that the state-owned enterprises would be undervalued if they went on the auction block right away. He compared the process to trying to sell an old house: investing in a new paint job and some renovations can increase the sale price well beyond the cost of the improvements. He outlined his views in an e-mail to Jackson:

> Let me note that I am a FIRM believer that privatization
> is the best route for almost all enterprises. My issue is
> the pace at which this should happen. Back to wearing
> my investor cap: if I am going to invest today in a com-
> pany that just went through all of those setbacks, I'm not
> going to be writing a very big check. The return I would
> demand for the risk I'm being asked to take would turn
> the net present value of future cash flows into a very
> small number. Using "public" money to get potentially
> viable entities back on their feet will allow us to get a
> much better price for the Iraqi people when the compa-
> nies do privatize. In short, you shouldn't sell low.

The path forward seemed clear enough to Corliss. At the end of the two-week analysis, he concluded that thirteen of the ministry's forty-eight companies had the most promise of actually turning a profit and thus should receive immediate attention. They would need money and management consultants to help with restructuring. He wasn't as sure about the others. Some might be salvaged over time. Others were so grossly unprofitable, their equipment so antiquated, their products so terrible, that they would never find a buyer. Those companies would have to be shut down. A decision would have to be made about the workers. Corliss thought it would be cheaper to pay the employees of those companies in perpetuity than to plow money into failing enterprises.

The vegetable oil company was not among the thirteen with promise. Corliss wasn't sure if it could be saved. He wasn't willing to write it off, but if the company was to survive, Aziz, the director, would need to find a way to turn a profit without the lucrative import subsidies. Other firms had far more potential. Among them were companies that produced cement, fertilizer, phosphate, and petrochemical products. Also on Corliss's list was an outfit called the al-Faris Company.

The al-Faris Company was located on Baghdad's western fringe, near the now-infamous Abu Ghraib prison. The operation consisted of a modest, one-story office, which had been stripped bare by looters, and a cavernous assembly line housed in a giant structure the size of several jumbo jet hangars. When I visited al-Faris, the company's director, Abdulrahman Azzawi, greeted me in a conference room furnished with a white folding table and a dozen plastic chairs. "It's all we have now," he said. As soon as I told him I was an American, he waxed on about his love of the United States. "If you have a good idea and you work hard, you can make a million dollars in America," he said. "I like that."

Although he had received his doctorate in Britain, Azzawi said he had been a member of the American Society of Mechanical Engineers until the 1991 UN embargo. "The American group is the best," he said. He intended to renew his membership as soon as the Iraqi postal service resumed mail delivery. Unlike with the State Company for Vegetable Oils, it was not immediately clear what al-Faris made. When I asked, Azzawi glared at me. "You have not heard of us?" he said. When I replied that I had not, he explained how his company had been repeatedly searched by UN weapons inspectors. Somebody apparently thought the giant building might be a good place to hide Scud missiles. "We had nothing to do with the mass-destruction weapons," he insisted. "Maybe other companies, but not us." I told him I wasn't interested in hidden missiles but in what his factory produced. Water-purification systems, he said, and heavy equipment for the oil industry. "There is very high demand for our products," he said.

The tap water in Baghdad had once been safe enough to

drink, but years of sanctions had restricted Iraq's ability to import chlorine for treatment plants, which eventually shut down. The municipal water was now pumped directly from the foul Tigris. New purification systems would be a hot item.

But nothing was rolling off the al-Faris assembly line. Most of the 1,200 workers were at home, save for a few guards and factory managers. The problem was electricity and raw materials. There were none.

Azzawi had a solution. He had $1.5 million in the bank. If the banks opened and he got authorization from the Ministry of Industry to access the company's funds, he would order a one-megawatt generator. He'd also import raw materials directly—at the prevailing exchange rate. "I will talk to my suppliers and work out a deal with them," he declared. "I just need my money."

Corliss thought it was a great idea. It sounded simple enough. Jackson and Carney supported it too. The only problem was that neither Corliss nor Jackson nor Carney had the final say. That power rested with Peter McPherson.

I met Peter McPherson a few days after my trip to al-Faris. I was escorted to his office on the second floor of the palace by a perky young CPA press minder—someone from the public-relations office was supposed to accompany reporters in the palace at all times—but to my surprise she left as soon as McPherson began talking. *Not a good sign,* I thought. Either he's really on message or he's really, really boring.

McPherson had taken a leave of absence as president of Michigan State University to serve in Iraq. Instead of the Oxford shirts favored by other senior CPA staffers, or the polo shirts worn by junior personnel who often traveled in the city, he was in a ratty green T-shirt and rumpled, baggy chinos. Bald and bespectacled, he had a modest spare tire. His skin showed no signs of a tan. In his mouth was an unlit cigar.

I reminded myself that despite his appearance, McPherson was far from an unkempt academic. He had directed the U.S. Agency for International Development for seven years under President Ronald Reagan. He had been a senior vice president at Bank of America. He had worked for the Internal Revenue

Service. And he had served as a special assistant to President Gerald Ford. It was in the Ford White House, where he was deputy director of the personnel office, that he forged a close professional relationship with Dick Cheney, who was then Ford's chief of staff.

A self-described conservative with an unshakable faith in the power of the free market, McPherson believed that the best way to promote economic development was through a vibrant private sector. He had never worked in the Middle East or in a post-conflict environment, but when a senior Treasury Department official called and offered him the job of CPA economic policy director, he didn't hesitate in accepting. Bremer was bringing democracy to Iraq. McPherson's mission, he was told, would be to bring capitalism.

The neoconservative architects of the war—Wolfowitz, Feith, Rumsfeld, and Cheney—regarded wholesale economic change in Iraq as an integral part of the American mission to remake the country. To them, a free economy and a free society went hand in hand. If the United States were serious about having democracy flourish in Iraq, it would have to teach Iraqis a whole new way of doing business—the American way.

In the months leading up to the war, while the State Department and Pentagon were feuding over how political authority should be devolved to Iraqis, USAID and the Treasury Department agreed to collaborate in promoting aggressive free-market reforms sought by the neoconservatives. After months of secretive discussions, USAID and Treasury officials came up with an ambitious plan for economic transformation. The plan was detailed in a confidential, 101-page document titled "Moving the Iraqi Economy from Recovery to Sustainable Growth," which specified the work that USAID wanted a private contractor to perform. The goal, according to the document, was to lay "the groundwork for a market-oriented private sector economic recovery." The plan envisioned the sale of state-owned enterprises through a "broad-based mass privatization program," the establishment of a "world-class exchange" for trading stocks, and "a comprehensive income tax system consistent with current international practice."

Iraqis, like many of their Arab neighbors, were wary of full

foreign ownership of domestic businesses and the privatization of the oil industry. But USAID and Treasury required the
contractor to promote investment laws that would be "blind as
to whether the investor is from that country or elsewhere."
The contractor also was to promote "private sector involvement . . . especially in the oil and supporting sectors." Notably
absent from the thick plan was much reference to consultation
with Iraqi leaders or even an interim Iraqi government.
USAID and Treasury knew what Iraq needed.

In the days after Saddam's government was toppled, if
you asked any Iraqi—from a man on the street to one of the
formerly exiled political leaders—what the country's biggest
economic problem was, the response was always the same:
unemployment. Nobody could be sure how many people were
out of a job, but it seemed that more than half of working-age
men were unemployed; estimates pegged unemployment at
about 40 percent. But the USAID-Treasury document outlined
no program to create jobs. The words *tax* and *privatize* were
mentioned dozens more times than the word *employment.*

USAID was helped in developing the plan by BearingPoint
Incorporated, a Virginia-based consulting firm. When it came
time to award the contract, valued at $79 million for the first
year, USAID chose BearingPoint. USAID's inspector general
subsequently scolded the agency for its handling of the contract, writing in a scathing report that "BearingPoint's extensive involvement in the development of the Iraq economic
reform program creates the appearance of unfair competitive
advantage." But the controversy didn't weaken the relationship
between USAID and BearingPoint. In September 2004, the
agency awarded the company a follow-on contract worth as
much as $225 million.

McPherson wasn't involved in drafting the 101-page plan.
But he didn't find anything in it to quibble about. His vision
for economic reform in Iraq hewed to the same philosophy.
Instead of using government money to create new jobs in an
Iraqi version of the New Deal, he favored a supply-side strategy:
reduce the role of government industry through privatization,
eliminate subsidies for electricity and fuel, cut tariffs, lower
taxes, promote foreign investment, and enact pro-business

laws. Those changes, he reasoned, would draw multinational firms, and even wealthy Iraqis, to set up businesses in Iraq that would create jobs for the unemployed. The key to economic growth, he believed, was "the development of a robust private sector."

"We need to shrink government employment," he said to me in that first interview, "not increase it."

McPherson landed in Baghdad a month after the city's liberation. He was eager to have BearingPoint get to work as soon as possible, but the company's consultants were not scheduled to land for several weeks. To McPherson, time was of the essence. He wanted to move forward right away with privatization and the elimination of subsidies. The faster you addressed those problems, he reasoned, the faster you would achieve economic growth. He also had a personal desire for alacrity. He had asked Michigan State's board of trustees for only 130 days of leave.

McPherson assembled his own brain trust. He brought over the deputy general counsel from the Treasury Department and two bright government economists, one from the White House's Council of Economic Advisers and the other from the Federal Reserve Bank of Boston. But McPherson didn't have the staff to tackle privatization. He had to rely on Corliss and Jackson.

As soon as he arrived, even before asking for the analysis of the state-owned enterprises that Corliss would perform in two weeks, McPherson announced his intention to move forward with privatization. At the Ministry of Industry, Carney, Jackson, and Corliss were still trying to understand how the place worked. On the CPA economics team, everyone was figuring out how to pay salaries to hundreds of thousands of government employees. "Here comes McPherson wanting to talk about privatizing state-owned industries," one member of the economics team said. "It struck us as so irrelevant."

There was also a legal roadblock. Article 43 of the second section of the Hague Convention of 1899—the first set of international treaties that attempted to create laws of warfare— requires an occupying power to respect all the laws of the occupied country except when it is necessary to promote public order and safety. Although the United States had the blessing of the United Nations Security Council, in Resolution 1483, to promote "economic reconstruction and the conditions for sustainable development" in Iraq, CPA lawyers were generally opposed to the sale of Iraq's industries, on the grounds that such sales violated the Hague Convention. What if a sovereign Iraqi government objected to privatization? You couldn't reverse the sale of a factory. Better to leave it to a future Iraqi administration, the CPA lawyers said.

Even more significant at the time was a practical challenge. There was no way Corliss, Jackson, and Carney could do it by themselves. Financial records would have to be scoured, offers posted and evaluated, financing arranged. When the trio met with a team of Germans to discuss how factories in the former East Germany had been privatized, the CPA team was told that the Germans had eight thousand people working on the project. "How many do you guys have?" one of the Germans asked.

"You're looking at all of them," Corliss responded.

The German laughed and asked again. "No, how many people work for you?"

"No, this is it. Three people," Corliss said.

"Don't bother starting," the German said.

Corliss quickly came to regard rapid privatization as a fool's errand. "So let's say that everyone within the CPA, every single bureaucrat in there, from Peter McPherson all the way down to little guys like me, all say privatization is the way to go. You then step out to the Iraqi ministry and you say, 'Guess what, guys? We're privatizing your factories. Starting today and starting with the vegetable oil factory. We're going to privatize it from our own funding.' The Iraqis would look at you and say, 'Really? Okay. Thanks. We'll get to work on that. We'll talk to you tomorrow.' And they'd walk off and say, 'Stupid, freaking Americans.' And they just wouldn't do it.

"We never were really in control. Now, again, why not? Well, there's 150,000 people within that ministry, all of which have their own little vested interests, and they've been there for years, if not decades. There were three of us responsible for the ministry. They sort of looked at us like clowns that kind of came in there and had ideas and concepts but never had any assets to back it up. We barked out orders at them and they just looked at us and said, 'Yeah. Sure. Sounds good. Great. You'll be back tomorrow, right? Super, we'll have some chai and we'll talk about it some more.'

"The point of all of this is we could choose to privatize or not to privatize. It didn't matter. We didn't have the power to privatize. We didn't have the power to do anything, 'cause we didn't have control of these assets. It's like one man walking into a country—a hugely militarized country—with a piece of paper and saying, 'This piece of paper now says I run the country,' and that country has twenty-four million people with weapons. They're just going to look at him and go, 'Oh, why don't you sit down over there in the corner, crazy guy?' That's what the Iraqis were like to us. They were like, 'What are you talking about? There's three of you. There's 150,000 of us. You haven't seen most of the factories. Why do you think that you're going to make any of the decisions?' So they just kept doing their thing, and we sort of played in our little, imaginary world over at the CPA."

McPherson soon began to grasp the difficulty of selling off the state-owned firms. Not only was the CPA's economic team too small, it was hard to imagine any investor braving an eleven-hour drive from Jordan (Baghdad's airport was closed to commercial traffic) to see a factory that was not operating because it lacked electricity and employees. He eventually concluded that an outright sale would have to wait until Iraq was stabilized.

But there was still something he could do in the interim. The state-run companies sucked up hundreds of millions of dollars a year in subsidies. Cement factories didn't have to pay for power. Petrochemical factories didn't have to pay for crude-oil inputs. And nobody had to pay market price for imports. Eliminating the subsidies, he figured, would result in a process of natural selection: viable companies would survive, and unprofitable ones would wither away. McPherson called it "shrinkage." As inefficient state companies shrank, or simply went out of business, he expected imports to increase and new private firms to flourish. Unemployment wasn't a concern for him, because the CPA had promised that anyone who worked for the government, even for a shuttered factory, would continue to get a salary. He deemed shrinkage "more practical, for at least a couple of years, than massive privatization."

To McPherson, looting was a form of much-needed shrinkage. If the theft of government property promoted private enterprise—such as when Baghdad's municipal bus drivers began driving their own routes and pocketing the fees—it was a positive development in his view. "I thought the privatization that occurs sort of naturally when somebody took over their state vehicle, or began to drive a truck that the state used to own, was just fine," he said. Fellow CPA officials were aghast. Hundreds of police cars had been stolen and turned into private taxis—good for the private sector but bad for law enforcement. The same problem plagued the Ministry of Trade's food-distribution system. Many of the trucks that had transported monthly rations were being used to haul private reconstruction supplies. "The Robin Hood philosophy might have sounded good to the economists inside the palace," one CPA ministry adviser said, "but when you looked at the real-world impact, it was lunacy."

McPherson also believed that his shrinkage strategy would help to address a vexing issue for his economic team. Nobody could be sure how much money various state-owned enterprises had in the bank—or how big their debts were. Bank records had been destroyed, as well as files at the Ministry of Industry. How much did the state oil company owe the al-Faris Company for products that had been delivered before the war? How much did al-Faris, in turn, owe the State Company for Iron and Steel Products? And what did that firm owe the government mining company? Sorting through everyone's assets and obligations would require a battalion of accountants. Borrowing a term suggested by Walt Slocombe, the architect of the dissolution of the army, McPherson called that challenge a "hopeless entanglement."

"There weren't records to bring to a table and sort out," he said. "If there had been, it's clear it would have taken a long period of time to reconcile.... And if you can't settle debt issues with companies, then they just sit there and you can't start new. Moreover, what was very clear was that they were all gonna chase each other's tails. The whole system was pretty clearly bankrupt."

To make matters worse, McPherson's team discovered that Iraq's state-run banks were $1 billion in debt. They had about $2 billion in deposits—about half was from state-owned entities—but only about $1 billion in assets. Whatever happened, McPherson was desperate to avoid a run on the banks, fearing that a slew of withdrawals would undermine what little public confidence existed in the Iraqi currency and in the overall economy.

McPherson's team met several times in his office to figure out a solution. No Iraqis were invited. Nor were Carney and his staff. McPherson viewed the latter as "special pleaders."

McPherson advocated a clean-slate approach. All debts and assets would be nullified. State-owned enterprises would start from scratch. Others on the economics team voiced doubts. They cited the precedent of Alexander Hamilton, who, as America's first treasury secretary, had insisted that the nascent federal government make good on its foreign and domestic debts. Post-Saddam Iraq should follow the same policy, they argued. McPherson refined his argument. The government would make good on private debts. After all, there was $1 billion in the banks to pay private depositors. But intragovernment debts, those among ministries and state companies, would be forgiven. To compensate state firms for their disappearing assets, McPherson promised to allocate $60 million from the 2003 budget to the Ministry of Industry. Carney, Corliss, and Jackson could figure out how to divvy up the money. To McPherson, it seemed more than fair.

When Corliss heard about McPherson's decision, "a hundred red flags" went up. *This is bad,* he thought. *This is really bad.*

McPherson's decision meant that the al-Faris Company, which had $1.5 million in the bank, now had nothing. So much for buying that generator to restart its assembly line. Cement companies were in the same position. They had cash in the bank, or so they thought, that they needed in order to resume production. At the same time, some of the country's most unprofitable companies would be left with a windfall. Most galling to Corliss was the case of the State Company for Cotton Industries. It had borrowed $75 million from a state-run bank to purchase a three-year supply of cotton. (There was literally a small mountain of raw cotton piled up next to the factory.) All of a sudden, that cotton was free. Instead of using it to produce cloth, factory managers sold it to neighboring countries and pocketed millions of dollars in under-the-table commissions.

"The very companies that matter most to us got hurt the most," Corliss said. "The very companies that were, in McPherson's terminology and mine, the dogs that you got to take out back and shoot benefited the most. . . . Who owes a bunch of money? Weak companies. Who had a bunch of money? Strong companies. So we just reversed that. . . . It was exactly the opposite of what we were trying to achieve."

Corliss also maintained that the $60 million that McPherson was allocating to the Ministry of Industry was not nearly enough. Preliminary assessments estimated damages from looting at the forty-eight state-owned companies at more than $400 million. Then there was the cost of buying raw materials and otherwise funding operations. *There's no way we can do this with $60 million,* he thought. He asked for a meeting with McPherson.

The two men met for dinner in the palace's gymnasium-size cafeteria. For over an hour and a half, Corliss explained why he thought McPherson's decision was wrong. "And his attitude at the end of it was just simply, 'You're going to spend forever unwinding these intercompany payables and receivables. They're going to play games on you, and you already told me the accounting is a mess. How in the heck do you think you're going to figure this out? . . . And by the way, Glenn, all of their deposits in the bank? There's no money in the bank to back that up. So if I don't implement this policy, all of your companies that have money in the bank are going to go to the bank to get their money, and guess what? It's not there. It's just not there.'

"And what I said to him? 'That's fine, sir. I agree with you. You made my life a lot more simple, and believe me, now I've got a clean working balance sheet. . . . But the problem is, sir, you've got all these wacky things. You've got the cotton company with $75 million worth of cotton. You've got the petrochem company that is owed money by all these other companies. And plus you have the problem of every company I now go to talk to, the first words out of their mouth is, "You stole my bank account." I can tell them the money was never there. They're not going to believe me. They're going to say, "You Americans stole my bank account," and that's what they're convinced of.' "

"I agree there's ramifications," McPherson said. "But you know, there's pros and cons to every decision. This is the decision we're making. We're moving forward."

As Corliss walked away, he announced that he wasn't giving up. "Sir," he said, "I'm going to try to convince you otherwise."

The next day, Corliss wrote a one-page e-mail to Carney and Jackson. He didn't pull any punches. On the cancellation of assets and debts, he wrote, "We will be saddling most of the Companies with negative working capital balances—a major red flag for investors and a drag on future performance of the Company. . . . This policy also says to the companies, 'any sales you made before June 1 but haven't been paid for yet were for naught. Sorry, but you got ripped off. Hope you didn't work too hard getting that deal done.' " He called the decision to devote just $60 million to the ministry "nothing short of a guaranteed death sentence for all but the strongest" state-owned enterprises. "I recognize that these are controversial opinions and I've made little attempt to communicate this diplomatically. Nonetheless, I believe it's a critical enough issue that one should not mince one's words. Furthermore, I have little interest in participating in destruction of otherwise viable Companies."

Two days later, Carney sent a note to McPherson titled "Fatal Flaws in Budget Policy Towards State-Owned Enterprises." He argued that the decision violated the Geneva Convention by undermining "assets of the Iraqi people." He also accused McPherson of drawing up the policy "without adequate Iraqi participation. Instead of transparency, with major concerned Iraqi Ministries and academics engaged, the policy seems to be the thinking of a small group in the Coalition Provisional Authority."

"We need to rethink this," he wrote in closing.

Carney left Baghdad for good the next day, his ninety-day commitment over. Before departing, he had a brief meeting with Bremer in the palace. "Good luck," Carney told Bremer, "and don't forget to rely on Iraqis."

With privatization abandoned in favor of shrinkage, McPherson turned his attention to other policies designed to create a capitalist utopia in the Middle East. He persuaded Bremer, who shared his dream of a vibrant private sector, to eliminate import duties. Saddam's government had charged taxes of as much as 200 percent on some imported luxury products. With no more fees, truckloads of cars, televisions, and air-conditioners were shipped into Iraq from every neighboring country. Baghdad's Karrada Street, the capital's main shopping boulevard, was lined with new vehicles and electronic appliances for sale. Curious Iraqis pawed the products. Wealthier ones removed the dollars they had been hiding under their mattresses and purchased the newly arrived goods, which had long been out of their reach. The scene was just what the press strategists at the White House had long sought: liberated Iraqis reveling in a free market.

Emboldened, McPherson became even more ambitious. He seized upon the tax code—without waiting for the Bearing-Point consultants—and took an ax to it. He slashed Iraq's top tax rate for individuals and businesses from 45 percent to a flat 15 percent. It was the sort of tax overhaul that fiscal conservatives long dreamed of implementing in the United States. No matter that most Iraqis never bothered to pay taxes. The details would be worked out later by BearingPoint, whose contract required them to develop a program to assign Iraqis taxpayer identification numbers.

The centerpiece of McPherson's agenda was a new foreign-investment law. Iraq, like almost all of its neighbors, restricted the degree to which foreigners could participate in the local economy. In most cases, a foreigner could own no more than 49 percent of a business. The rule, designed to protect indigenous firms, was out of sync with the globalizing world economy, but it played to the Iraqi public's conspiratorial, xenophobic fears that investors from Israel would seek to take over Iraqi companies. To McPherson, though, foreign investment was key to economic recovery. The way to create jobs, he reasoned, was to lure multinational firms into Iraq with the promise of being able to own not just 49 percent, but 100 percent, of the businesses they established. He figured that they would set up factories that would employ thousands of Iraqis, obviating the need for the CPA to resuscitate many state-owned firms. He pitched his idea to Bremer, who became an early convert. Others on McPherson's team also signed on. But the Governing Council was dubious. Members knew that the change would be controversial, and they didn't want to get blamed for selling the country to foreigners. McPherson and Bremer did a hard sell, bringing in economists from the World Bank, who explained that protectionist policies were the reason that the Middle East was lagging behind Africa in foreign direct investment. The discussions continued for weeks, with the council proposing various schemes to restrict the ability of foreign firms to sell goods, which McPherson and Bremer shot down. The deal eventually was sealed by Colin Powell, who told the council during a brief visit that it should support the change. The new foreign-investment law was announced a few days later, at an international banking conference in the United Arab Emirates. It was McPherson's happiest day since arriving in Iraq.

McPherson didn't see himself as an ideologue but as an American working in the best interests of the Iraqi people. He was there to dispense some bitter medicine, but he figured it was easier for him to do it than a fledgling Iraqi government, which probably would not want to squander political capital on liberalizing foreign investment or shrinking state businesses. He also forced Bremer and the neoconservative architects of the war to accept their share of tough-to-swallow news. When the CPA began running short of Iraqi currency to pay salaries to the Iraqis, McPherson decided to resume printing 250-dinar banknotes with Saddam's picture on them. Paul Wolfowitz objected, but McPherson stood his ground. He argued that if the CPA stopped paying salaries in dinars and dollars—and went exclusively to dollars—it would send a strong signal to Iraqis that their "currency was worthless." Later, McPherson presided over one of the most successful CPA projects: the printing of new currency, without Saddam's face, and a massive nationwide exchange program to swap old bills for new ones.

A month before McPherson left, Bremer told him he would no longer have to worry about private-sector development. That job would belong to Thomas Foley, an investment banker and a major Republican Party donor who had been President Bush's classmate at Harvard Business School.

A week after arriving, Foley told a contractor from Bearing-Point that he intended to privatize all of Iraq's state-owned enterprises within thirty days.

"Tom, there are a couple of problems with that," the contractor said. "The first is an international law that prevents the sale of assets by an occupation government."

"I don't care about any of that stuff," Foley told the contractor, according to her recollection of the conversation. "I don't give a shit about international law. I made a commitment to the president that I'd privatize Iraq's businesses."

When the contractor tried to object again, Foley cut her off.

"Let's go have a drink," he said.

THE GREEN ZONE, SCENE V

A Coalition Provisional Authority press briefing.
DATE: *February 25, 2004.*
SETTING: *Conference Room Three, Baghdad Convention Center.*
BRIEFERS: *CPA spokesman Daniel Senor and Brigadier General Mark Kimmitt.*

> QUESTION *(in Arabic from an Iraqi journalist): General Kimmitt, the sound of American helicopters, which fly so low to the ground, is terrifying young children, especially at night. Why do you insist on flying so low and scaring the Iraqi people?*
>
> GENERAL KIMMITT: *What we would tell the children of Iraq is that the noise they hear is the sound of freedom. Those helicopters are in the air to provide safety, provide security. Certainly our helicopter pilots do not fly at an altitude intentionally to distract the children of Iraq. They're there for their safety. They're there for their protection. And just as my wife, who is a schoolteacher, tells the children when they're sitting in the classroom that, when they hear the artillery rounds go off at Fort Bragg, she says, "Children, that's the sound of freedom." They seem to be quite pleased with that explanation. We would recommend that you tell the same thing to the children of Iraq, that that helicopter noise you hear above you ensures that they don't have to worry for the future.*

7

Bring a Duffel Bag

EVERY TIME I WALKED into the palace's main rotunda, my eye went immediately to a blue tarpaulin tacked to the wall. Only those who had arrived during the earliest days of the occupation knew what was behind it: a portrait of Saddam handing bricks to construction workers rebuilding the bombed-out palace after the first Gulf War. Two dusty, table-size scale models of the building sat nearby. One depicted the damage from the bombing; the other showed the larger, grander, rebuilt structure. A few months into the occupation, the models disappeared.

On one side of the rotunda, a metal detector stood next to three burly guards. That was the entrance to Jerry Bremer's office. On the other side was the Green Room, home to the Strategic Communications team.

Stratcomm, as it was called in the palace, was the CPA's public relations office. It was run by Daniel Senor, a lanky thirty-two-year-old with a receding hairline and a you're either with-us-or-against-us attitude toward journalists. He arrived in Iraq with Garner but stayed on after Bremer arrived. His press relations experience was limited to a stint as a spokesman for a senator, but Senor was an ardent Republican and soon became a trusted member of the viceroy's inner circle. He helped Bremer, a fellow Harvard Business School graduate, decide when to hold press conferences, which journalists to grant interviews to, and what photo opportunities were worth a dangerous trip outside the Green Zone.

As the occupation wore on, Senor became the most visible

CPA official after Bremer. Clad in a suit, he held televised press briefings several times a week in the Convention Center. The briefing room had been decorated by a White House image consultant, who was flown to Baghdad to specify the dimensions and location of the backdrop—a gold seal emblazoned with the words COALITION PROVISIONAL AUTHORITY. The consultant also had had two big-screen plasma televisions affixed to the wall so Senor could play video clips. While other CPA officials waited months for equipment and staff to arrive from the United States, the press room's needs were quickly met.

Behind the podium, Senor never conceded a mistake, and his efforts to spin failures into successes sometimes reached the point of absurdity. "The majority of Iraqis . . . do they want the coalition forces to leave? They say no," he once said. The CPA's own polls suggested just the opposite. Asked why Iraq had such interminable lines at gas stations, Senor insisted it was "good news"—more Iraqis were driving because the CPA had allowed the import of a quarter million new cars. He made no mention of the CPA's delays in getting Halliburton and other contractors to solve the problem by repairing refineries. When Senor was frank, it wasn't for publication. In April 2004, a few reporters asked him about a paroxysm of violence that had Americans hunkering down in the Green Zone. "Off the record: Paris is burning," he told them. "On the record: Security and stability are returning to Iraq."

Senor couldn't speak Arabic. When an Iraqi journalist asked a question, the cameras captured Senor lifting a pair of earphones so he could listen to a translation. His language handicap made some briefings almost comical. Basic queries posed by Iraqi reporters—When will you pay pensions? When will electricity production increase?—were often unsatisfactorily answered because the question or the response was mangled by an interpreter. Other requests for information about government services were punted to the Governing Council, to perpetuate the myth that it had real authority. The council's press office was inept, so the Iraqi reporters rarely received an adequate answer.

At his briefings, Senor talked about visits by congressional delegations and cabinet secretaries. There was another session for Arabic speakers, but it was conducted by a Brit who regurgitated day-old items from Senor's talking points, a slight that rankled many Iraqi journalists. "The Iraqis want to know what is happening in Iraq," a correspondent for one of Baghdad's largest newspapers groused after a Senor briefing. "But all he talks about is American politics."

Senor's priority was feeding the American media, particularly outlets favored by supporters of President Bush. Fox News, whose coverage of the occupation was generally sympathetic and supportive, was a favorite. (After the occupation ended, Senor joined Fox as a paid on-air commentator about Iraq.) On one occasion when I entered his office, only one of his three televisions was switched on. Like most televisions in the palace, including the one in Bremer's office, it was set to Fox. None of the other TVs in Senor's office was tuned to al-Iraqiya, the national channel, which Stratcomm was supposed to oversee.

Because Saddam's government had installed a network of terrestrial transmitters, al-Iraqiya was the one channel available everywhere in Iraq. Before the war, satellite dishes were verboten. The national channel was the only choice, despite its bland newscasts and prime-time paeans to Saddam. After his government fell, Iraqis predictably rushed out to buy dishes and tune into al-Jazeera and other pan-Arab stations. But the initial excitement soon wore off, and Iraqis were eager for news about their country. When they tuned in to al-Iraqiya, they rarely got it.

On an August afternoon, a thousand-pound truck bomb detonated in front of the United Nations headquarters. The blast shook homes five miles away. It was the biggest explosion in Baghdad since the war, and Iraqis scrambled to their roofs to find out what had happened. Seeing only a dark plume of smoke in the sky, they ran down to turn on the television. When my friend Saad clicked over to al-Iraqiya, it was airing an Egyptian cooking show. Saad, like seemingly everyone else in Baghdad, had a satellite dish. He switched to al-Jazeera, which had a live report about the incident. He watched al-Jazeera for the next few hours as it aired video footage from the scene. The on-the-ground reports were objective, but in follow-up commentary, self-proclaimed analysts branded the American occupation as illegal and all but praised the insurgents responsible for the attack.

"Do the Americans want us all to become jihadists?" Saad asked me later. "Why don't they try to compete with this filth?"

I got the answer from a veteran television producer named Don North.

North had been a cameraman in Vietnam, a bureau chief in Cairo, a media adviser to the Saudi Arabian military commander, and a journalism teacher in the Balkans. A few months before U.S. troops invaded Iraq, he got a call from Science Applications International Corporation (SAIC), a large defense contractor, offering him a job to help build an independent television station in Iraq. North, a silver-haired man whose foreign-correspondent gruffness was tempered by Canadian politeness, was pursuing a freelance career near Washington. He'd had his fill of wars and the Middle East. But the job in Iraq was too appealing. It was a combination of everything he had done since Vietnam.

SAIC had been contracted by the Pentagon to run the Iraqi Media Network (IMN), which would comprise the national television station, a national radio station, and a newspaper printed six times a week. SAIC had no experience running media operations in a post-conflict environment; it specialized in designing computer systems for the Defense Department and intelligence agencies. Nevertheless, the Pentagon offered the Iraqi media contract to SAIC without inviting other firms to bid. The contract was written by Doug Feith's office. Feith's deputy, Christopher Ryan Henry, had been a vice president at SAIC before joining the Pentagon. SAIC hired Robert Reilly, a former Voice of America director, to head the IMN project. During the Reagan administration, Reilly had headed a White House information operations campaign in Nicaragua to drum up support for the Contra rebels.

Don North's first task for SAIC was completed on American soil. He helped produce a documentary about Saddam's crimes against humanity that the U.S. government wanted to broadcast in Muslim nations to build support for the war. When it was finished, North asked his new bosses what he could do to prepare to run Iraq's television station. "But they said, 'Okay, Don, you can go do whatever you want right now. We'll see you again in Baghdad, after the fall of Baghdad,' " he recalled. "I said, 'Yeah, isn't there something we can be doing? Planning? I mean, in my experience it takes years to plan programming and structure for a new TV and radio station.'

" 'No. No. We got a few people that will be buying equipment. We're not quite sure what we'll find when we get to Baghdad, but don't worry about it.' "

When North arrived in Kuwait, he took stock of the equipment that SAIC had purchased. There were thirteen tripods, but all lacked a base plate upon which a camera could sit. The receiver for satellite transmissions didn't have a power cord. Nothing had instruction booklets. "It was like they bought everything from a flea market in London," North said.

A few days later, his backup plan, to use the broadcast equipment at the Iraqi Ministry of Information, went up in smoke when the military flattened the building with cruise missiles. As he was departing for Baghdad, North noticed that SAIC had purchased a few new video cameras, but when he tried to take one of them, he was told that the equipment had been promised to SAIC's security team.

Upon reaching Baghdad, he and two Iraqi exiles linked up with an army unit that had a radio transmitter. Within a day, they were broadcasting news reports and public-service announcements in Arabic. The setup was primitive: one of the Iraqi exiles listened to the BBC on a shortwave and wrote news blurbs that North edited and the other Iraqi exile read on the air. A week later, when Jay Garner was scheduled to hold his first news conference, North's team figured they should cover it. But when North asked his SAIC colleagues for a tape recorder, he was told there was none.

Once again, the Pentagon had failed to provide the resources necessary to accomplish the mission. SAIC received only $15 million. In a memo pleading for more funding, Reilly noted that al-Arabiya, a new pan-Arab news station, had an annual budget of $60 million. SAIC, he noted, was doing not just television but radio and a newspaper as well.

But it was never clear to North how SAIC was using even the $15 million it had initially received from the Pentagon. Reilly claimed to have spent $1.2 million on television and radio studio equipment before the war, but North didn't see much in the way of usable gear. Months later, the Defense Department's inspector general provided a partial explanation: SAIC charged the government for the purchase of an H2 Hummer and a Ford C350 pickup truck, and the cost of leasing a DC-10 cargo jet to fly the vehicles to Baghdad. Pentagon auditors weren't able to determine exactly how much the vehicles and the plane trip cost, but they estimated it to be more than $380,000. The auditors discovered that the purchase had initially been rejected by a Defense contracting officer, but SAIC circumvented him and obtained approval from Feith's office. The white Hummer, with air-conditioning and tinted windows, was used by SAIC personnel to drive around Baghdad. It quickly became a spectacle in the Green Zone. All of a sudden, the CPA's Suburbans seemed modest.

A month after North arrived in Baghdad, IMN was ready for its first television broadcast. More than two hundred Iraqis, many of whom had worked for the national television station before the war, had joined IMN as technicians, editors, and reporters. Some even brought in cameras and editing equipment they had taken home for safekeeping during the looting.

The IMN staff decided that the first broadcast would be a news report. But the night before they were to go on air, Dan Senor told North that his anchor, a well-known former exile who ran an opposition radio station, was unacceptable. Senor didn't want an exile. He also instructed North to take the newscast, which was to be prerecorded, to the home of Kurdish political leader Jalal Talabani so Talabani's wife could vet the program.

North compromised on the anchor by promising to add a woman who was not an exile. But he refused to prescreen the show for Talabani's wife.

"Dan, you're off base on these things," he told Senor. "These things are not going to fly. The Iraqis aren't going to allow it."

IMN recorded the newscast the next day. It opened with a brief prayer from the Koran. But just before the tape was to be broadcast, Senor came to the studio and told North to cut the prayer.

"On whose orders?" North said.

"This is from Washington," Senor said. "We are going to start off by separating religion from television programming."

"Wait a minute," North responded. "I've lived for a long time in Arab countries. It really is traditional that this be done."

"No," Senor said. "Those are orders."

North nodded and walked away. *It's not going to happen,* he thought. *Screw them.*

When he related the conversation to the Iraqis at IMN, they were adamant that the prayers be included. The newscast aired that night in its original form.

It was amateurish. The tape edits were rough, and the video had the quality of a homemade production. But it was an Iraqi newscast, and it immediately generated a buzz on the streets of Baghdad.

To North and his Iraqi colleagues, IMN was supposed to be like the BBC, a government-funded television-and-radio network that retained editorial independence. Iraqi journalists, with initial assistance from American advisers, would decide how to cover the news. But to some in the CPA, IMN was a propaganda tool: we're paying for it, so we can decide what airs. SAIC managers, North said, didn't want to rock the boat. If the CPA wanted to control what went on the air, that was just fine by them.

After the first few broadcasts, North asked Senor to set up a time for Bremer to be interviewed by IMN's anchor. Senor said he would try but that Bremer was very busy. Several days later, Senor noticed an IMN crew in the palace. Bremer had a free half hour, he said. You want to tape him? The reporter was an Iraqi who spoke little English, so Senor gestured to them to follow him and set up their equipment in Bremer's office. When the camera started rolling, Senor moderated the conversation, asking Bremer one softball question after another.

When North and his Iraqi staff viewed the tape, they deemed it agitprop. They decided not to use anything more than a brief clip of Bremer praising IMN as the "voice of Iraq." The next day, Senor asked North why he hadn't used the whole interview. "Well, Dan," North said, "if [former White House spokes-man] Ari Fleischer conducted the interview Dan Rather was promised with the president, would you expect CBS to air it?"

The incident only emboldened the CPA, which ordered IMN to cover endless daily press conferences and photo opportuni-ties, leaving the Iraqi journalists little time to report what North deemed "genuine news stories." Once live broadcasts became possible, CPA officials dictated that the news confer-ences be aired in their entirety.

The CPA also required IMN to broadcast an hour-long daily program funded by the British government. Called *Towards Freedom,* the program touted Iraq's liberation with puff pieces and rah-rah sound bites from American and British govern-ment officials. IMN staff worried that running government-produced fare before the evening news would ruin their credibility as an independent network. "We respectfully request to know whose political agenda is involved here," five IMN employees wrote in a letter of protest to SAIC managers. "Cer-tainly, it is not a professionally sound programming decision to use a mediocre propaganda program from abroad to super-sede our own news program! Following an exhausting hour of *Towards Freedom,* it is only the most dedicated news junkies who could tolerate it without seeking another channel."

Meanwhile, IMN limped along with gear inadequate for a college journalism program. When the DC-10 deposited the Hummer in Baghdad, North figured that SAIC had finally got-ten serious about funding IMN. He put in a request for a $500 satellite dish to downlink video clips from an international news agency for use on the nightly news. SAIC refused. The company also rejected a $200 requisition for North to print a training manual in Arabic.

A few days later, an SAIC official approached North and said, "We're going to get a wonderful new piece of equipment."

Great, North said. Might it be the camera batteries that we asked for weeks ago?

"Nope," the official said. "We're going to get a teleprompter."

"Where on my equipment list is a teleprompter?" North said. "Our announcers are doing fine, thank you, reading from paper. We need a teleprompter like we need a second asshole."

Oh, no, the official said. The teleprompter was for Bremer. It would be going into a television studio in the palace so he could deliver weekly addresses to the Iraqi people.

"What about my batteries?" North asked. The official didn't have an answer.

SAIC's contract, which was written by the Pentagon, did not require IMN to broadcast twenty-four hours of news a day as al-Jazeera and al-Arabiya did. Non-prime-time hours could be filled with movies, children's programming, and cooking shows. But, North said, a lack of planning for such programming resulted in the illegal airing of copyrighted Hollywood films confiscated from the palace of Saddam's eldest son, Uday.

Six months after the war, the State Department conducted a study of Iraqi television-viewing habits. Sixty-three percent of Iraqis with access to a satellite dish said they got their news from al-Jazeera and al-Arabiya. Twelve percent watched IMN. The IMN, North concluded by then, "had become an irrelevant mouthpiece for Coalition Provisional Authority propaganda, managed news, and mediocre programs." In Washington, President Bush talked about "engaging in the battle of ideas in the Arab world." But in Baghdad, North said, "We have already lost the first round."

When SAIC's contract ended, the Pentagon refused to give the firm an extension. Defense Department officials wanted a company with more experience in building media in post-conflict environments. In January 2004, the Pentagon announced that the new contract, worth $95 million for the first year, would be going to Harris Corporation, a manufacturer of telecommunications equipment. Harris had never set up a television station in a war zone.

Michael Battles arrived in Baghdad a month after the war with $450 in his wallet and plans to make millions through reconstruction contracts. He had none of the resources other business prospectors in Iraq had—no security detail, no caravan of supplies, no walled-off compound. He traveled from Jordan in a taxi, paid for with money a friend had loaned him. But Battles, who was thirty-three, had no shortage of chutzpah and connections. He had studied at West Point and worked for the

CIA. He had ridden rodeo bulls and run for Congress. He had contacts in Iraq and the White House.

His first stop was the Republican Palace. Back then, an American passport was all that was required for entry. As he walked the hallways, passing out his business card, he learned that the CPA was looking for a security firm to guard Baghdad's international airport. The CPA wanted to open the airport to civilian traffic in two months and needed a private contractor that could deploy armed guards and baggage screeners within a few weeks. Battles persuaded a CPA official to put him on a list of companies that would be invited to bid for the work. "For us," he said, "the fear and disorder offered real promise."

Battles looked like a guy you didn't want to mess with. He had the broad shoulders of a linebacker and the same bushy goatee favored by CIA operatives and Special Forces soldiers. But there was a little politician in him too. He'd grin, offer a firm handshake, and talk as if he knew everything about the business of private security.

He and his partner, a fellow former Army Ranger named Scott Custer, had never guarded an airport. They'd never even received a federal contract. Their firm had performed a security assessment of the Kabul airport for Afghanistan's Ministry of Aviation, but by the time the Iraq war began, their work in Afghanistan had ended. It was time to look for new opportunities. While Battles courted business in Baghdad, Custer paid the bills by teaching a counterterrorism class to public-utility managers in Reno.

The pair named their firm Custer Battles LLC, which drew snickers in Iraq. Custer told people he was a distant relation of George Custer, the general who was famously trounced at the Battle of the Little Bighorn. When Americans noted that Custer the general was defeated by the locals, Custer the contractor didn't have a good comeback.

Battles knew that he and his partner would need help to perform the airport job. He contacted four other firms, one of which was headed by Robert Isakson, a former FBI agent turned entrepreneur. Isakson, a middle-aged Alabamian with a bloodhound's nose for opportunity, ran a company that pro-

vided post-conflict management services. If you needed housing trailers, he could get them for you. Furniture? No problem.
Cooks and cleaners? Done. Isakson's firm, DRC Incorporated,
built roads, helicopter landing pads, and temporary housing
for NATO troops stationed in Kosovo. In 1993, DRC sent personnel into Somalia three days after U.S. troops landed, to provide housing, portable toilets, and food to soldiers and contract
workers. Before Battles had traveled to Iraq, he met with Isakson. As Isakson remembered it, Battles told him that Iraqi
ministries, not the U.S. government, would be issuing reconstruction contracts, and the only way to get them was to have
Iraqi partners. Battles, who said he had several Iraqi contacts,
offered to act as a broker for Isakson. "I know everyone there,"
he said.

Three weeks after Battles's visit to the Republican Palace,
the CPA issued a request for bids to guard the airport. Battles
called Isakson with a change of plan. Instead of brokering a
deal for DRC, Battles had his own deal. "We're going to bid for
it, but we want you to join us," he said. Custer Battles needed
Isakson's help to build living quarters at the airport and to
recruit dozens of guards on short notice.

Custer, who was still teaching in Reno, wrote the company's
bid on his laptop computer over three nights. The twenty-
three-page document promised that the firm would have 138
guards—"a full security and screening team for passenger
service"—on the ground within fourteen days. The firm also
pledged to hire guards only from "coalition of the willing nations." The proposal was articulate and audacious. Custer Battles described itself as a "leading international risk
management firm with extensive experience assisting large
organizations reduce and manage risk in extremely volatile
environments."

Two well-established private-security firms—DynCorp International and ArmorGroup International—also submitted bids.
But Custer Battles's was the cheapest. More important, the firm
promised to have guards on the ground weeks faster than any
other firm, even though it had no more than a dozen security
personnel on staff when the proposal was submitted.

Two days after the bid was delivered, the CPA informed

Custer Battles that it had won. The contract was worth $16 million.

"We got that contract because we were young and dumb and didn't know better," Custer said later. "Anyone with experience would have said they'd be there in eight weeks."

Franklin Willis, the CPA's deputy senior adviser to the Ministry of Transportation, was dumbfounded by the decision of the three-member selection panel. "They gave people three days [to bid]. They went up on the bulletin board with this very general request—I mean, here's this ten-square-mile airport—to provide security for civilian flights. One of the applicants, a very well known and skilled firm, said, 'I gotta know more information before I can possibly bid.' And so they disqualified them because they weren't responsive. Another said, 'We can do this but it will take six weeks to do a proper job.' So they were disqualified because they weren't going to be ready in two weeks. And then you had Custer Battles saying, 'We can do it. We can cover it.' So they said, 'Okay, we'll pick you.' "

"The whole thing smelled," Willis said.

As soon as the contract was announced, Battles e-mailed Isakson. "We got it!" he said. "Mobilize immediately."

Isakson flew to Jordan, where he bought furniture and arranged for a Saudi company to ship housing trailers to the airport. He dispatched his brother to Nepal to hire former Gurkhas, despite the pledge to employ guards only from coalition-of-the-willing nations.

Although Custer Battles had said in its bid that it had a loan "ready for activation" to fund start-up costs, the money didn't come through. So Battles canvassed the CPA.

"Bring a duffel bag," Willis said to Battles. When Battles got to Willis's office, two million dollars in shrink-wrapped bricks of brand-new hundred-dollar notes, flown in from the Federal Reserve of New York, lay on the desk. Willis didn't want to front the money, but CPA contracting officers had demanded it. Battles packed the bricks into a four-foot-long duffel bag and returned to the airport. A few hours later, he boarded a plane for Beirut to deposit the funds in a Lebanese bank.

Custer Battles had bitten off a big job. Baghdad's airport was a disaster. Iraqi soldiers had trashed the terminal as U.S. troops rolled into the city. They had even dropped grenades into the toilets. With scores of guards on the way, Custer Battles employees scrambled to clean up the mess and renovate the buildings. They installed showers in the bathrooms, converted part of the terminal into a dormitory, and transformed the airport kitchen into a mess hall.

They didn't have a payroll system or an office computer network, but they did manage to get the guards to Baghdad within the promised two weeks. Then Bremer decided not to open the airport. There were too many surface-to-air missiles in the hands of insurgents. But the CPA told the firm to stay at the airport. Custer Battles guards patrolled the empty terminal, and the CPA forked over another $2 million cash payment.

A few weeks later, Isakson said, he was approached by a Pakistani oil trader serving as an adviser to Custer Battles. The trader suggested they bid for "cost-plus" government contracts, which provide a reimbursement for expenses plus a fixed fee. When Isakson said that the profit margins were too low for him, the trader proposed using a shell company in Lebanon to inflate the cost of goods provided to the government to give the firm a 100 percent profit.

"If you do this, you're going to prison," Isakson said.

"Oh, no. We do it all the time," the trader replied.

"Not with Americans you don't," Isakson responded. "Count me out. I'm not doing that."

Over the following days, he said that Custer Battles's chief operating officer, Joseph Morris, also raised the subject of cost-plus contracts. Isakson repeated his line about going to prison. Then Custer mentioned it. "You do that and you're going to jail," Isakson said he told him.

At that point, Isakson's relationship with Custer Battles began to sour. He contended that it was because he didn't want to overbill the government. Custer Battles maintained that it was because the trailer camp Isakson set up was shoddy, a charge Isakson denied.

As the dispute was unfolding, Isakson brought his fourteen-year-old son to Baghdad. Isakson had been diagnosed with an autoimmune disease a few months earlier and didn't know how much longer he'd live. He wanted to spend as much time with young Bobby as he could.

A week after his run-in with Custer, Isakson said that Morris ordered him, his son, and his brother out of the Custer Battles compound. Company guards held the three at gunpoint before taking their weapons and identification cards and ejecting them from the airport. "You motherfuckers," Isakson shouted as he left, "you're scumbags." Without a place to stay in Iraq, the trio took a taxi back to Jordan. To get there, they had to drive through the dangerous cities of Fallujah and Ramadi.

A month after Isakson was forced out, Custer Battles won its first cost-plus contract. The firm was to assist the CPA in replacing Iraq's old currency by building camps in southern, central, and northern Iraq, where hundreds of private contractors involved in the exchange would be housed and fed. Custer Battles was also to provide trucks and other vehicles to transport the thousands of tons of new currency that had been printed overseas and flown into the Baghdad airport. The contract called for Custer Battles to receive a 25 percent profit on the cost of labor and equipment provided to the CPA.

It was then that Custer Battles created "sham companies" registered in the Cayman Islands and Lebanon to issue a series of false invoices that showed those companies were leasing trucks and other equipment to Custer Battles, according to a memo later written by the Pentagon's deputy general counsel. The prices were grossly inflated, allowing Custer Battles to reap profits far in excess of the 25 percent allowed under the contract, the memo said.

Two months later, Custer Battles representatives accidentally left a spreadsheet on a conference table after a meeting with CPA officials. There, in black and white, were the numbers showing that the company had billed the CPA $9,801,550 for work that had cost $3,738,592—a markup of 162 percent. There was the helipad in Mosul, for instance, that took $97,000 to build but was invoiced at $175,000. William "Pete" Baldwin, Custer Battles's facilities manager, wrote in an e-mail that "every line item on that invoice" was "false, fabricated, inflated." Even the scrap heap was ripe for profit: the company repainted Iraqi Airways forklifts found at the airport and then billed the CPA thousands of dollars a month for use of the equipment, claiming it was leased from abroad. All told, Custer Battles received $21 million from the CPA for the currency exchange.

Baldwin wrote his superiors during the currency exchange to warn them about the fraudulent and inflated invoices. Peter Miskovich, the manager of the exchange, also sounded the alarm. In a memo to Custer Battles's country director, he wrote that a $2.7 million invoice was based on "forged leases, inflated invoices and duplication of invoices." Records he had examined provided "prima facie evidence of a course of conduct consistent with criminal activity and intent," he wrote.

A few days before Miskovich wrote his memo, Isakson and Baldwin filed a whistleblower lawsuit against the company on behalf of the U.S. government. Custer Battles called the allegations of wrongdoing a baseless claim brought by a "disgruntled employee."

The lawsuit prompted the Pentagon to mount an investigation, and in September 2004, more than a year after Custer Battles was awarded the currency contract, the Defense Department announced that the firm would be barred from obtaining further military contracts. The department cited compelling evidence of "seriously improper conduct."

By then, however, Custer Battles had already received more than $100 million in contracts from the U.S. government.

Ben Thomas had been struggling to support himself in Florida as an ultimate fighter—the sport is similar to boxing except there are no gloves and no rules—when a friend suggested he apply for a job with a company called Custer Battles. *Nice name,* Thomas thought. The firm had just won a contract to guard Baghdad's airport, his friend said, and there was plenty of work to be had. Thomas wanted to keep fighting, but he was broke. The next day, he called up the company's human resources office and said the magic words: "I used to be a SEAL."

In the rush to hire private-security contractors in Iraq, nobody looked at résumés. If you had been in the army's Special Forces or been a Navy SEAL—the military's elite commandos— you were in. Word-of-mouth references were good enough.

Thomas was twenty-seven. He wasn't a hair over five foot six, but he looked as though he could take on a guy twice his size. He walked with a don't-mess-with-me swagger. On his rippled left biceps were tattooed the Japanese characters for sea-air-land commando; his forearm was emblazoned with a navy anchor. He cursed like a sailor but solicitously inquired about my mother's cancer treatment every time we talked. He was fascinated by Roman sculpture, but his laptop computer contained digital photos and videos of insurgent attacks and their bloody carnage. His online alias was DiabloBoy.

Before Thomas was hired, Custer Battles told him that he'd be performing "close protection," which meant that he would be a glorified bodyguard for a senior official. It sounded more exciting than patrolling the airport.

When he arrived in Baghdad in July 2003, Custer Battles issued Thomas a pistol and an M4 rifle. He received seven magazines, each capable of holding thirty rounds. But he got only twenty bullets. "If we're in an ambush, twenty bullets won't be enough," he said. An M4 can fire ninety bullets per minute on burst mode. With twenty bullets, he'd have just thirteen seconds of firepower.

"We've got a bullet shortage," a Custer Battles supervisor told Thomas.

His flak vest was no better. Designed for police officers in the United States, it could withstand a bullet from a pistol but not from an AK-47 rifle. In Iraq, everyone and his brother had an AK-47.

"Has it occurred to anyone here that this armor won't stop any bullet fired in Iraq?" Thomas said as he received his vest.

By the time he was ready to head into the field, Custer Battles had lost the close-protection contract. But the company had another job for Thomas. It had received written authorization to collect weapons seized by the American military. Thomas and another employee were to visit Special Forces safehouses and SEAL team observation posts to haul away Iraqi weapons.

He and a colleague drove around central Iraq in a truck. They picked up four hundred AK-47s plus belt-fed machine guns, cases of grenades, and a half million bullets. They even grabbed a few Russian-made ZSU-23 anti-aircraft guns. When Thomas asked Custer why they were becoming arms recyclers, he said he'd been told that the firm was bidding on a contract to train the new Iraqi army and that the weapons were needed for training. Thomas suspected that Custer Battles was shipping the matériel out of Iraq and selling it, but he did as he was told.

The Custer Battles camp consisted of trailers parked in a dusty lot on the airport grounds, which it was being paid to guard at the time. By Iraqi standards, it was comfortable enough. Thomas bought bottles of vodka for nine dollars apiece from the airport duty-free shop. He hung out by a makeshift pool, smoking cigars and watching videos. Every now and then, he'd get called to make a run into the city, to pick up supplies or escort a company official to the Green Zone.

One September morning, Thomas and three fellow Custer Battles employees were heading into downtown Baghdad in a sport utility vehicle. They had exited the airport on a side road that fed into the main expressway leading to the city center when they came upon a police checkpoint. Instead of waving the foreigners through, as most policemen in Iraq did, the men manning the checkpoint ordered the vehicle to slow. As Thomas and his colleagues drove through, one of the policemen turned his head. It was a giveaway, but Thomas, who was driving, hadn't been in Iraq long enough to recognize the head movement as a signal.

Seconds after driving through the checkpoint, they came upon rocks, gas cans, and other debris scattered on the street. To get around the debris, Thomas had to veer off the road to the left, drive by a small building, and turn right to get back on the road. He didn't hesitate. As he drove off the pavement, he heard an unusual sound. *Whack! Whack! Whack!*

Uh, shit, Thomas thought. *We're getting shot.*

He tried to hit the gas, but the SUV wouldn't move. It just made a loud banging noise. The three men with him bailed out and ran toward the building. Thomas rolled under the car. "This was before I learned the lesson that cars don't stop bullets," he said later.

From his vantage under the vehicle, Thomas estimated that a half dozen bad guys were shooting at him and his buddies. He could see just one of them, though. The muzzle flash gave the man's position away.

Thomas grabbed his M4, pointed it at the man he could see,

and pulled the trigger. He missed. Then he remembered a lesson from his military training. If you're trying to shoot someone from under a car, you've got to lie on your side to get a better angle. He rolled over, lined up the man's pelvis in his sight, and fired again. In the split second before he pulled the trigger, the man turned. Thomas shot him in the buttocks.

Thomas expected to fire again, but his target had crumpled in the dirt. "It was like God reached up and yanked him to the ground."

The rest of the shooters scattered. When the coast was clear, Thomas and his buddies went over to examine the downed man.

His hip was shattered and his abdomen was pulverized where the bullet had exited. "His guts were spewed out like someone had uncoiled him and spread him out," Thomas said.

It was then that Thomas confessed to his buddies that instead of the standard-issue ammunition used by the military and other security contractors, he had something special. The bullets he used were the same size as the standard ammunition—a little longer than an AAA battery—but they didn't have a copper finish. They were black. The company distributing the bullets, which had given Thomas a few boxes to take to Iraq, claimed that they were fundamentally different from the standard ammunition: instead of a lead core, these projectiles were made from a blend of several metals, including platinum, so they would pass through steel armor but would shatter in flesh, resulting in catastrophic injury.

The company's claims were disputed by several ballistics experts, including a surgeon at Stanford University who tested the bullets for the U.S. government. He maintained that the bullets had a lead core. What made them different, he said, was that they were packed with more gunpowder and had a soft point. Soft-point bullets, which lack a full metal jacket, are more likely to deform and mushroom as they enter flesh. Although the vast majority of police departments in the United States use soft-point bullets—because they are less likely to pass through the target and injure bystanders—their use on the battlefield was banned by the Hague Convention of 1899. The United States never signed the treaty, but the Pentagon has long abided by its provisions. Rank-and-file American soldiers use only full-metal-jacketed bullets.

If Thomas had been an active-duty soldier, he would have been court-martialed for having used nonstandard bullets. For private-security contractors, though, the rules were murkier. Custer Battles had a contract with the CPA. That contract didn't specify what bullets were permitted.

When military commanders heard about the bullets used in the shooting, they issued a memo to security firms warning against the use of nonstandard ammunition. But there was no effective way to enforce the rule—or any of the other regulations the military wanted to impose on security contractors. They were above the laws of war.

As word of the buttocks kill spread in the private-security community, so did demand for the bullets. Thomas gave away all he had. Others brought in more boxes in their suitcases.

"Out here, there are no rules," Thomas said. "You do whatever you have to do to protect yourself."

THE GREEN ZONE, SCENE VI

Books and magazines from back home were a precious commodity. It was considered bad form not to pass them on to friends when you were done. Mystery novels and thrillers were the most popular. Tomes about Iraq, the Arab world, and Islam gathered dust. After thinking about Iraq all day, the last thing you wanted to do was read about it at bedtime. But a few books on Iraq were well thumbed. A Halliburton employee found copies of the Complete Idiot's Guide to Understanding Iraq *while cleaning out CPA staff rooms at the al-Rasheed. When an Iraqi American interpreter offered to loan a senior CPA staffer a copy of Hanna Batatu's* The Old Social Classes and the Revolutionary Movements of Iraq, *a seminal work of regional history, the staffer declined. He pointed to a small book on his desk. "Everything I need is in here," he said. The interpreter picked up the book. It was a tourist guide to Iraq, written in the 1970s.*

8

A Yearning for Old Times

"**I DON'T KNOW HOW MUCH MORE** of this I can take," Walid Khalid moaned. Beads of sweat dripped from his face onto the counter, precariously close to the pizza he was making for me. "Why did I ever come back here?"

It was 130 degrees outside, and the electricity was off again. Without air-conditioning or a fan, his wood-fired oven had turned his restaurant into the seventh circle of hell. Everyone outside the Emerald City was receiving just twelve hours of power a day the summer after the Americans arrived. The lights would be on for three hours. Then there would be a three-hour blackout.

The men who ran convenience stores next to the pizzeria stopped selling perishables because they couldn't keep them cold. They set up their checkout counters on the sidewalk and lent patrons flashlights to browse the aisles inside the stores. Business was terrible. They had spent hundreds of dollars to import cases of Coca-Cola, a beverage unavailable in Baghdad before the war. But who wanted a warm Coke?

Walid and his neighbors groused about the blackouts all the time. "It's like we're living in the Stone Age," one of the shop-keepers remarked as he walked into the pizzeria.

"You're right," Walid responded. "It was never like this before."

Fifty yards away, inside the Green Zone, air-conditioners chilled buildings to a crisp sixty-eight degrees. The Emerald City wasn't connected to Iraq's electrical transmission grid. A diesel power station the size of a small house kept the appliances running in the Republican Palace. Others inside the walls—the private contractors, the CIA station, the military—had generators that were almost as big. The CPA deemed power to be "mission critical." Fuel tankers arrived from Kuwait every day, and a team of electrical engineers was always on call. "We've got twenty-four/seven reliability," one of the engineers boasted.

Electricity for those who lived outside the Green Zone came from plants across the country that fed into a national grid. The closest one to me was Baghdad South. After I ate my pizza, I wiped the perspiration off my brow and headed there.

Built in 1959 along the meandering Tigris River, Baghdad South told the story of Iraq's prosperity and poverty. Its four German-made, steam-powered generating units initially provided more than enough electricity to meet the capital's needs. As demand increased, Iraq turned in 1965 to the United States, acquiring two additional units from the General Electric Company. The plant's six towering smokestacks were symbols of the country's oil wealth. "Back then, we were the most advanced power plant in the Arab world," said Bashir Khallaf, Baghdad South's director.

In 1983, before Saddam's war with neighboring Iran had drained the national coffers, the four German generating units were replaced with made-in-the-USA turbines from GE. At the time, Khallaf said, the plant never had to operate at its 350-megawatt capacity because Iraq produced more electricity than it needed. New power plants and high-voltage transmission lines sprouted across the desert, paid for with abundant oil revenue. The city's neo-Baathist architects took advantage of the power glut, building tall concrete-and-glass apartment complexes and office towers that required elevators and massive air conditioners. The city became as electricity dependent as any Western metropolis.

The plant sputtered to a halt in 1991, after being hit by six U.S. bombs during the Persian Gulf War. According to UN assessments, American bombing during the war damaged about 75 percent of the country's power-generating capacity. Khallaf and other workers brought Baghdad South back to life

four months later, using spare parts and MacGyver-like ingenu-
ity. But the plant was nowhere as efficient as before. Duct tape,
baling wire, and scrap metal from the junkyard held the generating units together.

United Nations economic sanctions prevented Iraq from
importing new equipment for five years. Even after the sanctions were revised to allow Iraq to sell its oil for humanitarian
goods, including parts for power plants, bureaucratic hurdles
still restricted the flow of needed supplies. As equipment
broke, it either was not fixed or was replaced with jury-rigged
gear. With power in ever-shorter supply, government officials
didn't permit the plant to shut down for annual maintenance.
The once-modern facility gradually became a collection of
deteriorated pipes, broken gauges, and ramshackle devices.
Leaks in the steam pipes transformed the generating complex
into a giant sauna. The plant was one of the few places in Iraq
where you couldn't smoke; there was too much leaked fuel.
Before the 2003 war, Baghdad South was barely able to produce 185 megawatts. "We were like an old man losing his
energy," Khallaf said.

Baghdad's residents didn't notice. Saddam didn't want to
deprive his two most important constituencies, his cronies and
the generals who could launch a coup, all of whom lived in the
capital, so he ordered Baghdad to receive as much power as it
needed from the national grid. To meet the demand, other
parts of Iraq, particularly the Shiite-dominated south, were
starved of power.

On a trip to Baghdad in October 2002, four months before the
war began, I met a stout, bespectacled Dutchman named Mar-
cel Alberts. He worked for the United Nations Development
Program, and his job was to ensure that power-plant equipment purchased with Oil-for-Food funds was indeed for power
plants and not for making weapons of mass destruction.
Alberts traveled to every Iraqi generating station. He took copi-
ous notes and kept them in large white binders in his office. He
estimated that Iraq's national electricity demand was 6,200
megawatts during peak periods, but its maximum generating
capacity was only 4,400 megawatts—less than half of what the

country was able to produce in 1990. (One megawatt was enough to meet the needs of about 1,500 homes.) "When I see some of the power plants here, I'm surprised they're still running," Alberts told me. "The conditions are terrible."

Every three months, Alberts summarized his findings in reports that were sent to UN headquarters in New York and made available to every member nation. One such document, issued in 2002, noted that Iraq's generating units were "technically and economically obsolete," resulting in a 2,500-megawatt nationwide power shortage and lengthy blackouts.

Alberts wasn't alone in warning of a catastrophe. The Future of Iraq Project's infrastructure report predicted that the power sector would need $18 billion worth of repairs, and the CIA's nighttime satellite images of southern Iraqi cities showed shockingly few lights. "The telltale signs were there," said an American electrical engineer working in Iraq.

In March 2003, ten days after American tanks crossed into Iraq, the White House issued a press release proclaiming that Iraq produced 5,500 megawatts of power—1,100 megawatts more than Alberts's estimate. Before the war, the Bush administration set aside just $230 million for power-sector reconstruction in Iraq. "Iraq is a country rich with an educated populace, abundant and valuable natural resources like oil and natural gas, and a modern infrastructure system," the White House press release stated. "The United States is committed to helping Iraq recover from this conflict, but Iraq will not require sustained aid."

For the first two weeks of the war, Baghdad South chugged along as usual. Then one night, a massive power surge shut down the plant, as it did every other power station in central Iraq, plunging Baghdad into darkness and panic. Nobody—not U.S. military engineers, not Iraqi technicians—had any idea what had happened. Had Saddam ordered the lights out? Had the Americans bombed a power station? Months later, they would conclude that a loop of high-voltage lines encircling the capital was severed during the fighting, unbalancing the power grid and sending surges to every plant on the network.

With no idea what had caused the problem and with fight-

ing raging around the capital, Khallaf and other employees
decided to go home. They returned to work three days after
Baghdad fell to find a contingent of marines hunkered down
at the plant. A day later, officers from the U.S. Army Corps of
Engineers arrived. They saw the broken pipes, frayed wires,
and computerless control room, where the antiquated dials
were the size of wall clocks. "When I first looked around, I said,
'Holy moly. This is not good,'" recalled Lieutenant Colonel
John Comparetto, who was the army's chief electrical engineer
in Iraq. "I hoped it was an isolated incident. But it wasn't true.
It was typical."

It was then that Comparetto saw that the war planning had
been far too optimistic. "We were underestimating how bad it
was, no doubt about it," he said.

With no power on the national grid, he and Khallaf realized
that it would be impossible to restart Baghdad South quickly.
Electrical plants, like cars, need power to get running. Baghdad
South required about eight megawatts, far more than the
capacity of the army's largest portable generator. The engineers eventually came up with a solution: divert power from a
hydroelectric station, one of the few generating facilities in
operation. Two weeks later, Baghdad South was operating
again. But its output was 25 megawatts less than before the
war. Once other plants started, they faced the same problem.
The shock of the sudden shutdown, the lack of spring maintenance because of the war, and general fatigue had made an
already ailing system even sicker. Although Iraqi and American engineers turned on as many units as they could, they
could not get overall national output above 3,500 megawatts—
well below the 6,500 megawatts needed to satisfy the nation's
demand or even the 4,400 megawatts produced before the war.

Bremer hoped to increase generation to 4,400 megawatts by
authorizing emergency repairs funded with the $230 million
set aside before the war. He directed his electricity adviser to
aim for that target, and he began promising Iraqis that power
would soon return to prewar levels.

Then, with the stroke of his pen, he put the CPA into a no-
win position. Some CPA staffers thought that instead of divert-
ing the lion's share of power to Baghdad, Iraqis should share it

equally. It made perfect sense to the Americans: in a democracy, the government doesn't pick favorites. The CPA's electricity team consulted Iraq's Electricity Commission. "They thought we were nuts," said Robyn McGuckin, who worked on the electricity team. "They warned us that it would cause all sorts of problems." But nobody listened. Bremer signed an edict mandating that power be allocated equally across Iraq.

Residents of Basra and Najaf and the rest of the south got a few more hours of electricity a day. People were pleased, but it didn't win the CPA any admirers. Baghdad, however, was short-circuited. The capital, which was accustomed to receiving uninterrupted power, found itself without it for at least twelve hours a day. The blackouts began to foster almost overnight nostalgia for Saddam among people who had cheered his fall. "We figured the Americans, who are a superpower, would at least give us electricity," said Mehdi Abdulwahid, an unemployed oil engineer, as he sold drinks on a busy sidewalk. "Now we wish we had the old times back." Saddam, Abdulwahid said with a sigh, "was a ruthless man, but at least we had the basics of life. How can we care about democracy now when we don't even have electricity?"

Bremer was unmoved. He insisted that doling out power equally was the right thing to do, and it pleased Shiite politicians from the south whom he was trying to woo onto the Governing Council. The shortage in Baghdad, Bremer reasoned, would end as soon as production increased.

But that never happened. The production figures he received every morning showed little movement above 3,500 megawatts. As summer temperatures surpassed 130 degrees, thousands of angry young men rioted in Basra, which was receiving just twelve hours of power a day. It was more than they had gotten before the war but nowhere near enough. Taps were running dry because there was no power to operate water-pumping stations. The blackouts shut down gasoline pumps, causing miles-long lines at fuel stations.

The riots alarmed Bremer, who decided he needed one person to oversee Iraq's infrastructure. He chose Steve Browning, the U.S. Army Corps of Engineers specialist who had headed four ministries in the first weeks of the occupation. Browning was no electricity expert. He was a disaster-response specialist, but he had a knack for organization and leadership. He also had Bremer's confidence. And unlike most other CPA officials, he spoke a little Arabic.

Browning was a trim man with thinning hair. More of a listener than a talker, when he did speak, his voice was soft and unfailingly polite. If he was offered tea, he drank it, and when Iraqis came to see him, he was one of the few Americans who served them tea. "We have to always remember that we are guests in their country," he would say to his colleagues. "We have to respect their customs."

His new title was director of infrastructure. Roads, water systems, phone lines—all were in his purview. But the top priority was electricity. His marching orders were simple: find out what's going wrong and fix it.

Browning asked the CPA's electricity team to show him their plan to restore power to prewar levels. There was no plan. Nor was there a budget to allocate the ministry's operating funds. Every other aspect of Iraq's government was being micromanaged. The education advisers were going through textbooks line by line to determine what should be expunged. The health-care team was studying every single prescription medication used by the Health Ministry. Americans assigned to Iraq's Foreign Ministry were vetting every single Iraqi diplomat. But the Ministry of Electricity had been left on its own. Iraqi managers and technicians had been allowed to resume control of power plants. An American contractor was conducting emergency repairs at a few power stations, but the overall challenge of increasing output had been inexplicably handed off to the Iraqis. The CPA's four-person electricity team was taking a hands-off, advisory role. The group was led by a hydropower expert from the Army Corps of Engineers, though only a few of Iraq's generating stations had water-powered units; most ran on oil or natural gas.

Browning was dumbfounded. The CPA seemed to be treating the problem of restoring power as an afterthought.

"When I went to my first meeting between the Americans and Iraqis working on electricity, all I saw was finger-pointing," he recalled. "It was really quite embarrassing."

A few days later, Browning told Bremer that the viceroy's

pledge to return Iraq to prewar power levels was impossible "because there's no plan to get there."

Bremer's response was that the goal had to be met. If he was told what was needed, he would supply it, whatever it was.

Browning said it was possible to make enough emergency repairs to restore prewar levels in two months. He offered to lead the effort with two conditions: "that we weren't going to run wild and crank up power in the short term in a way that destroyed equipment for the long term," and that Bremer understood that after they reached the goal of 4,400 megawatts, plants would have to be shut down for maintenance.

Bremer told him that he wanted updates every morning at seven. It would be Bremer's first meeting of the day.

"Go for it," Bremer told Browning. "I'm counting on you."

Browning's first order of business was to move the electricity team from a closet to a large room next to the dining hall. Then he assigned a young British international-development specialist to assemble a budget for the ministry. Browning instructed Bechtel, the American engineering firm that had received the $230 million government contract for power-sector repairs, to focus its resources on meeting the goal. And he set out to form a new team. He pulled in two electricity specialists working for the U.S. Agency for International Development, grabbed an expert from the Army Corps of Engineers, and asked the top military commander in Iraq, Lieutenant General Ricardo Sanchez, for as many military engineers as could be spared. A week later, Sanchez ordered each of the twelve army brigades in Iraq to contribute two engineers to Browning's team. The engineers were sent to power stations across the country and told to work with the plant managers to conduct a detailed assessment of what repairs could be made in two months to increase output. Browning then summoned all the plant managers and army engineers to Baghdad for a two-day pep talk. He had them share their individual repair plans with the group. If a manager said that he lacked a certain part, Browning asked all the others if they had the item in their stockrooms. He sent them back with an exhortation to meet the deadline. "You are Iraqis," he told them. "You are smart and proud and resourceful. I know you can meet this challenge."

The army engineers sent reports to Browning, who compiled a daily update that was presented to Bremer and sent to Washington, where Paul Wolfowitz and Condoleezza Rice read it almost every day. When one plant had to shut down because of an accidental fire, which sent output tumbling for a week, Browning was inundated with messages from the highest levels of the United States government. *What's going on? Are we going to make the deadline?*

Browning's team reached its goal five days late, but still it was a cause for celebration. After working eighteen-hour days for weeks on end, they had pulled off a feat many in the palace had deemed impossible.

The glory didn't last long. Plants began shutting down for maintenance the following day. Within two weeks, the CPA was back where it had started: overall output dipped to 3,600 megawatts. Even more worrisome to Browning was Sanchez's decision to recall all the engineers, which deprived the CPA team of an on-site taskmaster and a reliable way to communicate with each plant. And Bechtel's funds, which were earmarked for emergency repairs, were running out.

If the CPA was serious about fixing Iraq's electricity system, Browning believed it would have to do more than just emergency repairs. It would need to spend hundreds of millions of dollars more to renovate and rebuild decrepit stations such as Baghdad South.

One morning, he raised the subject with Bremer.

When the CPA's bean counters had begun assembling a national budget for Iraq, they discovered that the country's income, almost all of which came from oil sales, was nowhere near enough to pay for its expenses. Saddam had dealt with the shortfall by withholding funding for ministries, and by not investing in the nation's infrastructure. Power plants such as Baghdad South never received new parts or upgrades. If the engineers there needed equipment, they often scavenged at the junkyard.

To Bremer, this was unacceptable. Building a stable democracy required a government that could balance its books and meet its obligations to the Iraqi people. Cutting back food and fuel subsidies would save money over the long term, but that wasn't something the CPA could do right away. Dismantling the safety net could spark unrest.

Bremer also worried about investment in infrastructure. Balancing the budget was only half the problem. He believed that if Iraq's economy was to flourish, foreign companies would have to invest in factories, oil wells, and mines. Perhaps investors would buy government-run companies as they privatized. Perhaps they would set up operations from scratch. Either way, they would employ thousands upon thousands of people, thereby resuscitating the economy. But before foreign companies would invest, they needed to be certain that their factories would have enough electricity and water. Simply getting back to prewar levels was not enough. Iraq had to produce enough electricity not just to meet the demand of the moment, but also for the power-guzzling factories of its future. The same theory held for security. Far more money was required to train existing police officers and to hire tens of thousands of new ones. The way Bremer saw it, there was no way to defer improvements in Iraq's security and infrastructure. Electricity was a catalyst in getting the country back on its feet. He hoped that with a modest upfront investment, Iraq would be able to increase oil production and attract enough foreign investment within a few years to balance its books.

David Oliver, the CPA's budget czar, calculated that Iraq needed to invest between $5 billion and $10 billion a year in its infrastructure, and that wasn't counting the money required to make up for years of Saddam's underinvestment. (Needs assessments conducted by the United States, the United Nations, and the World Bank eventually put the figure at $55 billion over four years.) Iraq didn't have the money. Oil revenue was barely enough to pay for the government's salaries, supplies, and other operating expenses. Oliver decided that approaching other nations for contributions would take too long. He nixed the idea of loans. Iraq already had tens of billions of dollars in foreign debt. To Oliver, there was only one solution: "The gap had to be filled with American money."

He went to Bremer, who supported infrastructure investment but didn't have a sense of how much it would cost until Oliver showed him a spreadsheet. Tens of billions of dollars.

Tens of billions of *American taxpayer* dollars. The sum exceeded the non-inflation-adjusted cost of the Marshall Plan, the $13 billion American initiative to rebuild Europe after World War II, and seemed to represent political suicide. After all, White House and Pentagon officials had promised Americans before the war that Iraqi oil revenue would cover reconstruction. Bremer told Oliver that he'd think about it.

Bremer regarded the prewar statements about reconstruction to be guesses based on sketchy data. It wasn't until CPA officials got a good look at facilities such as Baghdad South that the enormity of the problem became clear. Although he accepted Wolfowitz and Feith's advice on de-Baathification and other matters in his first weeks on the job, Bremer had never shared their view that Iraq would be an in-and-out operation. When he and Bush met in the Oval Office, the president had expressed an impassioned desire to transform Iraq into a model democracy in the Middle East. With search teams unable to turn up any weapons of mass destruction, the primary American justification for the invasion, the viceroy deemed the development of democracy to be no longer just an important goal. It was *the* goal. Iraq would have to become that shining city on a hill in the Arab world. And to accomplish that, the United States couldn't ignore Iraq's need for better infrastructure. In Bremer's mind, the logical progression was simple: improved infrastructure begets economic development, which, in turn, begets stability, a prerequisite for democracy.

He met with Oliver four days later. Poll all the senior advisers and compile a detailed list of Iraq's needs, Bremer told Oliver. The viceroy said he'd take care of selling it to the White House. He had political capital. If there was a time to use it, it was now. But be discreet, Bremer told Oliver. If word leaked that the CPA wanted to spend billions upon billions of dollars to rebuild Iraq, it could prove politically disastrous. The announcement would have to be choreographed in Washington.

Oliver informed the senior advisers that they had a week to submit their wish lists. Browning had the electricity staff assemble a realistic set of projects the CPA could accomplish. Others shot for the moon. One proposal called for rebuilding every mosque in the country. When Oliver added it up, it came to $60 billion. There was no way that would fly, so he began chopping. There was plenty of fat to slice. By the time he was done, the list tallied $35 billion.

He took it to Bremer, who had been holding intense discussions with the White House. The Pentagon was planning to send Congress a request for a massive supplemental appropriation to support the military operations in Iraq and Afghanistan. A request for reconstruction funding could be tacked onto that, the White House said. But Bremer figured that $35 billion was too much. He and Oliver made a decision to halve it. The new target was about $18 billion. Bremer asked Oliver to prepare a detailed budget at that level. It would be sent to the White House and, eventually, to Congress. Within the CPA, the $18 billion became known as the Supplemental.

Oliver carved up the $18 billion. Electricity was deemed the most important; it would get $5.7 billion. Water and sewage would get $3.7 billion. Oil would get $2.1 billion. The proposals Oliver had received from the senior advisers were just rough guesses. He told them to give him a detailed plan of how they intended to spend the money.

This is odd, Browning thought.

"We started with a number and built down," he recalled. "It wasn't the way I had ever assembled a budget before. It was, 'You have $5.7 billion. Now fill in the blanks.' It wasn't a very smart approach." There wasn't much time for Browning to consult with his Iraqi counterparts or international experts. Oliver needed the plan in a week.

Andrew Bearpark, a veteran British post-conflict reconstruction specialist who was the CPA's director of operations, had a bad feeling about the Supplemental. "The planning process was done with such secrecy and such speed that it was never going to be a particularly rational process in terms of creating projects you really needed," he said. "We were predestined for failure. There is a rate at which you can plan these things. If you do something in five minutes that you should spend five months on, you'll cock it up."

Bearpark was a chain-smoker with the mouth of a sailor who didn't suffer fools gladly, and he made no effort to hide his habit of an evening glass, or two, of Johnnie Walker. When work kept him late at his desk in his palace office, which was more often than not, he'd begin drinking. But, for all of his eccentricities, Bearpark had far more postwar development experience than anyone else in the CPA. Among his British colleagues, he questioned the basic premise of the Supplemental. "We've got a country whose infrastructure is not up to the standards of this region," he said. "It's not as good as Kuwait or Saudi Arabia or the United Arab Emirates. It's not up to the standards of a major oil-producing nation. We want it to be that good and therefore we're going to make it that good. We're American and we're going to throw money at the problem. Well, the world doesn't work that way." More planning needed to be done to ensure that the right kinds of power plants and hospitals were being built in the right places, he said. Projects needed to be scaled back to make them sustainable, to allow Iraqis to build them and operate them.

Bremer and Oliver listened to Bearpark, but they didn't heed his advice. The stars were aligned in Washington at that moment for the Supplemental. Waiting a few more months for additional planning might close that window, Bremer said. And, more important, he wanted the CPA to begin infrastructure projects as soon as possible. What better way to make the Iraqis love us than to give them electricity?

Browning wanted to use most of the money to build small power stations around the country. He figured that smaller plants, which would be located in cities and towns, would be less susceptible to insurgent attacks because the local population would have an incentive to protect the source of their own electricity. But more senior CPA officials wanted to fund large power stations built by American contractors. If they could show that American business would benefit from the Supplemental, Congress was more likely to approve it. Bremer also reasoned that big projects would generate more electricity overall, which would promote economic development.

The formal Supplemental request was fifty-three pages long and totaled $20.3 billion. Bremer asked for $4.2 billion to fund and equip Iraq's police and army, $900 million to build and repair hospitals, $800 million to upgrade the transportation and communications infrastructure, and $900 million for the development of "civil society." The $5.7 billion for power would yield 8,000 megawatts of electricity; it was enough, the CPA predicted, to meet Iraq's demands for the next three years.

The document was a glimpse of the country Bremer wanted to build, a country that looked a lot like the United States. There was $4 million to create a nationwide system of area codes and telephone numbers, $9 million for a national ZIP code project, $19 million for wireless Internet service, and $20 million for "catch-up business training" that would "develop and train a cadre of entrepreneurs in business fundamentals and concepts that were missing in the former Iraqi regime." A $200 million American-Iraqi Enterprise Fund would promote the development of a private sector in Iraq. Bremer even asked for $150 million for a "state of the art" children's hospital in Basra that would handle plastic surgery and pediatric oncology, despite warnings from the CPA's health team that Iraq did not have the resources to fund the ongoing operation of such a facility.

In September 2003, Bremer traveled to Washington to testify before four congressional committees considering the Supplemental. He compared the aid package with the Marshall Plan.

> The grants to Iraq the president seeks bespeak a grandeur of vision equal to the one which created the free world at the end of World War II. . . . Iraqis living in freedom with dignity will set an example in this troubled region which so often spawns terrorists. A stable, peaceful, economically productive Iraq will serve American interests by making America safer.
>
> When we launched military operations against Iraq we assumed a great responsibility that extends beyond defeating Saddam's military. We cannot simply pat the Iraqis on the back, tell them they are lucky to be rid of Saddam and then ask them to go find their place in a global market—to compete without the tools for competition. To do so would invite economic collapse followed by political extremism and a return to terrorism. If, after coming this far, we turn our backs and let Iraq lapse into

factional chaos, some new tyranny, and terrorism, we
will have committed a grave error. Not only will we have
left the long-suffering Iraqi people to a future of danger
and deprivation, we will have sown the dragon's teeth
which will sprout more terrorists and eventually cost
more American lives.

Five weeks later, Congress approved the Supplemental after
cutting out the ZIP codes, the wireless Internet service, and
several other small projects. The final total was $18.4 billion.

The night President Bush signed the Supplemental into law,
I saw Bremer in his office. It was almost ten o'clock. His tie was
loosened and his sleeves rolled up. Get ready for a big change,
he said. He predicted that funds from the Supplemental would
begin flowing into Iraq within weeks. "We're going to transform this place," he said.

Bremer's ambition wasn't confined to the Supplemental. It was
across the board. Over the summer of 2003, the CPA's Policy
Planning Office created a twenty-eight-page list of milestones
that were to be accomplished before sovereignty was returned
to the Iraqi people. The document was divided into three
phases: August to October 2003, November 2003 to January
2004, and February 2004 onward. The list of milestones
became the playbook for Americans in Baghdad.

The very first goal was to "defeat internal armed threats."
The task was assigned to CJTF-7—Combined Joint Task Force
Seven, the formal name for the U.S.-led military forces in Iraq.
All the bad guys were to be taken care of in the first phase, by
October 31. Power generation was to reach 5,000 megawatts by
January, even though Browning couldn't keep the system
above 4,000. The airport was to open by October, despite warn-
ings that the insurgents had hundreds of shoulder-fired anti-
aircraft missiles.

When it came to economic reform, Bremer and his policy
planners weren't daunted by the challenges Glenn Corliss and
Brad Jackson were facing with the Ministry of Industry. Privatization of state-owned enterprises was to begin by October. A
trust fund modeled after one in the state of Alaska was to be

established to provide Iraqis with annual cash rebates from oil sales. Monthly food rations were to be converted into cash payments by November. The food subsidies, along with below-market prices for gasoline and electricity, were to be eliminated after February. Iraq was to prepare to join the World Trade Organization, which meant the elimination of tariffs, the creation of new laws to protect businesses, and the entry of foreign-owned banks. "It's a full-scale economic overhaul," Bremer said. "We're going to create the first real free-market economy in the Arab world."

The political plan was just as bold. Bremer had rejected advice from Wolfowitz and Feith to cede more authority to the former exiles and had instead formed the Governing Council. The twenty-five-member body was Bremer's answer to the political-transition debate that had vexed Washington for months. The council was his showpiece: a multiethnic, multireligious group that included men in turbans and men in suits, women and tribal sheiks, Sunnis and Shiites, Arabs and Kurds. Council members looked good on paper and in pictures, but their on-the-job performance exasperated the CPA. The council had taken weeks to select a president, and then had opted for a rotating presidency among nine members, eight of whom were former exiles. Once the leadership was settled, many members stopped attending meetings. They used their new status to stake claim to riverfront villas and to travel overseas at government expense.

The council was just the first step in Bremer's seven-step transition plan to full Iraqi sovereignty. The other steps were the selection of a "preparatory committee" to devise a way to draft a constitution, the council's assumption of more day-to-day governing tasks, the writing of a constitution, popular ratification of the constitution through a national referendum, the election of a government, and, finally, the handover of sovereignty. Just when that would occur, Bremer did not say. He hoped it would happen by late 2004, but many of his aides expected the occupation to stretch into 2005. Whenever he was asked how long the occupation would last, he relied on the same vague sound bite: "We have no desire to stay a day longer than is necessary."

Bremer discussed elements of his plan on video teleconferences with senior members of the Bush administration, but there was no comprehensive, interagency discussion about America's exit strategy. He didn't share a draft with the State Department, the National Security Council, or the CIA. The first time Colin Powell saw the plan was on the editorial pages of *The Washington Post,* which published an op-ed by Bremer titled "Iraq's Path to Sovereignty."

The viceroy was adamant that his plan was the best. He rejected the idea of holding early elections, he said, because voter rolls and election laws didn't exist. But the real reason was that he feared Baathists or religious extremists might triumph. He nixed the idea of an interim constitution, invoking Saddam's reliance on temporary constitutions as an example the United States did not want to emulate. "Electing a government without a permanent constitution defining and limiting government powers invites confusion and eventual abuse," he wrote in the op-ed. And he shook his head at the notion of simply handing power over to the council. If Iraq was going to be a beacon of democracy in the region, he insisted, it needed a democratically elected government.

He continued to brush off Grand Ayatollah al-Sistani's fatwa stating that Iraq's constitution had to be written by elected representatives. But it was evident to anyone who spent any time among Iraq's Shiite majority, either in Baghdad's Sadr City neighborhood or in Basra or any other city in the south, that al-Sistani's religious authority was unparalleled. He was the spiritual leader. Every other cleric was subordinate to him. Inside the Emerald City, however, al-Sistani was just another old man in a black turban.

Some of the viceroy's political advisers did grasp the grand ayatollah's influence, but they still refused to heed his fatwa. To them, it was a matter of principle. They wanted to establish an American-style separation of church and state. Giving in to al-Sistani, they maintained, would set a dangerous precedent.

To veteran Middle East hands in the State Department, Bremer's plan sounded awfully unrealistic. Iraqi politicians had the same reaction. "It seems impossible," one Governing Council member said.

But Bremer was unmoved. "This is the only way to go," he told me. "I don't see any other option."

John Agresto arrived in Iraq with two suitcases, a feather pillow, and a profusion of optimism. His title was senior adviser to the Ministry of Higher Education, but he envisioned the job in grander terms. It was not just to oversee but to overhaul the country's university system. He wanted to introduce the concept of academic freedom and to open liberal arts colleges. He hoped to restock libraries with the latest books and to wire classrooms with high-speed Internet connections. He regarded the postwar looting, which had eviscerated many campuses, as a benefit. It provided "the opportunity for a clean start" and was a chance to give Iraqis "the best modern equipment."

Agresto was a lifelong Republican. The son of a Brooklyn dockworker, he was the first in his family to go to college. He went on to earn a doctorate in political science from Cornell University. After a brief teaching career, he joined the National Endowment for the Humanities during the culture wars of the 1980s. Along with Lynne Cheney and William Bennett, he hectored the higher-education establishment as liberal and lazy. After leaving the NEH, he spent eleven years as president of St. John's, a small, classical liberal arts college known for its Great Books curriculum. In 2000, he retired and set up a consulting company. In his spare time, he prepared homemade Italian sausage and relaxed with his wife in their cabin near the Pecos River in New Mexico.

A few weeks after U.S. troops rolled into Baghdad, Agresto got a call from his predecessor at St. John's, Edwin Delattre, who asked if he'd be interested in going to Iraq. A professor of philosophy at Boston University and an adjunct fellow at the American Enterprise Institute, Delattre had been approached about the Iraq job by John Silber, BU's president emeritus, who had been contacted by Jim O'Beirne, the White House liaison at the Pentagon. O'Beirne had figured that Silber, one of the few social conservatives in American academia, could recommend candidates who supported President Bush's decision to invade Iraq. Agresto most certainly did. He described himself as a "strong supporter" of the war.

But it was more than ideology that drove him to say yes. He was in graduate school during the Vietnam War. Although his draft status was 1A, his number never came up in the lottery. Going to Iraq, he reasoned, "was a way of finally serving" his country. *I'm almost sixty years old,* he said to himself. *I don't have that many years left to do good.*

"This is what Americans do: they go and help," he explained to me later. "I guess I just always wanted to be a good American." And, he said, he had "an inkling that this would be a never-to-be-repeated adventure."

Before he committed to go, he called Don Rumsfeld, whose wife had served on the St. John's board. He didn't have Rumsfeld's number at the Pentagon, so he left a message for him at home. "If there's any reason I shouldn't consider it, phone me back at once," Agresto said. He never got a call. But when he talked to O'Beirne again, he was told that Rumsfeld had weighed in on Agresto's selection. "Put a rush on it," the defense secretary had said.

Agresto knew next to nothing about Iraq's educational system. Even after he was selected, the former professor didn't read a single book about Iraq. "I wanted to come here with as open a mind as I could have," he said. "I'd much rather learn firsthand than have it filtered to me by an author."

His training from the Defense Department was no more extensive. "They taught me how to put on a gas mask, how to get the helmet snug, how to button up your flak jacket," he said. "That's it."

None of that fazed him. The televised images of Iraqis cheering as the statue of Saddam was toppled in Firdaus Square seemed like the Middle Eastern version of the Berlin Wall coming down. "Once you see that, you can't help but say, Okay. This is going to work," Agresto said.

In September 2003, he flew from Texas to Kuwait on a chartered 747 and then into Baghdad on an air force C-130, a propeller-driven cargo hauler that served as the CPA's personnel shuttle. The plane approached the airfield at a high altitude and then corkscrewed straight down to avoid insurgent missiles, leveling off just above the runway. Upon disembarking, Agresto was ushered into a heavily armed convoy for the journey along the treacherous eight-mile road to the Green Zone. It was his first taste of how security trumped everything—work, comfort, pleasure—in Iraq.

As a senior adviser, Agresto had no budget. If he wanted to accomplish anything, he'd have to cozy up to USAID, which had earmarked $25 million for Iraqi universities. He hoped to get millions more—hundreds of millions, even—from the Supplemental and from other nations. A needs assessment conducted by the World Bank and the United Nations estimated that Iraq required almost $2 billion to "ensure minimal quality standards of teaching and learning."

Much of the money was needed to repair and reequip looted universities. At Baghdad's Mustansiriya University, the pillaging began the day Saddam's government collapsed. In three days, the campus of yellow-brick buildings and grassy courtyards was stripped of its books, computers, lab equipment, and desks. Even electrical wiring was pulled from the walls. What was not stolen was set ablaze, spreading dark smoke over the capital. When Agresto saw the damage to Mustansiriya and the nearby College of Technology—where three thousand computers and every bit of laboratory equipment had been stolen in a four-hour period—he stopped thinking of the looting as the "opportunity for a clean start." Rebuilding the campuses would be his primary challenge. Without desks, books, or science labs, there was no way Agresto would be able to talk about academic freedom and a liberal arts curriculum.

A month after he arrived, representatives from donor nations gathered in Madrid to consider Iraq's reconstruction needs. Agresto put together what he hoped was a persuasive plea for international aid that included plans for "a nationwide electronic library network" and a "Western-style graduate business school." He asked for money for new textbooks, new classrooms, and for sixteen "Centers of Advanced Study" in fields such as biotechnology, conflict resolution, and information technology. The total price tag for Iraq to "take its rightful place in the world's intellectual, cultural, economic, and political communities" was $1.2 billion.

"We now have the opportunity to make a new start, and to supply Iraq with, for example, some of the best classrooms, laboratories, and libraries possible," Agresto wrote in the CPA's pitch to donors.

> It is not hyperbole to say that we have very few years to complete and very few months to begin the rebuilding of higher education in Iraq. The excellent faculty leaders who were trained in Europe and the United States in the fifties, sixties, and early seventies are at or near the end of their careers. Those who will follow in leadership have never been exposed to world-class research or international higher education. Without immediate, as well as in-depth, exposure to the contemporary scholarly world and the technology to participate in it, the needed experience to rebuild a quality teaching and research infrastructure for the coming generations will be lost. The lack of knowledge-based workers and world-educated leaders endangers the stability of Iraq and, by extension, the security of the rest of the world.

The donor nations pledged $400 million. Agresto was not disappointed. It was a start, he figured. There would be another conference in six months. He could ask for more money then.

Physical reconstruction was a means to an end for Agresto. What really excited him were Iraqis such as Asmat Khalid, the president of the University of Dohuk. A short, stocky, and gruff man, Khalid seemed to Agresto "more the head of a New Jersey truckers local than the founder and president of a major university." He had opened his university in the early 1990s, when U.S. fighter jets began enforcing a no-fly zone over Dohuk and the rest of Kurdish-controlled northern Iraq, keeping Saddam's army at bay and giving the Kurds de facto autonomy. Asmat wanted to start what he called a "College of Humanity," which would offer courses in political philosophy, democratic theory, Western civilization, the history of liberty, and human rights. No one would be allowed to graduate without passing the human rights course. There would even be a course in comparative religion. Agresto asked if Khalid would really introduce students to the Old and New Testaments in such a course. "Yes, of course," he told Agresto. And would he, Agresto asked, ever hire a Jew to teach the Old Testament course? Khalid didn't hesitate. "Of course," he said. "Why not?"

When the Pentagon asked him how long he'd stay in Iraq, Agresto didn't say three months, the minimum commitment required of CPA staffers and the response heard most often in the palace.

"For the duration," he replied.

PART TWO

Shattered Dreams

9

Let This Be Over

THE AL-RASHEED HOTEL WAS a concrete-and-glass monstrosity built by the Oberoi Group of India in the 1980s, before Saddam's manic spending spree on weapons to defeat Iran, and before the invasion of Kuwait made Iraq an international pariah. When the al-Rasheed opened, its 428 guest rooms had buttery leather chairs, color televisions, touch-tone phones, wall-to-wall carpeting, and marble-floored bathrooms. Downstairs, the Sheherezade Bar poured Johnnie Walker Black Label, the 1,001 Nights Disco teemed with dolled-up call girls, and a shopping arcade stocked French perfume. A medical clinic staffed with a European doctor tended to guests' aches and pains.

After the Kuwait war, United Nations sanctions forced the Oberoi Group to leave the country. Saddam's government took over the al-Rasheed and every other foreign hotel in the country, including the Ishtar Sheraton and Le Méridien, which was renamed the Palestine Hotel. The cash-strapped Finance Ministry eliminated the al-Rasheed's maintenance budget. For a few years, nobody noticed. Then the elevators broke, the linens frayed, and the toilets began to leak. By the time I paid my first visit to the hotel in 2002, the leather chairs had faded and cracked, the mattresses sagged, and I had to bribe the cleaning man for a roll of toilet paper. Most of the phones didn't work, and the televisions displayed only a half dozen channels, all of which were run by the government. Saddam's regime didn't allow CNN or the BBC in the hotel. My fellow guests and I suspected that Saddam's secret police had hidden bugs in the televisions.

A week before the war, the Pentagon warned American news organizations to vacate the al-Rasheed. A big bunker underneath the hotel put it on the target list. But those of us on the ground knew better. As decrepit as it had become, it still was the best place to sleep in town. The Americans would want to stay there when they came.

The first wave of American civilians—Jay Garner and ORHA—moved into the Republican Palace instead. Their security advisers said that the fourteen-story al-Rasheed, which soared over neighboring buildings, was too vulnerable to an attack. But as the palace began overflowing with people, the threat assessment changed: the CPA's security officers deemed the hotel safe enough to bed hundreds of employees who had been sleeping on cots in the palace, waiting for the housing trailers Halliburton was supposed to bring to Baghdad.

The job of running the al-Rasheed fell to Halliburton, which promptly rehired dozens of the hotel's prewar employees, including several I suspected were former intelligence agents. Little was done to renovate the rooms, but the company did reopen the disco and set up a sports bar in the basement bunker. The hotel became the place to party in the Emerald City.

Colonel Elias Nimmer yawned and rolled over. He had opened his eyes ten minutes earlier, at six o'clock, as the first sliver of the sun edged above the horizon and transformed the desert sky from deep indigo to light blue. His roommate was away, and Nimmer hadn't bothered to close the curtains before going to sleep. After almost three decades in the army, his body was accustomed to waking at sunrise.

When Nimmer stood at his west-facing window in Room 916, he could gaze down on an eight-lane expressway and, beyond that, the city's zoo and a surrounding park, a dusty expanse with wilting plants and decrepit buildings. To the left were the most famous monuments erected by Saddam: a giant ziggurat to commemorate the war with Iran, and a military parade ground bookended with massive arches in the shape of human arms—reportedly modeled after Saddam's own—hoisting crossed swords.

I need to get up, Nimmer thought. It was a Sunday, and he didn't have to report for duty at the Republican Palace until eleven, but he sensed that it would be a pleasant morning. He contemplated going for a walk before getting an early start at work. He was the chief budget officer for the CPA team that worked with Iraq's Ministry of Health. It was an exceedingly complex job, but Nimmer, a naturalized American citizen who was born in Lebanon and spoke Arabic, had plenty of experience. He had been the chief budget officer for the Walter Reed Army Medical Center in Washington. Before that, he'd managed a billion-dollar budget at Fort Detrick, the army's top medical research facility.

Nimmer was a beefy man with a square jaw, a pointy nose, and a swarthy complexion. His receding graying hair had been buzzed with army-regulation clippers. He yawned and thought about catching a few more minutes of shut-eye. *Should I or shouldn't I? Should I or—* A deafening explosion rocked the hotel, and the building shuddered. Nimmer jolted awake.

Oh my God, he thought. *They've finally done it.*

Instinct took over, and Nimmer rolled onto the floor. *Nobody ever fires one rocket. More are coming,* he thought. The safest place was on the ground, as far from the window as possible. He couldn't slide under his bed because he was too large to fit under the low box spring. He did the next best thing: he lay on his stomach between his bed and his roommate's. *It's like a trench down here. I'll be safe.*

It was October 26, 2003—six and a half months after American troops arrived in Baghdad. Insurgents had targeted the al-Rasheed with rockets a month earlier, but it had been a Wile E. Coyote affair. The projectiles had been launched from a makeshift stand in a residential neighborhood north of the Green Zone. One of them hit the top floor but caused little damage. Another landed in the garden. A third struck a house near the launch site. The hotel's narrow north façade wasn't the worry, nor the south, which abutted a mile-long expanse of Green Zone. The greatest points of vulnerability were the eastern and western faces—the two long sides with windows.

The CPA's security officers had dismissed the chances of a serious attack, assuming that the insurgents didn't have the skill or equipment to target the hotel with accuracy. But residents had been unnerved by the incident.

Sniper attacks and roadside bombings outside the Green

Zone had become more frequent. Car bombs had destroyed the Jordanian embassy and the United Nations headquarters, killing the head of the mission, Brazilian diplomat Sérgio Vieira de Mello. Intelligence officers began hearing of plots to kidnap foreigners. But the Emerald City, with its seventeen-foot-high walls and its checkpoints, was supposed to be safe.

Twenty seconds after the first impact, a second rocket crashed into a concrete awning outside Nimmer's window, shattering the glass and propelling debris into the room.

Nimmer began to pray. *Please God, let this be over.*

The third rocket followed the same trajectory as the second, except it streaked through the clear morning sky at a slightly higher angle. Like the others, it was an eighty-five-millimeter Katyusha, made in Russia. It had probably been sold to Iraq in the 1980s for use against Iran. Thousands had been looted from arms depots after the war.

A Katyusha travels at three times the speed of sound. If you're standing near one being launched, its sound resembles a high-pitched squeal amplified through a megaphone. If you're on the receiving end, you don't hear a thing until impact.

The third rocket flew through the shattered window of Room 916 and slammed into the wall to Nimmer's right. He saw a bright flash—as if someone had stuck a camera into his face—from the rocket's exploding phosphorous warhead. Then he felt a powerful burst of pressurized air from the blast wave. Scalding chunks of the rocket, pieces of wall plaster, slivers from the steel beams, and glass from the light fixtures pierced his flesh like shotgun pellets. The debris slammed onto his head, his back, his legs, singeing his skin.

Nimmer screamed. He thought he was going to die.

With his next breath, he tried to speak. "Help," he shouted hoarsely. "I need help in here."

Burning debris crackled around him. Electrical wires sparked. The room filled with smoke and the acrid odor of cordite. In the distance, he could hear shouting.

The hotel shuddered from the impact of another rocket. And then it was quiet.

"Is anybody there?" he wailed softly. "Somebody, please help me."

Nobody called out to him.

I better not shout anymore. I need to preserve my energy.

He tried to crawl, but only dug himself deeper into the debris.

I know they'll come for me. I have to save my strength.

Another rocket hit the hotel. And another. Nimmer counted seven more rockets after the one that got him.

He didn't know it at the time, but the rocket that flew through his window didn't explode in his room. If it had, he wouldn't have been alive to scream. It had punctured the wall and detonated in the bathroom. Much of the force of the blast had traveled away from him, demolishing the closet, the front door, and the hallway.

One of Nimmer's colleagues on the Health Ministry team, Lieutenant Colonel Charles Fisher, was living across the hall, in Room 915. The blast wave was so powerful that it threw him to the ground. In between the explosions, he could hear Nimmer's cries for help, which were growing fainter. *Oh, shit,* Fisher thought. *He's hurt pretty bad.*

"Elias," he shouted. "I'm coming to get you."

There was no response.

Fisher grabbed his rifle and his backpack, which contained his medical kit, and began to dig his way through the rubble blocking his door. Nimmer couldn't have been luckier. Fisher was a physician—not just any doctor, but the former director of critical care medicine at the Cleveland Clinic—and he was in the army's elite Special Forces.

When he reached the hallway, he found a wall of debris blocking Nimmer's door. He picked up what he could and threw it aside. When he entered Room 916, he came upon a 220-volt electrical wire dangling from the ceiling and sparking like an arc welder. Crawling under the wire, he began to dig toward Nimmer.

He's dead, Fisher thought at first. Rubble covered much of Nimmer's body. His white T-shirt was soaked with blood, and a large piece of wood had fallen on his head.

As Fisher cleared the debris, Nimmer moaned.

"Chuck, I can't move," he whispered. "I'm numb from the waist down."

Two South African security contractors shouted into the room from the hallway. "Anyone there?"

Fisher asked them to clear a path wide enough to remove the injured man and then enlisted them to help him carry Nimmer to the lobby. Fisher and the South Africans wrapped Nimmer in a blanket and hauled him down nine flights of stairs. With each bump, Nimmer yelped in pain.

The al-Rasheed's lobby was filled with panicked, disoriented CPA staffers. Paul Wolfowitz and his Pentagon entourage had been overnighting in the hotel. They milled around in one corner, surrounded by guards. Wolfowitz was dressed better than anyone else—in slacks and a light blue oxford shirt—but his hair was tousled and his face ashen.

The crowd parted as Nimmer's rescuers carried him into the lobby and eased him onto the marble floor. A medic began an intravenous drip, and Fisher conducted a fuller assessment of his friend. It didn't look good. He suspected not just brain damage and a skeletal injury but also serious abdominal and spinal damage.

A Humvee ambulance pulled up to collect Nimmer for the short ride to the Green Zone hospital. Fisher jumped in the back with him. Halfway there, Nimmer removed the crucifix from around his neck and pressed it into Fisher's hand.

"Chuck, I don't think I'm going to make it," he said. "Please give this to my wife. It's a family heirloom."

At the hospital, Nimmer was placed on a gurney and rolled into the emergency room. "He's immediate," Fisher shouted. "Roll him in."

After Fisher went off to search for the chief neurosurgeon, an orderly mistook Nimmer for an Iraqi prisoner of war and wheeled him into a holding area for Iraqis who had been shot by American troops.

"You don't understand," he screamed. "I'm a fucking U.S. Army colonel. I don't belong with these people."

Then he passed out.

Surgeons removed two large Starbucks-size cups' worth of shrapnel from Nimmer's legs and back. They extricated bits of metal from his vertebrae that had caused the temporary paralysis. Examining his left ear, they discovered that the drum had been blown out. They treated burns on his face caused by the unspent rocket fuel.

Fifteen hours later, he was on a medevac flight to an army

hospital in Germany. He would eventually be sent to Walter Reed. He would endure a dozen more surgeries. It would be harrowing, painful, and depressing at times, but he would recover.

The Emerald City never would.

Fifteen hours before the attack, Major General Martin Dempsey had stood at the center of the Fourteenth of July Bridge and proclaimed that "safety and security have been achieved" in Baghdad. As a U.S. Army band played Iraq's national anthem, he and three members of the Baghdad City Council cut a blue ribbon strung across the roadway.

"Go ahead, it's open!" an Iraqi policeman yelled. Hundreds of children and adults sprinted over, cheering and clapping.

The bridge, named after the July 14, 1958, revolution that overthrew the British-backed monarchy, spanned the Tigris southwest of the Republican Palace. It fed into an eight-lane expressway that flanked the al-Rasheed on the west before connecting to the main highway north to Mosul. Both the bridge and the expressway, which bisected the Green Zone, had been closed since the day the Americans arrived.

But as summer gave way to autumn, the U.S. military's "Force Protection" team, the unit responsible for securing the Emerald City, grudgingly agreed to reopen the bridge and the expressway. Seventeen-foot-high blast walls had been placed around the Green Zone's perimeter, reducing the chances that someone on the bridge could take a potshot at the palace. Blast walls also lined both sides of the expressway, forming an aboveground tunnel through Little America. Americans crossed the expressway using an underpass near the al-Rasheed.

Iraqi politicians had been complaining that the closure was causing miles-long traffic jams on other roads and bridges. Although insurgent attacks in the capital were on the rise, the CPA was still clinging to the idea that the country was becoming safer by the day. When Force Protection officials objected, CPA staffers noted that the city's zoo and a surrounding park, which was on the other side of the expressway from the al-Rasheed, had been opened a month earlier without incident.

At five-thirty the next morning, a white pickup truck towing a trailer loaded with what appeared to be a blue electrical generator drove down the expressway and turned into the park opposite the al-Rasheed. The driver stopped in a clearing with a line of sight to the hotel. He, and possibly an accomplice, opened the side panels of the supposed generator. Inside was a crudely welded array of forty rocket tubes. Half were French-made. The other twenty were manufactured in Russia. The launcher was booby-trapped, and a battery-operated timer was activated.

Afterward, Dempsey told Wolfowitz that the attack revealed the weakness of the forces opposing the American occupation. The launcher was a makeshift contraption. Only one hotel occupant, a psychological operations specialist on the Strategic Communications team, was killed. The hotel was damaged but far from destroyed.

Many in the Green Zone drew the opposite conclusion. To them, the attack demonstrated that the Emerald City was no longer an oasis of safety. The insurgents had struck at the heart of American power in Iraq and killed a CPA staffer. Dempsey and other generals eventually conceded that months of surveillance and planning probably had preceded the assault.

The sight of bloody Americans sprawled on the lobby floor scarred many in the CPA. They had never before witnessed the impact of their war. A few staffers ran outside to retch.

The Fourteenth of July Bridge and the expressway were once again closed off to Iraqis, but security officers, fearful of a copycat attack, still decided to shutter the hotel. The rockets had damaged the plumbing and electrical systems anyway. Some floors were covered with a foot of water or scorched by small fires.

Hotel residents had no choice but to move back into the palace. Some slept in their offices. Halliburton and the army set up cots in the gargantuan ballroom, in the hallways, even in the closets. The building came to resemble a large orphanage. Morale plummeted as CPA staffers, who already had been complaining about having to share rooms in the hotel, were forced to sleep with hundreds of their colleagues and line up at Porta-Potties.

The only upside was that people felt safer. The palace was

far enough inside the Green Zone that insurgents couldn't get a straight shot at it, and the foot-thick walls seemed like protection against future rocket attacks. But two days after the al-Rasheed assault, insurgents lobbed mortars into the Emerald City. They did it the following day too, and for many of the remaining days of the occupation. They rarely hit anything of significance. Instead of calibrating successive shots to improve accuracy, the insurgents would set up their mortar tubes across the Tigris and let several rounds fly in rapid succession before they sped away. American radar could pinpoint the origin of a shot within seconds, but the army didn't automatically retaliate because it wasn't clear if the attacks had been launched from populated areas. The army didn't want to drop an artillery round in the middle of a bazaar.

Whether the insurgents actually hit anything, the simple act of tossing a few mortars inside the bubble sowed anxiety among residents of the Emerald City. Danger was everywhere.

Whenever there was a mortar attack, loudspeakers in the palace boomed. "Take cover! Take cover!" Staffers called it the Giant Voice, and it was always a minute or two late. Usually by the time the announcement echoed through the marble hallways, the mortars had already landed. But everyone went through the motions anyway. They strapped on their flak vests and helmets and ran toward the basement shelter.

The almost daily bleating of the Giant Voice began to fray nerves. Many staffers had difficulty sleeping. Others took to smoking and drinking. Visits to the Combat Stress Clinic increased. Some CPA personnel started popping tranquilizers and antidepressants.

It wasn't just that they felt scared. The attack on the al-Rasheed and the mortar barrage shattered the illusion inside the Emerald City that Iraq was becoming safe. From the earliest days of the occupation, the CPA had labored under the assumption that Iraq would be a quiescent terrarium in which to cultivate democracy and a free market. Peter McPherson's economic development strategy assumed that the country would be safe enough for multinational firms to establish factories. John Agresto's higher-education strategy assumed that he and his team would be able to travel to every university.

Jerry Bremer's political strategy assumed that governance specialists could drive around the country to promote democracy. Reports of insurgent attacks were brushed off. The bad stuff, they assumed, was happening in Fallujah, in Ramadi, in Tikrit—the so-called Sunni Triangle.

The assaults on the Green Zone were the first chinks in the armor. "It was a rude wake-up call," a CPA friend told me. "All of a sudden, we realized that the security situation was nothing like what we had been led to believe. And people began asking themselves, If things are getting worse, not better, how can we possibly do all these ambitious things we hoped to do? That's what really freaked people out."

The CPA's daily security reports took on an alarmist tone. Every issue brought a new BOLO warning—Be On the Look Out—for suspicious cars, for fake badges, for booby traps. The few shopping excursions or dinners at fancy restaurants outside the bubble ceased. CPA staffers began carrying weapons in the Green Zone.

There were always rumors of another attack in the works, except the next time it wouldn't involve rockets or mortars, but car bombs and waves of armed insurgents storming the palace. The population of Iraqis in the Green Zone was increasing by hundreds a day, according to one rumor, a sure sign that legions of bad guys had infiltrated the supposedly secure bubble.

Americans began to question the allegiances of their Iraqi interpreters and secretaries. One internal assessment estimated that as many as 60 percent of the Iraqis working for the CPA were compromised. The problem was that the Americans did not know which ones were. The Americans believed that Iraqis assumed to be loyal to the CPA had the lives of their families threatened by insurgents, who wanted to know where Americans went when they left the Green Zone. The Iraqis had no confidence that the CPA would protect them if they reported threats. More often than not, CPA security officers believed, the Iraqis gave the insurgents the information they sought.

Force Protection began posting signs around the palace warning people not to leave sensitive material in places where Iraqis might see it. Rather than becoming more involved in CPA operations, Iraqis were pushed to the margins.

"You couldn't share things with your Iraqi colleagues. You couldn't travel outside the Green Zone. You couldn't stay at the al-Rasheed," a CPA friend told me. "We felt like we were under siege." He paused. "You can't run a country that way," he said. "You can create the illusion that you're running things, but you can't actually do it."

THE GREEN ZONE, SCENE VII

On a balmy Wednesday night in May, six weeks before the handover of sovereignty, dozens of CPA staffers gathered around the palace pool for yet another farewell party. Jerry Bremer wanted his subordinates to return home in small groups, to avoid the perception that Americans were deserting Iraq en masse. The ambitious ones angled to be on the latest possible flight. Others couldn't wait to head to the airport. Either way, they wanted to have one last round of drinks with their buddies. Every night in May and June was consumed with goodbye events—at the pool, at the al-Rasheed, at the Chinese restaurants.

It had been a quiet night. No mortar thunderclaps. No messages from the Giant Voice warning people to take cover.

Then came the gunshots. A pop-pop-pop *in the distance. Alex Dehgan, a State Department employee at the pool party, dismissed it as a firefight between soldiers and insurgents. So did his colleagues.*

But the popping grew louder, more intense. It seemed to be coming from every direction. Orange tracer rounds arced into the night sky. Bursts of AK-47 fire echoed across the Tigris.

Dehgan began to panic. This is it, *he thought.* The full-on assault. They're going to crawl over the walls.

He and everyone else by the pool scurried indoors. Some ran into the basement shelter. Others retreated to their offices but stayed away from the windows. They began to wonder if they'd have to leave by helicopter, like the last staffers at the American embassy in Saigon.

Hours later they heard the news: Iraq had defeated Saudi Arabia 3 to 1 in a soccer match, earning a berth at that summer's Olympics in Athens.

Baghdad was celebrating.

10

The Plan Unravels

IN A PALATIAL VILLA on the Tigris River, members of Iraq's Governing Council milled about an ornate receiving room the size of a basketball court. There were former exiles in Savile Row suits, women wearing colorful head scarves, Shiite religious leaders with black turbans identifying them as descendants of the Prophet Mohammed, a tribal sheik in a gold-fringed black cloak. Butlers offered shot glasses of sweet tea, a welcome dose of warmth on a chilly autumn morning. Young aides ferried chirping mobile phones to their bosses. Weathered Kurdish militiamen and thick-necked former U.S. Special Forces soldiers stood guard in front of the house, a former residence of Saddam's half brother.

After fifteen minutes, Jerry Bremer walked into the room with a gaggle of guards and a half dozen aides. From afar, he appeared the same as ever: pressed blue suit, manicured hair, vigorous gait. Those who looked more carefully saw that his face seemed drawn, the wrinkles on his forehead deeper, the bags under his eyes bigger.

It was November 15, 2003. He had just returned from emergency consultations at the White House and the Pentagon—a trip so hastily arranged that he left Iraq aboard an air force medical evacuation flight. He had summoned the council to discuss the outcome of his discussions in Washington.

As he entered, the usually jovial Governing Council members were chatting in somber tones. Three days earlier, American troops had mistakenly riddled a member's vehicle with bullets as it entered the Green Zone. Although only one Iraqi was wounded, angry members resolved to stop using their Green Zone chambers. When Bremer said that he wanted to talk to them, they told him he'd have to leave the Emerald City and drive to the home of Jalal Talabani, the corpulent Kurdish politician who held the council's rotating presidency.

Bremer normally met with the council on Wednesdays, not Saturday mornings. But everything about this gathering was different. The council, a motley assortment of political veterans and neophytes, had recently become more assertive. They regarded the occupation as troubled, and they saw themselves as saviors. But Bremer still viewed them as lackeys. He thought they were disorganized, craven, and self-centered, but they were also his frontmen, and he needed their imprimatur on big decisions so it would appear that the Iraqis concurred with their occupiers.

After a round of pleasantries, he got down to business. He had an offer that he assumed Iraq's political leaders would not refuse, an offer that would change the course of the occupation.

Bremer's seven-step path to sovereignty had run aground.

Step one was the formation of the Governing Council. That was done. Step two was the establishment of a "preparatory committee" to determine how a constitution should be written. That also had been accomplished. Step three was the Governing Council's assumption of more day-to-day governing tasks. That was occurring in fits and starts. Step four was the writing of a constitution—and that's where the plan had stalled.

Grand Ayatollah al-Sistani's fatwa called for the constitution to be drafted by elected representatives. Although Bremer had pledged that the charter would be "written by Iraqis for Iraqis," he was adamantly opposed to holding elections because he feared a roomful of popularly elected Iraqis might not produce a document that endorsed a separation of mosque and state, provided equal rights for women, or enshrined any of the other elements sought by the White House, which wanted to be able to point to Iraq as a model of an enlightened democracy in the Arab world. The viceroy and his political advisers were counting on the preparatory committee to stand up to al-Sistani by endorsing drafters who were appointed, not elected.

Bremer's unwillingness to give in to al-Sistani was fueled by his Governing Council. Shiite members kept telling Bremer and his advisers that they'd take care of al-Sistani. They claimed that the fatwa simply meant that al-Sistani didn't want foreigners involved in the drafting. Once the ayatollah understood that Iraqis would be doing the writing, he'd drop his objections. The Shiite council members, particularly the leaders of the two largest religious Shiite parties, didn't want a cleric, no matter how popular he was, to inject himself into politics. It was the same concern Bremer had, but it had little to do with principle; the Shiites feared a loss of power and legitimacy if they had to vet policies with al-Sistani.

Sunni council members, both Arabs and Kurds, were also concerned about al-Sistani, but for yet another reason: they didn't want the government to be beholden to a Shiite, ayatollah or not.

Bremer and the council, which had chosen the preparatory committee, expected that the committee would give them cover not only by endorsing the idea of appointed drafters but also by specifying how those drafters should be selected. But the committee's report blindsided Bremer and his council; it called for a constitution to be drafted by elected representatives. The twenty-five-member committee included judges, lawyers, and professors, not political hacks, and it comprised nearly as many Sunnis as Shiites. A majority of the members were secular-leaning academics. But even they didn't want to cross al-Sistani. The vote for elections was twenty-four to zero. "It was very difficult, if not impossible, to disregard the fatwa of Ayatollah al-Sistani," Yass Khudier, a former judge and a member of the committee, told me a few days after the report was submitted.

Bremer and his political advisers called several Governing Council members and said they needed to fix things. The council leaned on the committee, and eventually a new report was submitted. It proposed three possibilities for choosing drafters: a national election, direct selection by the council, or town hall meetings across the country that would be limited to academics, political leaders, tribal sheiks, clerics, and other notables in each community. The committee did not rank the three options, but it was no secret that most of the group still supported elections. With the options arrayed on the table, it was time for the Governing Council to pick one. Since the council had been so dismissive of al-Sistani, Bremer expected the group to either appoint the drafters or set up town hall meetings.

Once the constitution had been written, there would still have to be a national referendum to approve the document and the election of a government. If the handover of sovereignty was to occur by the end of 2004, the Iraqis would have to get moving.

Bremer's plan required the council to do his bidding at every stage. To Bremer, it didn't seem like an unreasonable expectation. Members of the council, however, didn't see things the same way. The council's most prominent members were former exiles who had been wanting to run Iraq from the day Saddam was deposed. They regarded themselves as legitimate national leaders who commanded Iraq's largest political parties. Other members, who were not prominent politicians but who nevertheless had been appointed by Bremer to cultivate a new crop of post-Saddam political figures, began to grow into their roles. Members such as Ghazi al-Yawar, a tribal sheik, and Mowaffak al-Rubaie, a neurologist, joined the former exiles in demanding more power and independence for the council.

By September 2003, council members began to voice opposition to Bremer's seven-step plan. They argued that the occupation was doing more harm than good. Scores of angry Iraqis were joining the nascent insurgency. Some were doing it because they felt dishonored by the presence of foreign troops on Iraqi soil. Others were taking up arms because they blamed the Americans for the lack of security, jobs, and electricity. Mindful of the growing anti-American sentiment, council members called for an end to the occupation. They said that the council should assume sovereignty and administer the country until elections could be held.

"We're in a very dangerous situation," Adel Abdel-Mahdi, a senior Shiite politician, told me at the time. "What prevents us from moving forward is this idea of occupation. Iraq cannot be governed if Iraqis don't get more responsibility." A restoration of sovereignty, Ahmed Chalabi said, "would make the Americans look like liberators again" and would reduce attacks against U.S. troops. "Iraqi people," he said, "don't understand the logic of occupation."

Council members made their case to Bremer, who rebuffed them. Unbowed, they chose a different tack. The United States was pushing for yet another UN Security Council resolution aimed both at getting more international support for Iraq's reconstruction and at encouraging UN personnel to return to Iraq after the devastating truck bombing of its headquarters in Baghdad. Members of the Governing Council began lobbying the French, the Russians, and the Germans to support a rapid transfer of sovereignty. One council member traveled to Paris at Chalabi's behest to raise the issue with the French government, and Chalabi himself flew to the United States to press the council's case on Capitol Hill and at the United Nations.

Bremer was incensed that Chalabi, whom he regarded as an opportunist, would turn against his American patrons and embrace the French. He saw the council's request as a smarmy power grab. A rapid handover of sovereignty to the council "would be a mistake," Bremer told the Senate Armed Services Committee in late September. "No appointed government . . . can have the legitimacy necessary to take on the difficult issues the Iraqis face as they write their constitution, elect a government and, I might add, undertake a major economic reconstruction effort. The only path to true Iraqi sovereignty is through a written constitution, ratified and followed by free democratic elections."

Eager to embarrass the United States and wrest control from Washington, France and Russia seized upon the Governing Council's request for sovereignty to force changes in the UN resolution that Americans were pushing for. The changes demanded so alarmed Bremer that he sent a message to President Bush three days before the Security Council was to vote on the resolution, urging Bush to withdraw it. The gist of the note, according to one person who read it, was that Bremer had reached the conclusion that the resolution was fundamentally flawed, that it would give the UN and the French too much say in America's business. When Powell saw the note, he became apoplectic. He had been working around the clock to persuade France, China, and Russia to support the document, or, at the very least, not to veto it, and he had thought he had a deal. He told the White House he wasn't going to pull the resolution.

The resolution wasn't even Powell's idea. It had been conceived by the White House as a way to help win passage of the Supplemental in Congress. Democrats were demanding that the Bush administration do more to get the United Nations back in Iraq and to encourage other countries to help pay for reconstruction projects. The resolution was supposed to accomplish both goals.

After a final bout of American arm-twisting, the Security Council unanimously adopted the resolution. The document contained two concessions to appease the French and the Russians. It stated that the Governing Council would "embody the sovereignty of the State of Iraq." It also set a December 15 deadline for the council to present a timetable for writing a constitution and holding elections.

The White House called it a victory, but the resolution turned out to be nothing more than words on paper. No other nation stepped up to send troops or write checks. The United Nations refused to send its staffers back to Iraq because the country had become too dangerous. And the Governing Council didn't receive any additional power from Bremer.

The only provision of significance was the December 15 deadline. Now the United Nations was also cracking the whip on the Governing Council to hurry up with the constitution.

The council, however, remained deadlocked. Sunni and Kurdish members were willing to appoint drafters or hold town hall meetings to select them, but most Shiites on the council refused. Despite their earlier promises, the Shiites had been unable to persuade Grand Ayatollah al-Sistani to amend his fatwa. All talk of standing up to al-Sistani evaporated. The Shiite members knew that the ayatollah had far more legitimacy among the Iraqi people than they did.

Bremer kept trying to persuade the Shiites to select an option other than elections. But they dug in their heels.

"The Iraqi people must be able to choose the people who

are going to write their constitution," Adel Abdel-Mahdi told Bremer at a council meeting. "There is no other way."

It sounded hauntingly similar to Bremer's remark a few months earlier, when I had asked him about his political plan. "This is the only way to go," he had said.

When it came to dealing with fellow Americans, Robert Blackwill was rarely a diplomatic diplomat. Colleagues at the State Department, even people who considered him a friend, used words such as *overbearing, arrogant,* and *imperious* to describe him. When he was ambassador to India, he chewed out so many embassy staffers, often in full view of their colleagues, that State opened two internal investigations into his management of the embassy. "He was a bully," said one veteran Foreign Service officer who worked for Blackwill in New Delhi. "He was rude and abusive."

But, the same officer noted, Blackwill "was a brilliant man." Raised in Kansas and educated at Wichita State University, he joined the Foreign Service at twenty-seven and rose through the bureaucracy with alacrity. In the 1980s, he was the chief U.S. negotiator at talks with the Warsaw Pact on reducing conventional forces in Europe. At the end of the decade, as the Berlin Wall fell, he served as President George H. W. Bush's special assistant for European and Soviet affairs. One of his subordinates was a bright young political science professor named Condoleezza Rice. Blackwill sat out the Clinton years at Harvard's Kennedy School of Government, but returned to government in 2000 as a top foreign policy adviser to George W. Bush's presidential campaign. When Bush won, Blackwill expected to get a senior job at State, the Pentagon, or the NSC. But one never materialized, partly because of concerns about his management style. India was his consolation prize.

When he returned from India in the summer of 2003, he was sixty-four years old. His silver hair was receding and his face had grown doughy, but he remained as feisty as ever. Rice offered him a chance to work for her as the NSC's policy planning coordinator. He'd get to help shape American foreign policy in Afghanistan, Iraq, and other hot spots. When Blackwill started in August, Bush, Rice, and other senior White House officials were on vacation. He began by looking at Iraq and reading everything relevant he could obtain: classified cables, CIA reports, internal memos. The more he read, the more alarmed he became. Bremer's seven-step plan, Blackwill concluded, was untenable. If an election were held to select the drafters, as al-Sistani was demanding, the occupation wouldn't end until 2006. That was too long for Iraq, and it was too long for the White House.

When Rice returned from vacation, Blackwill made his case to her. Bremer's plan needed to be reworked, he said, and the NSC needed to get more involved in coordinating Iraq policy. Rice had not immersed herself in the details of Bremer's strategy. Bremer reported to Don Rumsfeld, whom Rice assumed was delving into the nitty-gritty of the CPA. Bremer had been happy with Rice's hands-off approach. As far as he was concerned, he worked for the president and he answered to Rumsfeld, not to Rice or anyone else in Washington.

Convinced that the rules had to change, Blackwill tried to persuade Rice that the White House needed to take charge. Rice called Powell, who had just returned from Iraq. Powell said he didn't believe that Bremer's plan was viable. Rice then queried Rumsfeld and Wolfowitz, who were coming to the same conclusion.

Rice went to Bush and lobbied for greater White House control. She was discreet in her characterization of Bremer's performance. She knew that the president had immense respect for Bremer, particularly for the risk he was taking by serving as the viceroy, and even treated him like a cabinet secretary and a friend. They held video teleconferences at least once a week, and during Bremer's first trip back to Washington, in September, the president and the first lady had invited Jerry and Francie to the White House for dinner. But Bush's bond with Rice ran deeper. He agreed to set up an NSC task force called the Iraq Stabilization Group, headed by Rice, that would take charge of key policy decisions and put Bremer on a short leash.

The White House announced the formation of the Iraq Stabilization Group on October 6. In a background briefing to reporters, Rice downplayed suggestions that she was reining in Bremer or cutting out Rumsfeld. "It is to facilitate Bremer," she said. "It's an effort to make sure Washington is not part of the problem." Bush said that the group was "aimed at the coordination of interagency efforts." He explained away reports of violence in Iraq and blamed the media for ignoring good-news stories. "Listen, we're making good progress in Iraq. Sometimes it's hard to tell it when you listen to the filter," the president said. "The situation is improving on a daily basis inside Iraq. People are freer, the security situation is getting better."

The next day, a testy Rumsfeld told reporters that he had not been consulted by Bush or Rice about the Stabilization Group. It was a rare display of disunity among the president's war cabinet. In Baghdad, Bremer kept his mouth shut, not sure what the changes meant.

He got his answer in late October, when he was summoned to Washington for consultations. When he had made the rounds of the capital in late September, nobody in the upper echelons of the Bush administration questioned Bremer's assertion that Iraq needed a permanent constitution before the occupation could end. They didn't press him on his timetable to hand over sovereignty or for details on how the $18 billion Supplemental would be divvied up. But on this visit, it was evident that the Teflon had worn off. Rice and Blackwill told Bremer that his plan no longer seemed viable. They asked if the open-ended occupation was fueling the insurgency. Bush didn't want American forces to be embroiled in a bloody guerrilla war as Americans headed to the polls the following November. Think about ways to speed up the process, Rice and Blackwill told Bremer.

Bremer got the same message from Powell and Rich Armitage at State. And the Pentagon crew was even more adamant. Rumsfeld's office gave Bremer a memo drafted by Wolfowitz and Feith that proposed a new plan: sovereignty would be handed over to an expanded version of the Governing Council by the following spring. Bremer objected, saying that there needed to be some kind of legal framework before a transfer of power could take place. "I don't think it would be responsible to turn over sovereignty to a nonelected Iraqi body with no constitution in place," Bremer told Rumsfeld. "We'd risk Iraq falling into disorder or civil war, with no constitution to shape Iraq's political structure and to guarantee individual and minority rights."

Before he left, Blackwill pulled Bremer aside. The two men had known each other for thirty years, since the days when Bremer was a special assistant to Secretary of State Henry Kissinger and Blackwill the chief aide to State Department counselor Helmut Sonnenfeldt. Bremer and Blackwill had mediated between their bosses, both strong-willed Central European intellectuals. They became friends, although they eventually drifted apart as their assignments took them to different countries.

"Jerry, I don't think this is going to work," Blackwill said.

Bremer told Blackwill and everyone else that he wanted to talk to the Governing Council one more time. He held out hope that they would finally agree to appoint drafters.

When he got back to Baghdad, Bremer met with Meghan O'Sullivan and Roman Martinez, two of his three top political advisers. The third, Scott Carpenter, the head of the CPA's "governance team," was on holiday in New Hampshire at the time. Although the CPA lacked a stable of veteran Middle East specialists from the State Department—Bremer hadn't asked for many of them and Powell hadn't sent many—there were a handful at the viceroy's service: Hume Horan, a former ambassador to Saudi Arabia who spoke Arabic better than anyone else at State; Chris Ross, a former ambassador to Syria and Algeria; Ron Neumann, a former ambassador to Bahrain; and Ron Schlicher and Tom Krajeski, two Arab-world experts who had run State's Iraq desk. But Bremer kept all of them at a distance. He limited his inner circle to O'Sullivan, Martinez, and Carpenter—none of whom had any prior experience in Arab affairs or any knowledge of Arabic.

Martinez, a handsome young Cuban American with wavy brown hair, was twenty-four years old. He had graduated from Harvard in 2001 and then spent a year studying at Cambridge, where he wrote a thesis on Winston Churchill's anticommunist philosophy. In the fall of 2002 he joined Doug Feith's Office of Special Plans, the Pentagon unit that touted Ahmed Chalabi as Iraq's savior. I first met Martinez in April 2003 at one of Chalabi's homes in Baghdad. Although we ate dinner at the same table, Martinez never told me what he did. I thought he was a spy.

O'Sullivan was a tall, slender, thirty-four-year-old redhead. After receiving her doctorate from Oxford, she had joined the Brookings Institution, a left-leaning think tank in Washington, where she advocated a leaner-but-smarter regime of sanctions on Iraq. In 2001, when her Brookings colleague Richard Haass became the State Department's director of policy planning, she told him that if the United States went to war in Iraq, "I want to be a part of the effort to rebuild the country." The following year, as the prospect of war became a near certainty, O'Sullivan joined Haass at State, and when ORHA was assembled, Powell asked her to go to Iraq with Jay Garner. But her stance on sanctions had angered many neoconservative Iraq hawks, who complained to Cheney, who, in turn, told Rumsfeld to remove her from ORHA. When Powell heard that she had been black-balled, he called Rumsfeld and demanded that the order be rescinded. O'Sullivan was allowed to rejoin ORHA, but her role was supposed to be limited to humanitarian relief. When Bremer arrived, she deftly shifted herself onto the governance team. Her tenacity and tirelessness impressed Bremer, who assigned her to vet candidates for the Governing Council. Pleased with her work, he increased her responsibilities and included her in high-level decision making.

Scott Carpenter was a former legislative assistant to Pennsylvania senator Rick Santorum. He had worked for the International Republican Institute on democratization projects in Eastern Europe before joining the State Department as a political appointee in the Bureau of Democracy, Human Rights and Labor. He was sent to ORHA after Garner asked Rumsfeld for "the best minds in the nation" to draw up a political transition plan for Iraq. Rumsfeld passed the request to Liz Cheney, the vice president's daughter, who was an assistant secretary at State. She dispatched Carpenter, who had not been involved in the Future of Iraq Project or in the department's other initiatives with Iraqi exiles but, unlike some of his State colleagues, was a firm believer in Bush's effort to promote democracy in Iraq and the broader Arab world. Carpenter "really wasn't what I wanted," Garner said later.

Why did the viceroy surround himself with such unseasoned advisers? Like the president, Bremer valued loyalty above all else. Some of the veteran Arabists, who were at the end of their careers, didn't share his tireless dedication. Others seemed beholden to the State Department, and he worried that they would share internal CPA discussions with their colleagues in Washington. There was also a practical reason: the gray-haired veterans rarely stayed for more than three or four months. The trio of Martinez, O'Sullivan, and Carpenter was there the day Bremer arrived, and they remained in Iraq until the month he left. None of them had been at their previous jobs long enough to develop prior allegiances. And they were all looking to make a name for themselves in Baghdad.

But their lack of experience led to a fundamental miscalculation. They tried to right Saddam's wrongs by engaging in social engineering, favoring the once-oppressed Shiites and Kurds at the expense of the once-ruling Sunnis. It was the easy and obvious strategy, but it was fraught with danger. The Shiites and Kurds had political leaders who were known to the Bush administration; the Sunnis did not. The Shiites and the Kurds had been the victims of the Sunnis, who were willing accessories to Saddam's despotism. The result was a Governing Council that had strict quotas: thirteen Shiite Arabs, five Sunni Arabs, five Sunni Kurds, one Christian, and one Turkmen. To some Iraqis, who placed national identity over religious or ethnic affiliation, it looked like the Americans were adopting a version of the troubled political system in Lebanon that divided government posts among several religious groups. "We never saw each other as Sunnis or Shiites first. We were Iraqis first," said Saad Jawad, a professor of political science at Baghdad University. "But the Americans changed all that. They made a point of categorizing people as Sunni or Shiite or Kurd."

To make matters worse, the CPA chose five relatively weak Sunnis to sit on the council. The governance team, at the behest of the Shiites and Kurds, excluded low-level Baath Party members from consideration, further alienating Sunnis who were already reeling from Bremer's decision to fire many Baathists and dissolve the army.

The deference to the Shiites and Kurds also meant that when Grand Ayatollah al-Sistani issued his fatwa, Bremer's trio of young advisers accepted the assurances of Shiite council members that they would get the cleric to change his position. The veteran Arabists in the palace knew better. But Bremer didn't listen to them.

By mid-October, even before Bremer's fateful trip to Washington, Martinez, O'Sullivan, and Carpenter began to realize that the seven-step plan, which they had helped develop, was in trouble. They wrote a memo to Bremer outlining various options to get the Governing Council to appoint drafters. If the council refused, the trio suggested that Bremer consider promulgating an interim constitution and then holding elections. The viceroy bristled.

On November 4, just a few days after Bremer returned to Baghdad, Martinez and O'Sullivan tried again. They knew about the pressure in Washington, and they were worried about the Pentagon plan to hand over power to an expanded Governing Council without an interim constitution. They sent Bremer two memos. The first urged him not to overrule the council if it refused to appoint drafters. The second recommended that he drop his demand for a permanent constitution and settle for an interim document. It also called for the CPA to hand over sovereignty in the summer of 2004 to an interim government selected through national elections. This time, Bremer didn't dismiss the suggestions.

Two days later, Bremer met with the council's nine presidents in his Green Zone villa to make one last attempt to get them to agree on something other than elections to select the drafters. What about caucuses in each province? What about a large national convention? They refused to budge.

Bremer realized that his seven-step plan—conceived in the ambitious, idealistic early months of the CPA—was dead. He asked Martinez and O'Sullivan to flesh out their proposal to draft an interim constitution.

When Blackwill arrived in Baghdad on November 8, he wanted an update. Other than a missive from Bremer criticizing the Pentagon's plan, written in the palace basement during a mortar attack, none of the constitutional strategy memos had been forwarded to Washington. When Blackwill heard that Martinez and O'Sullivan were calling for an interim constitution, he sat down with Bremer and urged him to embrace the new plan. Handing over sovereignty by the middle of 2004, Blackwill said, was very important to the president.

On November 10, Bremer wrote a letter to Rumsfeld, copied to Condi Rice and Colin Powell: "Based on my conversations with the Governing Council last week, I have concluded the time has come to readjust our planned program for Iraq's political transition." He wrote, "It would be a mistake" to force Shiite members of the council to cross al-Sistani. Instead, the United States should support the creation of an interim constitution, something he had long opposed, which "would ensure an honorable end to the occupation."

A few hours after Bremer sent the letter, Rice called him. She wanted him to brief the president in person. She told Bremer to come back to Washington as soon as possible.

The only plane departing from Baghdad that night was a medical evacuation flight to Ramstein Air Base in Germany. Normally, the viceroy would have waited for his own C-130 transport to fly him to Amman, where he'd hop aboard a U.S. government Gulfstream jet with reclining leather seats for the flight to Andrews Air Force Base, outside Washington. But there was no time. Bremer sat in a canvas jump seat amid litters of wounded soldiers, some of them moaning in pain, in the frigid cargo bay of the C-141 Starlifter. He wrote out his White House presentation in longhand. Martinez sat next to him and typed it into his laptop, creating a series of PowerPoint slides.

Bremer landed at Andrews at eight o'clock the next morning. He had just enough time for a quick shower at the base before rushing off to the White House, where Bush, Cheney, Rumsfeld, Powell, and Rice were seated in the Situation Room. They were joined by CIA director George Tenet and White House chief of staff Andrew Card. At Rice's request, aides and assistants were kept out. The meeting was too sensitive.

The CPA's new plan was straightforward: an interim constitution would be written by the spring of 2004; elections would be held in the summer; sovereignty would be handed over as soon as an elected government was in place; and a constitutional convention would be held in early 2005. Rice and Powell voiced concern about trying to hold elections in less than a year. Bremer told the group that elections experts consulted by the CPA had determined that "rough and ready" elections could be held in six to nine months. It wouldn't be ideal. There wouldn't be time to conduct a census so district lines could be drawn, but it would meet international standards for fairness. After a lengthy discussion about the feasibility of elections, Bush adjourned the meeting. They would resume discussions the following day.

The next morning, Bremer called O'Sullivan in Baghdad and told her he needed to know exactly how long it would take to organize elections. He asked her to check once again with the International Foundation for Election Systems, which had assured her earlier that elections could be held within six months.

This time, the IFES team equivocated. It could be six months, they said, or it could be a year. They couldn't give her an exact time.

When Bremer heard that, he decided to change the plan yet again. Although O'Sullivan, Martinez, and Carpenter regarded elections as a prerequisite to ending the occupation, hinging the handover of sovereignty on a shifting date wasn't what the White House wanted. What if violence increased and IFES judged it too dangerous to hold elections? When O'Sullivan had mentioned in a meeting in Baghdad a few days earlier that the election might not occur until the late summer of 2004, Blackwill had said, "That's a little too close to another election." The U.S. presidential election would be in November.

Bremer grudgingly deleted the proposal for elections. But that raised a pressing question: How would the interim government be chosen? He, Carpenter, and Martinez decided to resurrect a proposal they'd made to the Governing Council for choosing constitution drafters—holding caucuses in each province. Bremer's new plan called for caucuses to select delegates to a national convention, which would choose an interim government. To prevent the Governing Council from manipulating the process, its role in organizing the caucuses would be limited. Each caucus would have a fifteen-member organizing committee that would choose who could participate. Only five committee members would be selected by the council. Of the remaining ten, five would be picked by each province's own ruling council, and five would be picked by the city councils in the province. It sounded complicated, but Bremer and his team were convinced that it was the most democratic way to pick a government short of elections. They still wanted to leave Iraq with the nearest thing to a representative government.

Blackwill and his staff questioned the complexity of the caucus plan. Blackwill told O'Sullivan and Martinez that it would "work perfectly, but you have to go door-to-door in Iraq and knock on the door and say, 'We hate to bother you, but can we have your afternoon to explain the caucus system to you?' And then you'd have to go over to the next house." But Bremer and his team were insistent. It was the closest to their ideal. Blackwill and the others backed down. Bremer had already ripped his seven-step plan to shreds. If he wanted caucuses, fine. He could have his caucuses.

When the meeting resumed in the Situation Room, Bremer described the new plan. It called for a handover of sovereignty by June 30, 2004, more than four months before Bush faced reelection. It was just what the president and Cheney wanted to hear.

The next morning, Bremer and his aides headed back to Baghdad. The death of the seven-step plan was depressing, but they had cause to be upbeat. They had blocked the Pentagon's plan to hand over sovereignty to an expanded Governing Council without an interim constitution. Bremer had also beaten back Blackwill, who hadn't wanted caucuses. Not only was the president happy, Bremer thought, but the Iraqis would be overjoyed to have sovereignty in less than eight months.

He arrived in Baghdad on November 14 and summoned the council's nine presidents to his villa that night to brief them on the new plan. As Bremer talked, the Iraqis began to realize that they had won.

As soon as Bremer finished, the members stood and congratulated him, and one another. Ahmed Chalabi launched into a speech about the importance of returning Iraq's sovereignty.

Carpenter interjected. Bremer hadn't delved into the details
of how the caucuses would be organized. Perhaps, Carpenter
suggested, "we should walk through this in detail."

Chalabi and Bremer cut him off.

"We need to keep our eye on the ball here," Chalabi said.
"The goal is sovereignty—it's ending the occupation and the
insurgency."

Bremer agreed, and the self-congratulatory speeches continued. The details would be addressed the following day, at Jalal
Talabani's villa.

In Talabani's dining room, members sat shoulder to shoulder—
the table was smaller than the one in the council's chambers—
but everyone managed to fit because nobody wanted to be a
backbencher. A drab green cloth covered the table. At its center
was a bouquet of white and yellow silk roses and several boxes
of tissues. Gold curtains over the windows prevented the guards
and aides waiting outside from observing the proceedings.

Talabani had parked himself at the head of the table. To his
right was Chalabi. To his left was Bremer, with Carpenter, Martinez, and O'Sullivan standing behind him, ready to pass notes
and whisper instructions.

Bremer began by going over the new plan. It had been transformed into a three-page agreement that he and Talabani
would sign as soon as the council voted to approve it. Council
members had copies, in English and Arabic, and they read
along as Bremer addressed each point. The first two sections—
on the process of creating an interim constitution and allowing American troops to remain in Iraq after a handover of
sovereignty—went smoothly. But when Bremer got to the formation of the interim government and the complicated method
of selecting who could participate in the caucuses, Adel Abdel-
Mahdi objected.

"This will split our people," he said. "We will not accept it."

Abdel-Mahdi was the political chief of the country's largest
Shiite party, the Supreme Council for Islamic Revolution in
Iraq, known by the acronym SCIRI. He was one of the most
skilled and most mercurial politicians in the room. In his
teens, he had been a Baathist. Then he became a communist,

and then an Islamist, though I never regarded him as a hard-core Islamist. He didn't believe women had to be subservient to men or that sharia should be the law of the land, but many in his party did, and he represented their views with vigor. He was in his fifties but appeared a decade older. A chain-smoker with a sizeable gut, he had suffered during Saddam's reign. Several of his relatives were tortured and executed. He eventually fled to France, where he had joined other exiles seeking political change.

The United States government had long been wary of Abdel-Mahdi's party. It had been based in Iran when Saddam was in power, and many in Washington believed that its leadership was riddled with Iranian agents and that many members were on Tehran's payroll. But it represented millions of Shiites and was a political force that the United States couldn't ignore.

At least, that's what everyone thought. It was never clear just how popular SCIRI was. Before the war, SCIRI and another Shiite party, Dawa, were the two largest Shiite opposition groups. But after the fall of Saddam, new political, religious, and social forces had appeared in the Shiite-dominated south. A young firebrand cleric named Moqtada al-Sadr had been attracting tens of thousands of followers, many of them disaffected young men drawn to his strident calls for the Americans to leave. Small political parties had sprung up in cities across the south.

Abdel-Mahdi was worried about losing control of the caucuses. Under the CPA's system, the Governing Council would choose only five of the fifteen members of each province's coordinating committee. The other positions would go to local politicians. Many local leaders across the south were not members of SCIRI. Abdel-Mahdi feared that members of his party would get shut out of the process. He proposed that the council be able to select eight of the fifteen members. Local officials could choose the remaining seven.

Bremer turned to Carpenter, Martinez, and O'Sullivan. They urged him to reject Abdel-Mahdi's proposal. If we're serious about making the new government more representative, we can't let the council exercise a veto over who gets to participate in the caucuses, Carpenter argued. Bremer agreed.

But Abdel-Mahdi refused to back down. Concerned about losing SCIRI's support, Martinez and Chalabi pulled Abdel-Mahdi aside for a chat. They urged him to reconsider.

Abdel-Mahdi said he needed more time to discuss it with leaders of his party. Martinez and Chalabi proposed a compromise: in order for a person to participate in a caucus, eleven of the fifteen caucus members would have to agree. That would give the five Governing Council appointees effective veto power. Abdel-Mahdi said it was a step in the right direction, but he asked Martinez and Chalabi for more time to talk to SCIRI officials.

When they returned to the meeting, Bremer asked Abdel-Mahdi if he was willing to support the agreement.

"We need more time to discuss this," Abdel-Mahdi said.

Bremer shot him a look of exasperation. Other members began whispering to each other. Carpenter, Martinez, and O'Sullivan huddled behind the viceroy.

Several members suggested waiting a day so Abdel-Mahdi could talk to his party, but Bremer and his team refused. There was a great deal on the table, and the council needed to approve it.

Dan Senor, Bremer's spokesman, hadn't waited for the agreement to be signed to call a news conference. Hundreds of journalists were assembled in the Convention Center, eager for the details of the new plan. Senor reminded Bremer that the press was expecting an announcement.

Bremer's trio of political advisers found the council's desire for consensus maddening. This was no way for a democracy to operate. They should call a vote, Carpenter said to his colleagues. Let Abdel-Mahdi vote against it. The rest of them will support it.

Martinez had been traveling for the better part of a week. As the council dithered, he grew angry. He and his colleagues had trashed their seven-step plan to give Iraqis the sovereignty they so desperately wanted, and now the council had the temerity to object to the terms?

He passed a note to Bremer urging him to take a hard line and call a vote.

The viceroy silenced the room.

"Frankly, I'm disappointed in the council's deliberations,"

Bremer said. The CPA "has come a very long way to meet your interests. If we don't reach agreement today, I will have to answer questions from the press. . . . If I speak to the press, I'll have to explain that we were unable to agree because the Governing Council is standing in the way of returning sovereignty to the Iraqi people and is trying to control the process by which the interim government will be chosen."

Some members gasped. He had never strong-armed the council that way before.

Talabani called a vote. Twenty members supported the plan. Abdel-Mahdi and two others opposed it.

Bremer instructed Talabani to talk to the press. A half hour later, he stood in front of a phalanx of cameras to announce the November 15 Agreement.

"This is a feast for the Iraqi people," Talabani proclaimed. "This is what Iraqi people were dreaming to have."

Abdel-Mahdi didn't appear at the press conference. He had stormed out of the villa after the meeting.

Ten days later, Abdel-Mahdi and his boss, Abdul Aziz al-Hakim, SCIRI's top leader, climbed into an armored Toyota Land Cruiser and told the driver to head south—to the city of Najaf and the home of His Eminence, the Grand Ayatollah al-Sistani.

Al-Hakim met with al-Sistani for more than an hour. Al-Sistani began by offering condolences to al-Hakim. His brother, an ayatollah who had been SCIRI's spiritual leader, had died in a car bomb attack in Najaf in late August. Al-Hakim thanked the ayatollah for his sympathies and then turned the conversation to the November 15 Agreement. He outlined his concerns with the caucus system, arguing that there was a grave risk of manipulation by local politicians. Al-Sistani listened carefully, and afterward he seemed to agree with al-Hakim's concern. Al-Hakim didn't tell al-Sistani what to do—you don't say such things to a grand ayatollah—but he hoped that the cleric would issue a statement criticizing the terms of the CPA's caucus plan. After leaving the meeting, al-Hakim told reporters that al-Sistani had expressed "deep concern over real loopholes" in the plan "that must be dealt with, otherwise the process will be deficient and will not meet the expectations of the people of Iraq."

Al-Hakim's description of al-Sistani's position sent a jolt of panic through the Republican Palace. One of Bremer's aides called Jalal Talabani and told him to hustle down to Najaf to set the record straight with the grand ayatollah. Talabani went the next day, but al-Sistani's views were set. The cleric spelled out his concerns to Talabani. As he left al-Sistani's house, Talabani couldn't suggest that he disagreed with him. That would have been political suicide. "I see the views of his Grace as logical and reasonable, and I agree with them," Talabani said.

Two days later, al-Sistani made his position public through a handwritten response to questions submitted by Anthony Shadid of *The Washington Post.* "The mechanism in place to choose members of the transitional legislative assembly does not guarantee the establishment of an assembly that truly represents the Iraqi people," al-Sistani wrote. "This mechanism must be replaced with one that guarantees the aforesaid, which is elections, so the assembly will emanate from the desire of the Iraqi people and will represent them fairly without its legitimacy being tarnished in any way."

With those few words, al-Sistani killed the caucuses.

Nobody was unhappier than the original supplicants to al-Sistani, Abdel-Mahdi and al-Hakim. They didn't want elections. They wanted caucuses, but with more council control. The grand ayatollah hadn't tweaked the plan. He had smashed it. SCIRI would have to put itself before the voters, a far riskier gambit than caucuses, even under Bremer's terms.

Bremer and his political team hadn't expected al-Sistani's rejection, but they weren't willing to give up without a fight. They sent emissaries to the ayatollah, and they tried to get the council to uphold the agreement. It was déjà vu. Al-Sistani wasn't backing down, and the council wasn't going to contradict the grand ayatollah. Carpenter, Martinez, and O'Sullivan tried to come up with adjustments to the caucus plan that would satisfy al-Sistani, but the ayatollah's aides rejected all of them. He believed that elections were possible. His proxies suggested that food ration cards could double as voter registration cards. If that was impossible, he wanted to hear it from someone other than the Americans.

At al-Sistani's behest, al-Hakim sent a letter to United Nations secretary-general Kofi Annan in December asking for the world body to determine if it was feasible to hold elections before the planned June 30 handover of sovereignty. The request alarmed Bremer and his political aides, who feared losing control of the process to foreigners. But in Washington, Bob Blackwill saw a path to compromise. For him, sticking to the June 30 deadline was of paramount importance. With the caucus plan imploding, he viewed the United Nations as America's best hope in Iraq. He began lobbying Rice, Powell, and others in the administration to back al-Hakim's request.

The fight between Blackwill and the CPA over UN involvement was so acrimonious that when he returned to Baghdad in January, he no longer trusted aides in the palace to transmit his secure messages to Rice in Washington; he brought his own communications team from the White House. While his aides fought with CPA staffers for suitable office space in the palace, Blackwill dressed down Martinez and O'Sullivan "for keeping stuff away from me, for playing a game of Merlin the Magician." He told them that he had been sent to Baghdad by the president, just like Bremer, and that he expected to be brought into discussions about the formation of an interim government. And he told them to get over the caucuses. "They're dead," he said.

Blackwill's choice to lead the United Nations team was former Algerian foreign minister Lakhdar Brahimi. Bremer's political advisers regarded Brahimi as an anti-American Arab nationalist who might manipulate the process in ways that did not serve American interests. But Blackwill was insistent. He was impressed with the work Brahimi had done as the UN's point man in Afghanistan after the United States ousted the Taliban. He eventually invited Brahimi to the White House for meetings with Rice, Powell, and, finally, Bush.

In mid-February, Brahimi came through for the United States. After a weeklong visit to Iraq, where he met with al-Sistani and most members of the Governing Council, he announced that it would not be possible to hold elections before the June 30 handover of sovereignty. A week later, al-Sistani issued a handwritten statement dropping his demand for elections by June.

With caucuses dead and elections impossible, the question

of how to select an interim government remained unresolved. Brahimi favored holding a round-table meeting of Iraqi leaders or a larger national conference similar to the *loya jirga* he had helped to convene for Afghanistan. Members of the Governing Council disagreed, saying that they ought to be anointed as leaders of the interim government. Bremer and his political advisers wanted anything but the council, largely because handing power to a body it had so roundly criticized would make it look as if the CPA had failed. Blackwill wanted to ensure that whatever the process, the United States would retain veto power over who was chosen.

Brahimi ultimately decided that a round-table meeting would not provide enough control to the United Nations or the United States, and that a national conference could not be organized in time. He also rejected the idea of handing power to the Governing Council. Faced with no other good choice, he said that he should select the interim government himself, in consultation with Iraqi leaders and the CPA.

Bremer and Blackwill readily agreed, largely because it would give them the influence they sought. But for Carpenter, Martinez, and O'Sullivan, who had wanted to leave with a government chosen by Iraqis, the decision was a bitter one. After months of wrangling and planning, the interim government would be picked in the equivalent of a smoke-filled room.

Adel Abdel-Mahdi, the catalyst for the sea change in the plan, was also dissatisfied with the outcome. Although he would eventually be tapped to be the finance minister, the events of November 15 continued to gnaw at him.

"If Bremer had only given us an extra day, none of this would have happened," he said ruefully. "We could have had the democratic government that the Americans promised us when they went to war."

THE GREEN ZONE, SCENE VIII

The corkboard in the bar at Ocean Cliffs, the British housing compound, was the Green Zone's version of the Hyde Park Speakers' Corner. There was a photograph of President Bush dressed as Marlon Brando in The Wild One, *in a leather jacket and touring cap, sitting atop a motorcycle. "Be afraid," the caption read, "because paranoia is patriotic."*

Another parodied a poster for the movie Jackass. *It depicted the Bush administration's foreign policy team in a shopping cart, flying off a cliff.*

Other postings involved less graphic design acumen. A handwritten sign admonished YEE-HAW IS NOT A FOREIGN POLICY.

11

A Fool's Errand

IF NOT FOR THE OLIVE GREEN shipping containers emblazoned with bright red crosses stacked across the street, I never would have found the Green Zone's hospital. It looked like dozens of other marble-and-sandstone villas surrounding the Republican Palace. The front portico was two stories high, the windows were tinted, and towering date palms lined the sides and rear. A modest placard next to the portico, resembling the type of shop-front sign that a jeweler or a tailor might post, identified the building.

Once inside, however, there was no mistaking the three-story edifice for anything other than a modern American military hospital. It had five operating theaters, ten emergency room trauma stations, and seventy-six beds. There were respirators, computerized heart monitors, and a CT scanner. Neurosurgeons and burn specialists were at the ready to treat wounds from roadside bombs.

The hospital was free of the fine desert sand that was everywhere in Iraq. The white tile floor was always scrubbed, as were the walls and windows. Only the military-issue boots worn by the emergency room doctors were dirty. Instead of light brown suede, they were black and crusty with blood.

Iraqis called it the Ibn Sina Hospital, after a pioneering physician in the early Islamic world. The Americans called it the "Twenty-eighth Cash," a reference to the army unit that ran the facility—the Twenty-eighth Combat Support Hospital—which deployed more than 350 physicians, nurses, and support staffers to the Green Zone.

Before the war, the hospital had been a private clinic for Saddam's relatives and Baath Party leaders. Once the Americans arrived, it remained a private facility, limited to soldiers, CPA personnel, and private contractors. The only Iraqis admitted were those accidentally shot by American troops.

Despite its selective admission of Iraqis, Tommy Thompson, the secretary for health and human services, used the hospital as a backdrop to laud the CPA during a visit to Baghdad eleven months into the occupation. The facility, he announced under the portico, was an example of how the United States had begun to "reestablish Iraq as a center of excellence for medical protection and medical care."

None of that excellence was evident outside the Emerald City.

Yarmouk Hospital, a campus of two-story concrete buildings erected around a concrete courtyard, was a five-minute drive from the Green Zone, just a few blocks off the road to the airport. It was one of Baghdad's largest and busiest medical centers, but after visits to more than a dozen other hospitals across Iraq, I regarded Yarmouk as a fair representation of the country's health-care system. It was, quite simply, a disaster.

Nothing was clean. The bedsheets were soiled, the floors were streaked with blood, the toilets overflowed. The rooms lacked the most basic equipment to monitor a patient's blood pressure or heart rate. Operating theaters were without modern surgical tools or sterile implements. The pharmacy's shelves were bare. In the emergency room, a few bloodstained gurneys cast dim shadows on the floor. There was no defibrillator, no respirator, no blood transfusion equipment, and no syringes of epinephrine.

I visited the hospital for the first time a few hours after a suicide car bomber leveled the Jordanian embassy. The ward echoed with the screams of men whose limbs had been blown off but who had not received anything to dull the pain. I smelled blood, shit, and corpses that had been stored without refrigeration. Despairing relatives huddled around loved ones who had been so burned and maimed that they wouldn't survive the night. I touched the hand of a lanky young man, Abbas Ali, whose abdomen and legs were covered in what seemed to be third-degree burns. He winced but did not cry. Over and over, he repeated the words, *"Bismillah ar rahman ar rahim. Bismillah ar rahman ar rahim."* (In the name of God, the beneficent, the merciful.) A doctor told my interpreter that Abbas wouldn't live for more than a day or two. "There's nothing I can do," he said. "We don't have the equipment to treat him."

The story of Yarmouk Hospital was the same as that of nearly every other public institution in Iraq. In the 1970s, it had been one of the best medical centers in the Arab world. Jordanians, Syrians, and Sudanese traveled to Baghdad for operations. That changed, of course, after the invasion of Kuwait and the imposition of sanctions. Although Saddam eventually won the right to sell his oil in exchange for food and humanitarian supplies, the hospital never had enough medicine. The government blamed the United Nations for screwing up the purchase orders. The United Nations blamed the government for ordering the wrong items and for steering contracts to cronies instead of to reputable suppliers. The Bush administration believed that Saddam's government, which was trying to generate international support to overturn the sanctions, was deliberately depriving Yarmouk and other hospitals of needed supplies.

However bad the place was before the Americans arrived, it got much, much worse when the U.S. Army rolled into the city. A tank shell struck the hospital the day Saddam's government fell, knocking out the generator and sending doctors fleeing home. With nobody to watch over the building, looters carted away not just all the beds, medicines, and operating room equipment, but also the CT and ultrasound scanners. When doctors returned to work, they struggled to provide basic first aid with makeshift implements.

Once the Americans arrived, the job of rehabilitating Iraq's health-care system fell to Frederick M. Burkle, Jr., a physician with a master's degree in public health and postgraduate degrees from Harvard, Yale, Dartmouth, and the University of California at Berkeley. Burkle was a naval reserve officer with two Bronze Stars and a deputy assistant administrator at the U.S. Agency for International Development. He taught at the

Johns Hopkins School of Public Health, where he specialized in disaster-response issues. During the first Gulf War, he provided medical aid to Kurds in northern Iraq. He had worked in Kosovo and Somalia. And in the lead-up to the invasion of Iraq, he had been put in charge of organizing the American response to the expected public health crisis in Iraq. A USAID colleague called him the "single most talented and experienced post-conflict health specialist working for the United States government."

A week after Baghdad's liberation, Burkle was informed that he was being replaced. A senior official at USAID told him that the White House wanted a "loyalist" in the job. Burkle had a wall of degrees, but he didn't have a picture of himself with the president.

Burkle's job was handed to James K. Haveman, Jr., a sixty-year-old social worker who was largely unknown among international health experts. He had no medical degree, but he had connections. He had been the community health director for the former Republican governor of Michigan, John Engler, who recommended him to Wolfowitz. Haveman was well-traveled, but most of his overseas trips were in his capacity as a director of International Aid, a faith-based relief organization that provided health care while promoting Christianity in the developing world. Prior to his stint in government, Haveman ran a large Christian adoption agency in Michigan that urged pregnant women not to have abortions.

A silver-haired man with a ruddy complexion and a modest paunch, Haveman wore glasses and a lapel pin depicting an American flag crossed with an Iraqi one. His voice had the twang of a Midwesterner and the courtesy of a man from small-town America.

In the two months between Burkle's dismissal and Haveman's arrival, the Health Ministry was handed off to Steve Browning, the U.S. Army Corps of Engineers specialist who headed four ministries in the first weeks of the occupation and who would later get the job of increasing electricity production. Browning had no medical experience, but he knew enough, and he had talked to enough experts, to draw up a list of priorities. Preventing disease, providing clean drinking water, and improving care at hospitals were at the top. So, too, was obtaining drugs and medical supplies. Hospitals and clinics were out of antibiotics, painkillers, and other medicines. Determining if the government-owned company responsible for ordering and distributing drugs and supplies had the needed goods in stock, and finding a way to get those products shipped to hospitals, became top priorities.

A few days after Jerry Bremer landed in Baghdad, he wanted to visit a hospital. His handlers assumed that his doing so would be a good photo opportunity. On the way to one, Browning rode with Bremer in his armored Suburban. Browning figured he could use the time to discuss his plans for the ministry and the need for a massive infusion of foreign aid, but Bremer talked at length about Operation Smile, an American charity that sends physicians overseas to provide reconstructive surgery to children with facial deformities. At first Browning nodded politely, but when Bremer kept chatting about Operation Smile, Browning cut him off.

"Look, you need to understand the situation on the ground," he said. "We're trying to prevent epidemic diseases. We're trying to just provide some decent drinking water for people. . . . We're trying to restore basic service in hospitals . . . and to push out the pharmaceuticals and medical equipment. It's ludicrous to talk about something like Operation Smile."

If someone else had dismissed the viceroy in that way, it would have been a pack-your-bags moment, but Browning was something of a made man. He was regarded as one of the CPA's most talented managers. And everyone seemed to know that, no matter what else Iraq's hospitals lacked, they had generators because of Steve Browning.

A month after Baghdad's liberation, an angry crowd had converged upon the Health Ministry. As Browning waded into the mob to ascertain their grievances, a tall, thin man who looked like an Iraqi Abraham Lincoln began beating his own chest. When Browning approached him, the man held up a photograph of a tiny infant. It took some minutes for Browning's interpreter to explain: The infant was the man's daughter. There had been a power outage, and the hospital in which his daughter was born didn't have a working generator. She had died in her incubator.

Browning drew up a proposal that night to buy new generators for every major hospital in Iraq. He took the document to Jay Garner, who approved it on the spot.

To address the problem of getting medicines from government warehouses to hospitals, Browning deputized Chuck Fisher—the Special Forces physician who would later rescue Elias Nimmer from the al-Rasheed—with czarlike powers to pull cartons of drugs off the shelves and send them to hospitals by military convoy. Forget the paperwork or the pretense that Iraqis had to be the frontmen, Browning said. People needed medicine, and the Americans had to deliver.

When Browning heard that Haveman had been tapped to take over the CPA's health team, he tried repeatedly to get in touch with him while he was still in the United States. He wanted to give Haveman a briefing so he'd have a head start. Haveman never called back.

Haveman arrived in Baghdad with his own military aide, his own chief of staff, and his own priorities. He emphasized to the press the number of hospitals that had reopened since the war and the pay raises that had been given to doctors instead of the still-decrepit conditions inside the hospitals or the fact that many physicians were leaving for safer, better-paying jobs outside Iraq. He approached problems the way a health-care administrator in America would: He focused on preventive measures to reduce the need for hospital treatment. He urged the Health Ministry to mount an antismoking campaign, and he assigned an American from the CPA team, who turned out to be a closet smoker, to lead the public-education effort. Several members of Haveman's team noted wryly that Iraqis faced far greater dangers in their daily life than a little tobacco. The CPA's limited resources, they argued, would be better used raising awareness about how to prevent childhood diarrhea and other fatal maladies. I was reminded of a comment made by my Information Ministry minder before the war, when I asked him why a pack of cigarettes cost only about thirty cents.

"Ali, your government keeps complaining that it doesn't have enough money," I said. "Why don't they tax the cigarettes like they do in America?"

"In our country," Ali said, "it would not be wise to tax a tranquilizer."

Medical care in Iraq had long been free. In Saddam's welfare state, the government picked up the tab. That was anathema to Haveman, who insisted that Iraqis should pay a small fee every time they saw a doctor. He also decided to allocate almost all of the Health Ministry's $793 million share of the Supplemental to renovating maternity hospitals and building 150 new community medical clinics. His intention was "to shift the mind-set of the Iraqis that you don't get health care unless you go to a hospital." A noble goal, no doubt, but there was no money from the Supplemental set aside to rehabilitate the emergency room and operating theaters at Yarmouk and other hospitals, even though injuries from insurgent attacks were the country's single largest public health challenge.

A massive cog in Iraq's health-care wheel was Kimadia, the state-owned firm that imported and distributed drugs and medical supplies to hospitals. It would have made a Soviet central planner proud. It had thirty-two thousand employees, an annual budget of $600 million, and unparalleled influence over the health-care system. Kimadia selected which medicines to import, chose which countries and companies would get Iraq's business, warehoused the products, and distributed them to hospitals and clinics. Everything was paid for with government funds. In Saddam's Iraq, medicine was supposed to be free, but it rarely was. More often than not, government hospitals and clinics lacked vital drugs. Those who could afford it bought medicine from private pharmacies, which often sold items that had been imported by Kimadia and then fenced on the black market by warehouse employees.

Bureaucrats at Kimadia, not doctors or hospital administrators, decided which medicines, and how much, to send to hospitals and clinics. Dispensary shelves would be overflowing with one antibiotic but empty of another. Sometimes this was due to incompetence; the other drug would be sitting in the warehouse. Other times it was because Kimadia hadn't purchased enough. It would buy a five-year supply of one drug while failing to order dozens of others. Contracts were given to firms in countries supportive of Saddam instead of to suppliers who provided the best price or quality.

"Kimadia was filled with thieves and incompetents," said

Scott Svabek, an army procurement officer on the CPA's health team. "It was corrupt and dysfunctional."

To Haveman, the answer was to privatize it. But before he sold off Kimadia, he wanted to attempt something he had done in Michigan. When he was the state's director of community health, he sought to slash the huge amount of money Michigan spent on prescription drugs for the poor by limiting the medicines doctors could prescribe for Medicaid patients. Unless they received an exemption, physicians could order only drugs that were on an approved list, known as a formulary.

Haveman figured the same strategy could bring down the cost of medicine in Iraq. The country had 4,500 items on its drug formulary, meaning that Kimadia was supposed to stock 4,500 different products. If private firms were going to bid for the job of supplying drugs to government hospitals, they needed a smaller formulary. A new formulary would also outline new requirements about where approved drugs could be manufactured. It would be a way to get Iraq to stop buying medicines from Syria, Iran, and Russia, and to start buying from the United States.

He asked the people who had drawn up the formulary in Michigan if they wanted to come to Baghdad. They declined. So he beseeched the Pentagon for help. His request made its way to the Defense Department's Pharmacoeconomic Center in San Antonio. A few weeks later, three formulary experts were on their way to Iraq. They arrived eleven days before the November 15 Agreement.

The group was led by Ted Briski, a balding, middle-aged pharmacist who held the rank of lieutenant commander in the navy. Haveman's order, as Briski remembered it, was: "Build us a formulary in two weeks and then go home." By his second day in Iraq, Briski had come to three conclusions: First, the existing formulary "really wasn't that bad." Second, his mission was really about "redesigning the entire Iraqi pharmaceutical procurement and delivery system, and that was a complete change of scope—on a grand scale." Third, Haveman and his advisers "really didn't know what they were doing."

Haveman "viewed Iraq as Michigan after a huge attack," said George Guszcza, an army captain who worked on the CPA's

health team. "Somehow if you went into the ghettos and projects of Michigan and just extended it out for the entire state—
that's what he was coming to save."

Briski and the two other experts nevertheless set about
designing a modern formulary. They took the 4,500-item list
and slimmed it down to about 1,600 entries. But simply creating a new list wasn't sufficient for Briski. The Iraqis, he
decided, needed a way to manage the formulary, so he drew up
plans to form a committee of pharmacists that would update
the list every few months. By choosing which drugs should be
purchased, the committee would wrest a little power from
Kimadia. Briski viewed his work as part of a larger plan to
improve drug distribution. For the new formulary to succeed,
Kimadia would have to be privatized or it would need a complete overhaul.

Haveman told him not to worry. He had big plans for Kimadia. He was going to create an efficient, market-based system to
distribute drugs. It was part of his strategy to refashion Iraq's
socialist health-care system into one that looked more American, with co-payments and primary-care clinics. Making it happen would require a fundamental redesign of health policy in
Iraq, but it was the CPA's mission, as he saw it, to tear down
the old and build anew.

Then came November 15, and the announcement that the
United States would hand over sovereignty to the Iraqis by the
following June. Everyone in the palace would be going home
by then, if not sooner.

Bremer held an all-hands meeting of CPA staffers on
November 16. He didn't mention that, in the name of political
expediency, he had torpedoed his grand plans to have the
Iraqis write a constitution and hold elections before a transfer
of power, but everyone knew what had happened. CPA
staffers, Bremer said, now needed to focus on "building capacity" among Iraqis to run their government. It was time to scale
back plans and expectations. Put Iraqis in charge, he said, and
pursue only those projects you can accomplish by June.

Haveman stopped talking about privatizing Kimadia. There
was no way the CPA could pull it off by June. With an outright
sale off the table, Haveman and his loyalists decided not to pur-

sue other ways to restructure Kimadia. Haveman wanted his ministry to be the first one handed back to the Iraqis.

When Scott Svabek, the procurement officer, asked for $8.4 million to renovate Kimadia's offices and to purchase telecommunications equipment for the headquarters in Baghdad to communicate with warehouses across the country, Haveman's chief of staff denied his request. Haveman did endorse a suggestion from his subordinates to strip Kimadia of its drug-purchasing function and give it to a new procurement team established within the Health Ministry. The reorganization was intended to reduce opportunities for corruption: if Kimadia's venal managers weren't in charge of buying, they'd have fewer chances to take kickbacks. But by the time the CPA implemented the new structure, the handover of sovereignty was just a few months away. Members of the procurement team, who had been selected from within Kimadia, never left their old offices, and they continued to take orders from their old bosses.

"They did not believe that it would last, and [believed] that if they were somehow associated with these procurement teams above and beyond attending meetings, they would be forced out," Briski said. "A big chunk of what was going on was this whole idea that the Americans are not here forever. We're going to wait them out and they're going to leave and . . . so we're going to end up going right back where we were before."

Briski and others who worked for Haveman paid little attention to the political winds. They had come to Iraq to fix things, and they came to conclude that the United States needed to devote more resources and stay longer to get the job done. "How could we have fixed Kimadia?" Briski said a year after returning from Iraq. "We needed dozens of pharmacists, procurement experts, and logisticians working for two years."

To Haveman, that was a nonstarter. "Do you bring in another fifty people to run Kimadia? No. It might take another seven years to fix it, but it will be the Iraqi way," he said. "Is it perfect? No. Can they handle it? Yeah."

But Haveman's critics, including more than a dozen people who worked for him in Baghdad, contend that more could have been done with the resources at hand during the fifteen-month occupation. Rewriting the formulary was a distraction, they said. Instead, the CPA should have focused on restructuring Kimadia, but not privatizing it, and on ordering more emergency shipments of medicine to address shortages of essential drugs. The first emergency procurement did not occur until early 2004, after the Americans had been in Iraq for more than eight months.

But Haveman did meet one big goal. Health was the first ministry to be handed over. When Bremer did so, in March 2004, three months before the transfer of sovereignty, he praised Haveman for his "real, practical accomplishments."

The new Iraqi minister of health, Aladdin Alwan—a talented and eloquent former World Health Organization official selected by UN envoy Lakhdar Brahimi—didn't share Bremer's assessment. Alwan's staff told him that 40 percent of the nine hundred drugs deemed essential by the ministry were out of stock in hospitals. Of the thirty-two drugs used in public clinics for the management of chronic diseases, twenty-six were unavailable.

Alwan beseeched the United Nations for help, and asked neighboring nations to share what they could. He sought to increase production at a state-run manufacturing plant in the city of Samarra. And he put the creation of a new formulary on hold. To him, it was a fool's errand.

"We didn't need a new formulary. We needed drugs," he said. "But the Americans did not understand that."

THE GREEN ZONE, SCENE IX

From afar, it seemed like a funeral. But there were no funerals in the Green Zone. The dead were sent home aboard giant C-17 Globemasters.

The sound of a bagpipe wafted from a white tent in the palace's front garden. Guests sat on folding chairs and engaged in small talk. Jerry Bremer was there, as were a score of Iraqi staffers. White roses and yellow carnations adorned the center aisle. More flowers, and brass candelabras, decorated the altar.

Three Western women wearing floor-length Kurdish dresses walked in, one after another, followed by a fourth woman in a shimmering white gown, escorted across the lawn by a Halliburton construction foreman. "Here Comes the Bride" flowed from an electronic piano. It was the Emerald City's first—and only—wedding: George Adair and Sheryl Lewis, junior staffers in the Governance Office, were tying the knot.

George and Sheryl were an item before they arrived in Baghdad. They'd met while studying for their master's degrees at George Mason University, in Virginia. A few months into the occupation, they decided to apply for jobs with the CPA. It seemed like an adventure.

When they got to the palace, they were assigned bunks in the north wing, in a communal room with two hundred other staffers. They pushed their twin beds together, but they couldn't be intimate. One middle-aged man regularly walked around the room in nothing more than his tight white briefs, snapping photographs of sleeping women. Sheryl didn't want to get caught in a compromising position.

So they skulked around the palace, looking for discreet places to get busy.

"We found plenty," Sheryl said.

"Unoccupied offices with a locking door," George said.

"And bathrooms," Sheryl said.

"And automobiles," George said.

"And the women's locker room at the gym," Sheryl said. "It had a locking door."

Taking Sheryl out of the Green Zone for a night on the town was out of the question, so George escorted her to the al-Rasheed. To the sports bar. To the coffee shop. To the disco.

Sometimes they went to the army base at the airport to shop at the PX and eat at the Burger King. At the palace, they strolled by the pool, on the roof, in the garden. And they went to Moe's, the bar at the Halliburton employee trailer park named after Homer's watering hole on The Simpsons. The Halliburton guys had all sorts of booze you couldn't find anywhere else in the Green Zone: tequila, vodka, Budweiser. They were the logistics guys. They could get anything into the Emerald City.

When he decided to propose, George asked a friend to send him a ring from the United States, which the friend shipped by DHL. The next day, a DHL plane was struck by a missile as it took off from the Baghdad airport. All future cargo flights, including the one with the ring on board, were put on hold. George asked Sheryl to marry him in the courtyard of the al-Rasheed—without the ring.

Iraqi staffers in the palace were so excited by the prospect of a Green Zone wedding that they did whatever they could to help. One woman loaned Sheryl a gown. Another purchased the invitations. A third arranged for the flowers.

Still ringless as their December 3 wedding date approached, the couple found a jeweler in the al-Rasheed's shopping arcade who had two silver wedding bands for sale.

They had wanted to have the ceremony in the palace chapel, the room with the giant mural of a Scud missile, but it had been converted into a dormitory after the attack on the al-Rasheed. The chapel had been moved to the white tent. They settled for a garden wedding.

At the ceremony, one of their colleagues from the governance team read Robert Frost's "The Road Less Traveled." After they were pronounced man and wife, and had kissed, they walked out under an arch of crossed Nepalese kukri knives held by the Gurkhas who guarded the palace. The newlyweds then climbed into a Humvee with the words JUST MARRIED scrawled on the hood in shaving cream. They rode to the al-Rasheed, where they hosted a reception complete with cake and open bar, before retiring to a suite next to the pool normally reserved for dignitaries. The next day, they left to honeymoon in Dubai.

The day after they returned to Baghdad, they received the package with Sheryl's engagement ring.

12

We Cannot Continue Like This

EIGHT GUNMEN WAITED ON EITHER SIDE of the Sajjad Mosque in southwestern Baghdad. Their prey wasn't a big shot politician, a businessman, or a religious leader, but a humble, fifty-three-year-old factory director. When he drove by on his way to work at eight in the morning, the gunmen cut off his white Isuzu Trooper, shot his driver in the chest and leg, then dragged the factory director out of the vehicle. They threw him to the ground and fired five times, ending with a bullet to his head.

Iraq's largest newspaper had printed a small story identifying the victim as Faez Ghani Aziz, the director-general of the State Company for Vegetable Oils. I had met Aziz just a few weeks earlier, after Tim Carney had urged me to visit the company's decrepit factory. Why, I wondered, would someone want to rub out a factory director? It was late July 2003, a little more than three months since the fall of Baghdad, and well before people working for the government were being marked for assassination.

Then it struck me: Aziz had been wading into treacherous waters. He had been talking, albeit quietly, about privatization.

I had recently traveled with Jerry Bremer to a special meeting of the World Economic Forum in Jordan, where he outlined his vision for a free-market Iraq before hundreds of business executives. "Markets allocate resources much more efficiently than politicians," Bremer said in his keynote address, delivered inside a giant tent erected on the grounds of a posh resort at the Dead Sea. "So our strategic goal in the months ahead is to set in motion policies which will have the effect of reallocating people and resources from state enterprises to more productive private firms."

As we returned to Baghdad aboard a U.S. military transport plane, he discussed with such fervor the need to privatize government-run factories that his voice cut through the din in the cargo hold. "We have to move forward quickly with this effort," he said. "Getting inefficient state enterprises into private hands is essential for Iraq's economic recovery."

A couple of days later, I went to the vegetable oil factory to ask Aziz what he thought of Bremer's strategy. He wholeheartedly agreed. "We need outside investors," he told me. "We cannot continue like this."

Aziz never shared those views with his colleagues at the factory—he knew it was dangerous to talk about laying off employees—but he drew the line at expanding the already bloated workforce. Dozens of men who had been dismissed before the war had been demanding their jobs back, but Aziz refused to rehire them. Two days before his death, a man walked into Aziz's office with a grenade and threatened to pull the pin if his job was not reinstated. Although Aziz managed to restore calm, scores of job seekers held a protest the next day in front of the ministry's temporary headquarters.

"These people were saying, 'Either you let us back to work or we're going to do something,'" recalled Luay Ali, the ministry's security director. Ali had no doubt that Aziz was killed because he had opposed rehiring the workers. "There is a very clear connection," he said.

Aziz's killing sent a wave of panic through the Ministry of Industry. The Iraqi interim minister and his advisers had been eager to start the process of privatization, figuring it would be a quick way to enrich themselves. They had, for a while, been far more aggressive in promoting privatization than Tim Carney, Glenn Corliss, or Brad Jackson, the American advisers to the ministry. But Aziz's death changed all that. If one of their own could be killed for simply refusing to hire new workers, what would happen if they allowed tens of thousands of workers to be fired by private investors? All of a sudden, no one in the ministry wanted to talk about privatization.

Two weeks after Aziz was killed, Tom Foley arrived in Baghdad to head up a new CPA department: the Office of Private Sector Development. Foley's mission, as he defined it, was to privatize all of Iraq's state-owned enterprises within thirty days.

The first resistance he encountered was in the Republican Palace itself. His aides and the CPA's legal department informed him that selling off Iraqi government assets, such as factories, would likely violate the Hague Convention of 1899, the treaty governing "the laws and customs of war on land." Article 55 of the treaty states that an occupying power "shall be regarded only as administrator and usufructuary of public buildings, real estate, forests, and agricultural estates belonging to the hostile State" and must "safeguard the capital of these properties."

When Foley approached Iraqis at the Ministry of Industry about privatization, they recoiled. Aziz's death had made the issue radioactive. Mehdi Hafedh, the minister of planning, who was regarded as one of the most forward-thinking Iraqi leaders, told Foley that inefficient state-run firms had to be sold, but not right away. "It will be too destabilizing," Hafedh said to Foley.

Foley was undaunted. He hit the phones, trying to persuade his friends on Wall Street to invest in Iraq's industrial sector. They were no more enthusiastic than the Iraqis. He turned to the Governing Council. They, too, turned him down.

Then came November 15 and the announcement that sovereignty would be returned to the Iraqis by June. There was no way to privatize that quickly. Even if some firms could be sold before the handover, Bremer and his keepers in Washington had lost their appetite to do so. They didn't want anything to derail the transfer of power.

A contractor from BearingPoint, the consulting firm hired to assist the CPA with economic reconstruction, gave Foley a white paper suggesting that he lease the factories to private investors instead of selling them outright. "That's what we did in Kosovo," the consultant told Foley. "It could work here, too." Foley grudgingly agreed to the leasing scheme, and so did the Governing Council. The Ministry of Industry announced in

February 2004 that it would accept bids to lease thirty-five separate factories. But the investors had to promise not to fire a
single employee.

The response was tepid. The insurgency was gathering
strength. Electricity was inadequate. The airport wasn't open
to commercial flights. And who knew if a new Iraqi government would uphold deals made by the CPA? By the time
Bremer left, not a single factory had been leased.

After Foley had been in Baghdad for a few months, Bremer
concluded that he wasn't the right guy for the job, but he was a
friend of the president. Bremer told people in the palace that
Foley was "untouchable."

Finally, in early 2004, Bremer came up with a new job for
Foley. He would travel the world with former secretary of state
James Baker III to persuade other nations to forgive Iraq's
debt.

Once Foley left, he was replaced by his deputy, Michael
Fleischer, a businessman from New Jersey. Although Fleischer
had served as a State Department officer in Africa in the 1970s,
he had no previous experience in promoting free enterprise in
a socialist economy. But he had connections: his brother Ari
was Bush's press secretary.

The November 15 Agreement was the writing on the wall for
the neoconservative experiment in Iraq. But several senior
CPA staffers refused to succumb as Jim Haveman and Tom
Foley had. They clung to their pet projects. There were seven
and a half months until the end of June, enough time to make
a few big changes.

The collective to-do list was long. The Strategic Communications team wanted to establish an Iraqi Federal Communications Commission. Advocates for gender equality wanted to
open women's centers across the Shiite south. The governance team wanted new members to be appointed to the mini–
governing councils in each province. The security policy team
wanted to ensure that all militias were demobilized. Bremer
wanted to appoint inspectors general to root out corruption in
every ministry. And everyone, it seemed, wanted Bremer to
promulgate another law.

The neoconservatives who succeeded economics czar Peter McPherson weren't willing to give up on everything. If they couldn't sell off state-run firms, they figured they could at least try to eliminate the pervasive subsidies across the economy. Why sell gasoline for five cents a gallon? Why distribute electricity for free? Why offer fertilizer so cheaply that farmers would smuggle it into Syria and Jordan to resell it instead of using it on their fields? Why give everyone monthly food rations, regardless of need? Subsidies accounted for more than half of Iraq's annual budget—the food rations alone cost $5 billion a year—and resulted in a grossly inefficient, Soviet-style system of economic allocation. The CPA's economists realized that reducing subsidies, which would result in higher prices, would be unpopular and would likely trigger unrest, but they also were convinced that it was the CPA's responsibility to wean Iraqis from government handouts. They figured that the Iraqi government that would take over from the CPA wouldn't have the intestinal fortitude to take such steps.

Instead of doubling the price of fuel or fertilizer, the economists came up with what they thought would be a far less risky strategy to start cutting back on subsidies. Every month, Iraqis received government food rations: sacks of rice, beans, flour, sugar, tea, and other staples. Under the CPA plan, the government would get out of the business of ordering and distributing food and instead offer people cash payments equivalent to the cost of the food. The private sector, they believed, would distribute food far more efficiently, saving the government hundreds of millions of dollars a year. A sovereign Iraqi government could decide to go even further and cut back on payments to the wealthy through a means test.

As with privatization, the economic rationale was sound, but the practical concerns were enormous. Six days after the November 15 Agreement, the CPA's senior adviser for labor and social affairs told Bremer that the plan had "the possibility of huge humanitarian problems." Bremer was a strong advocate of monetizing the monthly rations, and opposing the change was regarded as career suicide in the palace, but the adviser was Jim Otwell, the feisty firefighter who had earlier clashed with Bernie Kerik. Although he was a rank-and-file firefighter—he rode on Engine 32 in Buffalo—he became the senior adviser for labor and social affairs by the fall of 2003 because the U.S. Department of Labor failed to send anyone to Baghdad to fill the post. Otwell's experience with the firefighters' union in Buffalo made him the closest thing to a labor expert in the Green Zone.

Otwell told Bremer that the responsibility for collecting the rations and apportioning them was typically handled by Iraqi women. If the CPA switched to cash, there was the possibility that men would pick up the payments and then squander the funds on other things. There also was the margin of error, not an insignificant factor in a country of twenty-five million people. "Let's say we get this ninety-nine percent right and only one percent don't get their payments," he told Bremer. "Now we've got two hundred fifty thousand hungry, mad Iraqis who used to get something. We thought we had a problem before."

The CPA's economic team had no shortage of ambition. They began studying the feasibility of giving each family a debit card loaded with the cash value of all the rations they were due. The cards would be automatically replenished each month. Otwell was aghast. Nobody in Iraq used credit cards. There were no automated teller machines. Phone service and electrical power were unavailable for much of the day. How did the CPA expect merchants to process debit cards? Who would purchase the processing equipment? To Otwell, it was another crazy ivory-tower scheme invented in the Emerald City.

Bremer was unmoved by Otwell's warnings. Monetization made sense, he decided, and it would be enacted by June 1— thirty days before the handover of sovereignty. But Otwell didn't back down. He sought out senior members of the British contingent in the CPA. They were receptive to his concerns and began lobbying Bremer and the American military. In the end, it was the U.S. military command that shot down the plan. The troops were already stretched thin fighting the insurgency. They couldn't handle food riots, too. If changing the ration system wasn't a prerequisite for relinquishing power, it didn't need to happen. Members of the economic team saw it differently: a little pain now would prevent bigger problems in the future. But expectations had changed. What was best for Iraq was no longer the standard. What was best for Washington was the new calculus.

A few weeks after he arrived in Baghdad, twenty-four-year-old Jay Hallen realized he'd never meet his goal of reopening the stock exchange by December 31. He had become infected with the same pre–November 15 ambition, as had almost everyone else in the palace. Hallen had decided to build what he called "a whole new stock exchange from the ground up," with a computerized trading system, a board of directors, a securities and exchange commission, licensed brokers, and a revised financial markets law. Despite American enthusiasm for the plan, Iraqis had cringed. Their top priority was reopening the exchange, not setting up computers or enacting a new securities law. Brokers and traders wanted to go back to work. Investors wanted to buy and sell. "People are broke and bewildered," broker Talib Tabatabai had told Hallen. "Why do you want to create enemies? Let us open the way we were."

Tabatabai, who held a doctorate in political science from Florida State University, believed that Hallen's plan was unrealistic. "It was something so fancy, so great, that it couldn't be accomplished," he said. "But he didn't listen to us."

Hallen was convinced that major changes had to be enacted. "[Iraqi] laws and regulations were completely out of step with the modern world," he said later. "There was just no transparency in anything. It was more of a place for Saddam and his friends to buy up private companies that they otherwise didn't have a stake in."

Hallen turned to the Financial Services Volunteer Corps, a nonprofit American organization that helps build stock markets in developing nations. The FSVC, comprising government and private-sector specialists, agreed to send a six-person delegation to Baghdad in November to meet with Hallen and a group of Iraqis. At the meeting, which was relocated to Jordan after the attack on the al-Rasheed Hotel, the American volunteers agreed to help Hallen with his to-do list. One of the participants took up the task of rewriting the securities law. Others offered assistance with training brokers and purchasing computers.

As the law was being written, Hallen began firing Iraqis. The old stock exchange employed eighty-five people—far more than he needed for the new, computerized exchange. Instead of keeping all of the former employees, as other CPA staffers had done with the government agencies they supervised, Hallen was determined to create a lean, American-style exchange with just forty salaried positions. He met with each of the old employees and then chose forty-five to sack. "It definitely ruffled feathers," he said. "It was not an easy time, because people in Iraq are not used to getting fired."

Hallen nominated nine Iraqis to serve on the exchange's board of governors. To ensure the board's independence, he needed to find at least four who would not be involved in the exchange's day-to-day operations, but he didn't know many Iraqi businessmen beyond those involved with the stock market. For recommendations he turned to two Iraqis he trusted. As he met candidates, he screened them for proficiency in English—he later said that this was for his personal benefit—and for "a very American style of thinking in terms of business and capitalism."

He eventually assembled what he thought was an outstanding group, until an Iraqi friend told Hallen he was making "a big mistake." Most of the candidates Hallen had selected were Sunni Arabs. It was an understandable oversight—most of the wealth and business expertise in the old days was in the Sunni community—but even so, Shiite and Kurdish leaders were bound to be upset. Hallen struck a few Sunni names from the list.

Opening the exchange also required money to buy the computers, to fund the construction of a trading floor, to lease a building, and getting money meant Hallen had to compete against other CPA staffers and their pet projects. "Some could argue that the country had so many needs, like electricity and security, so who cares about the stock exchange?" But Hallen believed that his project was just as deserving. He began to lobby his boss, and everyone else involved in disbursing funds, to pay for the exchange. In the end, he got the money he needed.

By the spring of 2004, the securities law was ready. It had

been vetted by the CPA's lawyers and several cabinet agencies in Washington. On April 19, Bremer signed it, and simultaneously appointed the nine Iraqis selected by Hallen to become the exchange's board of governors. Another five Iraqis were named to the new Securities and Exchange Commission.

The stock exchange's board selected Talib Tabatabai, the American-educated broker who had been so critical of Hallen, as its chairman. The new securities law that Hallen had nursed into life gave the board control over the stock exchange's operations, but it didn't say a thing about the role of the CPA adviser. Hallen assumed that he'd have a part in decision making until the handover of sovereignty. Tabatabai and the board, however, saw themselves in charge.

The board hired back the forty-five workers whom Hallen had fired. The stock exchange didn't need more employees, but it didn't make sense to create enemies of fellow Iraqis. Who knew what a pink-slipped worker might do?

Tabatabai and the other governors also decided to open the market as soon as possible. They didn't want to wait several more months for the computerized trading system to be up and running. They ordered dozens of DryErase boards to be installed on the trading floor. They had used blackboards to keep track of buying and selling prices before the war, and that's how they'd do it again.

Tension between Hallen and the board grew. Hallen regarded the board as "stubborn and resistant to change." Board members couldn't understand why Hallen wouldn't leave them alone. It was their country, after all. The board balked at paying bills for services ordered by Hallen that they felt were unneeded; Hallen believed that the board was refusing perfectly reasonable expenses, such as guards to prevent squatters from occupying the stock exchange. "It was not a pleasant business," Hallen said.

On June 22, Hallen left Iraq. Two days later, the stock exchange opened. Brokers barked orders to floor traders, who used their trusty whiteboards. Transactions were recorded not with computers but with small chits written on in ink. CPA staffers stayed away, afraid that their presence would make the stock market a target for insurgents.

When he returned to the United States, Hallen told an inter-
viewer from the Association for Diplomatic Studies and Training that his work in Iraq "was not the crowning achievement of
my career."

"When I think about how I felt when I left, I was unhappy,"
he said. "But when I look back on it . . . and put it in perspective
and look at everything I was up against, I feel differently. I was
by myself for five months in a nearly impossible situation.
At times it really felt impossible, trying to pull everything
together. When I look at how things are, I feel very proud
because I knew I was instrumental in bringing things to where
they are today, even if things didn't turn out the way I wanted
them to. If I hadn't done my job, maybe nothing would've happened at all."

I asked Tabatabai what would have happened if Hallen
hadn't been assigned to reopen the stock exchange. He smiled.
"We would have opened months earlier. He had grand ideas,
but those ideas did not materialize," Tabatabai said of Hallen.
"Those CPA people reminded me of Lawrence of Arabia."

But even T. E. Lawrence had known when to back down. As
Tabatabai spoke, I thought of one of Lawrence's most apropos
quotations, and wondered if anyone in the palace had bothered
to read him:

> Do not try to do too much with your own hands. Better
> the Arabs do it tolerably than that you do it perfectly.
> It is their war, and you are to help them, not to win it
> for them. Actually, also, under the very odd conditions
> of Arabia, your practical work will not be as good as,
> perhaps, you think it is.

THE GREEN ZONE, SCENE X

American military personnel stationed in the Republican Palace rarely had a kind word to say about the CPA. The soldiers, many of whom were majors and colonels, had been in uniform for more than two decades and resented being ordered around by CPA staffers in their twenties. Some of the soldiers had done tours in Kosovo, Haiti, and Somalia, and a few had even served in Vietnam. They knew a thing or two about post-conflict nation building. But to the CPA's young turks, the soldiers were drivers, guards, and errand boys. The civilians made policy; the soldiers implemented it.

Since the soldiers weren't supposed to drink, they didn't hang out at the bars or the al-Rasheed's disco. They kept to themselves, smoking in the rear portico, exercising in the gym, and playing cards in their trailers. They maintained that things would be a whole lot better if they were in charge. The acronym CPA, they joked, stood for Can't Produce Anything.

In early 2004, a contingent of marines was assigned to guard the palace. They erected concrete barriers to limit traffic around the compound and strung new coils of razor wire atop the blast walls. They set up more observation posts and established a sign-in table, where those without plastic CPA badges had to hand over a piece of identification in exchange for a visitor's pass, which had to be displayed at all times while that person was on palace grounds.

Behind the desk was a white DryErase board upon which the marines drew cartoons. One day the board depicted a gravestone inscribed with the words COMMON SENSE. *Underneath was a caption: "Killed by the CPA."*

13

Missed Opportunities

DRIVING ANYWHERE IN BAGHDAD before the war took about fifteen minutes. A network of wide expressways and boulevards crisscrossed the city. Motorists could zip along at the speed limit or faster. Everyone stayed in his lane and stopped at red lights. Traffic policemen—in white shirts, white hats, and white gloves—manned busy intersections. The traffic was light because the importation of cars was restricted. If an Iraqi wanted a car, he put his name on a list at the Ministry of Trade. If he was lucky, he'd get a letter five years later informing him that a car was ready for purchase—at a subsidized price. Perhaps it would be a Toyota, a Volkswagen, or a Russian Lada. He took what he could get. Of course, the car everyone wanted was a Chevy Caprice, or any American-made, eight-cylinder gas-guzzler. Saddam hated Washington, but the Iraqis loved Detroit.

After the war, the most noticeable change in Iraqi life was the traffic. The stoplights went out. People started driving on the wrong side of the road, secure in the knowledge that cops were no longer reporting for work. Cars barreled down sidewalks. People who always wanted to make a left turn in front of their house but couldn't because of a concrete median simply hired construction workers to jackhammer away the obstruction.

Lawlessness was only part of the problem. The American military closed off streets near its bases in the city, regardless of whether they were vital thoroughfares. To protect the Green

Zone, the military shut down one of the bridges spanning the Tigris and two expressways connecting western and northern Baghdad with the city center. The sight of barricaded roads was a daily reminder to Iraqis that they were under occupation, and those barricades did more to stoke anger at the Americans than almost anything else.

But the biggest problem had its roots in a well-intentioned CPA policy. Peter McPherson, Bremer's economics czar, abolished duties on imports, including a tax on cars that could be as much as 100 percent of the cost of the vehicle. Within days, savvy entrepreneurs brought truckloads of used cars to Baghdad from as far away as Germany and the Netherlands, and Iraqis who had socked away money under their mattresses bought their first car, or, in many cases, a second car for the family. The CPA estimated that a half million cars were shipped into Iraq in the first nine months of the occupation, more than doubling the number of vehicles on the road. Iraqis were happy—until they had to get somewhere or fill up the tank. Yes, they were living atop the world's second-largest oil reserves, but Iraq's refineries could not produce enough gasoline to fuel all the new cars. Gas lines stretched for miles, prompting the CPA to pay Halliburton millions of dollars a day to truck in gasoline from Kuwait and Turkey. But even with gas in the tank, the volume of new cars on the roads made routine trips interminable.

Iraqis weren't the only ones grousing. American soldiers grew increasingly nervous about getting stuck in traffic. Although the traffic police had returned to their posts a few months into the occupation, the CPA forbade them to levy fines. The traffic cops had been notoriously corrupt, forcing motorists to fork over money instead of issuing them summonses to appear in court. The CPA was standing on principle, even if declawing the cops meant that traffic would continue to crawl.

To Major General Martin Dempsey, the commander of the First Armored Division, the army unit in charge of Baghdad, the solution seemed clear. He decreed that a new traffic law be drawn up. The order trickled down the ranks to a captain named John Smathers, a personal-injury lawyer from Maryland.

Smathers was a reservist attached to the military's civil affairs team working with the CPA to administer Baghdad. He was forty-five, though he had the trim physique of a soldier a generation younger. The only giveaway was his graying hair and his intense, no-nonsense demeanor. He had already received three Bronze Stars for his service in Iraq. He fended off an ambush in southern Baghdad the day after the city's liberation. Over the next few weeks, he and his quick-reaction team captured two of the fifty-five Iraqis most wanted by the Pentagon; foiled a bank robbery, recovering $6.3 million in cash; and found ten artifacts stolen from the Baghdad Museum.

As a former county prosecutor, Smathers knew a fair bit about traffic laws. His first step was to read a translated copy of Iraq's code. After poring through it, he judged it a disaster. Traffic officers could seize a driver's car without a judge's permission. They could collect fines on the spot. They could jail a driver for two years for simply uttering an insult. "There was no definition of what powers the police had, other than whatever they wanted," Smathers said.

With the help of an Iraqi judge he befriended, Smathers began rewriting the law. It took him three weeks. His finished draft was fifty-three pages long, more than twice the length of the original law, and it embodied all of the earnest intentions and parochial biases of the American occupation. He limited officers to issuing tickets payable at a courthouse. As collateral, they could seize a driver's license. If drivers wanted to dispute citations, they could do so at new traffic courts established under the law.

To Smathers, the old law was riddled with sloppy definitions and loopholes. Since he didn't know enough about traffic law to rewrite those sections himself, he logged on to the Internet and searched for a document to serve as his model, a document he knew well: the State of Maryland's motor vehicle code. After reading the Maryland law, he engaged in a flurry of cutting and pasting. The Iraqi law, he noticed, didn't have a ban on following another vehicle too closely. Section 21-310 of the Maryland code had just the wording he needed. It became Article 18, Paragraph 11, of his draft: "The driver of a motor vehicle may not follow another vehicle more closely than is reasonable and prudent, having due regard for the speed of the other vehicle and of the traffic on and the condition of the highway." He did the same borrowing for regulations on speeding, unsafe lane changes, and the failure to yield. If it was good enough for Baltimore, it was good enough for Baghdad.

As he went about drafting the code, the personal-injury lawyer in Smathers seized upon the fact that the original law had no provision for people to sue the police for misbehavior. He saw this as a glaring omission. He opened his laptop and typed out a paragraph:

> If a police officer, acting within the scope of his duties as an employee of the Ministry of Interior, uses excessive force to make an arrest and causes personal injury to another or unnecessarily damages the property of another, then the injured person or owner of damaged property has a civil cause of action against the Ministry of Interior, in civil court, to recover compensatory damages for (1) the value of medical services rendered; (2) lost wages; (3) pain and suffering; and (4) the lesser of the cost of repair of damaged property or the value of the property. If the police officer acted intentionally and with malice, then the person may also recover punitive damages.

Smathers regarded his crafting of the new law as a model of an enlightened occupation. He had consulted with an Iraqi judge and had stuck to the general framework of Iraq's old law, but he had added the necessary safeguards against abuses of power. He proudly carried the document to the Republican Palace and gave it to the team of CPA staffers working with Iraq's Ministry of Justice. They were to vet the proposed law before it was sent to Bremer's office for final approval.

They read his draft and called him back for consultations. As soon as he walked in, it was clear to him that they didn't share his enthusiasm. They had dozens of other legal matters to address: reopening courts, rehabilitating prisons, revising laws addressing serious crimes. A new traffic law seemed so trivial. Besides, they noted, who would train the police, set up the new courts, and process the fines? The CPA was already stretched thin. "Nobody was saying it was a bad idea," one of the CPA participants recalled. "It was a matter of priority and timing." But they didn't dismiss Smathers outright. They knew that a general wanted the law. They finally told him to return in a few weeks. They'd have to consult with the Council of Judges and the Interior Ministry, which supervised the traffic police.

A few weeks later, in early February 2004, the CPA staffers met with a group of high-ranking traffic officers. Smathers showed up with a folder filled with copies of his draft. The Iraqis, who had read a translation, were equal parts angry and incredulous. They couldn't believe that the Americans would involve themselves in such minutiae, and they were none too pleased with the prospect of losing the power to shake down motorists.

Smathers had expected the Iraqi police to dislike his revisions. "It puts power in the hands of the people," he said later. "It holds the police accountable. It stops them from making money on the side. I really didn't know how these guys were paid before, but a lot of them were rich. They had twenty cars . . . and I wasn't going to allow that."

The Iraqis proposed that they draft their own version. They promised to do it within two weeks. The CPA staffers agreed. The days of ordering the Iraqis around were supposed to be over.

Smathers felt burned. *The Americans hate my plan because it wasn't invented in the palace,* he thought as he walked out. *And the Iraqis hate it because it will take their power away.*

"The people working in the CPA were debaters who wanted a hundred percent best solution for any problem," he told me. "Sometimes the sixty percent solution today is better than the hundred percent solution six months from now. And that's what those people needed. They needed *something.* They needed *some* kind of action even if it's a little bit of one to show them that you're doing something. And what got sent from Washington was a bunch of debaters. They'd sit around in the Green Zone and debate. Well, I don't know about this. Let's try this. And then they'd debate it for months and months and months and months, and nothing would happen."

Smathers never made it to the next meeting. On February 21, a convoy in which he was traveling was ambushed south of Baghdad by a band of insurgents. His interpreter was killed, and his sport utility vehicle flipped over. Smathers broke his arm in two places and busted his knees. He was evacuated to an army hospital in Germany later that day.

While he was recovering, the Iraqi traffic officers returned to the Green Zone to present their draft. They had written it in Arabic but had gotten an Interior Ministry employee to translate it into English for the benefit of the CPA staffers. The document was laden with what seemed to be nonsensical prohibitions. Standing on the seats of a moving car was forbidden. So was talking to the driver. The draft even banned smoking in cars. The CPA staffers weren't sure what to make of it. Iraqis smoked more than almost anyone else on the planet. What were the traffic officers thinking? Their draft was even sillier than Smathers's.

It turned out that the Iraqis didn't mean to prohibit smoking in all cars, just on public buses. It was a translation error— the sort of goof that bedeviled so many of the CPA's attempts to administer a country where few of the administrators spoke the language of the administered. The CPA team thanked the Iraqis for the draft and promised to include elements of it in the new law. And then they set about melding the original Smathers draft with the Iraqi one. It was at the very bottom of the to-do matrix in the general counsel's office, but it finally did get finished, vetted, and signed by Bremer.

The final document included much of what Smathers had written, but it contained dozens of new provisions as a sop to both the Iraqis' and the CPA's micromanagement tendencies.

- Pedestrians walking during darkness or cloudy weather shall wear light or reflective clothing.
- The driver shall hold the steering wheel with both hands.
- Long-distance driving may cause drowsiness or fatigue. To avoid this, rest should be taken for five minutes for every one hour of driving.

The traffic code became CPA Order 86.

Before Bremer left, he signed a hundred orders in all. Some

were essential. Order 96 established rules for elections. Order 31 modified the penal code. Order 19 guaranteed freedom of assembly. But many others were aspirational or just plain unnecessary in a nation wracked by a violent insurgency. Order 81 revised Iraq's laws governing patents, industrial design, undisclosed information, integrated circuits, and plant varieties. Order 83 revised the copyright law. Order 59 detailed protections for government whistleblowers. Order 66 created a public-service broadcasting commission.

Many in the Emerald City assumed that if you wanted to change something, you changed the law, just like in the United States. But Iraq didn't work that way. Solving traffic snarls had little to do with a new law. Traffic lights had to be fixed. Traffic officers needed to be trained. Cars had to be registered. Imports had to be regulated. A decree wasn't a substitute for the laborious, on-the-ground work of rebuilding a nation.

The Iraqis, of course, just disregarded the new traffic code. It was never distributed to officers or announced to the public. After Bremer left, I asked Sabah Kadhim, a senior official at the Interior Ministry, what would happen to the traffic law. He laughed. "Our main concern is terrorism," he said. "You have to be practical. We haven't reached the state where we can implement traffic laws. It's great in theory, but in reality, we are not focusing on it. We have no resources to enforce it, and it's not our priority."

Moreover, Kadhim said, laws promulgated under the occupation were suspect. "There is a question mark there," he said. "We will have to evaluate it. We need to enforce traffic laws in an Iraqi way. The Americans inside the Green Zone acted like they lived in New York, not in Baghdad. Good work is not going to bring good results unless you tailor it to a country's concerns. Outside solutions won't work here. It has to be an Iraqi solution. They should have let the Iraqis develop these laws themselves rather than imposing laws imported from America."

The November 15 Agreement called for an interim constitution to be written by February 28. In early January, with Bremer and the council still focused on the stillborn caucuses,

Roman Martinez and two colleagues from the CPA's governance team met with two former exiles who had extensive
legal experience: DePauw University law professor Faisal Istrabadi, and Salem Chalabi, an international lawyer who had
studied at Yale, Columbia, and Northwestern, and looked like a
younger version of his uncle Ahmad Chalabi. The council had
already received two proposed drafts, one written by a Kurdish
politician and the other by an aide to a Sunni Arab member,
but the CPA believed that both were riddled with problems.
The two Iraqi lawyers agreed, but told Martinez not to worry;
they were writing their own document with the council's blessing. They promised that their draft would include a bill of
rights guaranteeing personal freedoms unheard of in the Arab
world.

Instead of foisting an American document on the Iraqis,
Bremer and his aides decided to allow Istrabadi and Salem
Chalabi to proceed. From that moment on, the Iraqis had the
pen. If the CPA wanted changes, the Americans would have to
go to the Iraqis and make a case for additions or deletions. It
was a jarring reversal for Americans who had been used to getting their way and for Iraqis who had grown accustomed to
Bremer having the final say on everything.

The shift was a sign that Bremer and his CPA had finally
started to understand that the Americans needed to play a supporting role, stepping in only to prevent the Iraqis from making colossal mistakes. He and his aides had learned that
creating a plan in Washington and ramming it down the
throats of Iraqis didn't work. And they also came to understand
the enormous influence of Grand Ayatollah al-Sistani. Too
much American involvement in the drafting of the interim
constitution ran the risk of inciting the ayatollah's opprobrium.

At one of the first meetings in the palace to inform other
CPA departments about the drafting process, the governance
team delivered an admonition: This is their document. We're
going to play a limited role. Of course, that didn't stop CPA officials from weighing in and trying to make changes. Istrabadi's
passion was a bill of rights, which he designed as a bulwark
against another dictatorship. His original draft included ex-
plicit rights to privacy, free expression, a speedy trial, educa-

tion, health care, and social security. He also wrote that government authorities could not search private residences without a
warrant. That provision alarmed CPA officials working with
the ministries of Interior and Justice. Iraqi security forces were
fighting an insurgency. Would they have to request a warrant
if they received a tip that someone was assembling roadside
bombs in his house? The CPA officials lobbied members of the
governance team to push for a change, which they did. Ultimately, Istrabadi agreed to water down the provision and allow
warrantless searches in "extreme exigent circumstances."

The Istrabadi-Chalabi draft didn't address several of the
most contentious issues among Iraqis: the role of Islam in government, the status of the autonomous Kurdish region, and the
rights of women. Those would have to be hashed out among
council members.

Bremer issued only one ultimatum: if the document enshrined Islam as the sole source of legislation, as the two
largest Shiite parties wanted—meaning that sharia would be
the law of the land—he would veto it. The viceroy also stepped
in to help hammer out a compromise over Kurdish rights. The
Kurds had had effective autonomy in three northern provinces
since 1991 and they were not about to give that up. They were
willing to accede to a "voluntary union with Iraq" if they could
keep their Kurdish Regional Government, which would have
the power to veto any laws passed by the federal government
in Baghdad. The Kurds also wanted their autonomous zone to
include the historically Kurdish city of Kirkuk, which Saddam
had resettled with thousands of Arabs. In addition, the Kurds
insisted on maintaining their *peshmerga* militia and retaining
revenue from oil pumped in Kurdish areas.

The Pentagon, the State Department, and the White House
had long been opposed to ethnic federalism in Iraq. Bremer
had supported that policy until early January, when he realized
there was no way the Kurds would embrace an interim constitution that did not provide for at least a multiprovince Kurdish
zone with its own administration. Bremer sought a compromise. He flew to the north for consultations with Kurdish leaders, where he struck a historic federalist bargain: the Kurds
could maintain their three-province regional government,

which would have far more power than other provinces—it could, for instance, reject some laws passed by the central government—but the Kurds would also accept the central government's authority over a number of issues, including fiscal, defense, and foreign policy. It was Bremer's finest hour in Iraq, breaking away from his masters in Washington to pursue a pragmatic policy based on Iraqi reality.

Bremer's aides had sent cables about the Kurdish negotiations to keep the White House and the Pentagon in the loop, but as soon as Bremer announced his deal with the Kurds, Condi Rice and Paul Wolfowitz balked. They insisted that references to the Kurdish Regional Government be stricken from the interim constitution and that federalism be based solely on provincial lines. After seeing if the Kurds would budge—they wouldn't—Bremer stood his ground with Washington. Rice and Wolfowitz eventually backed down, allowing Bremer and the CPA to head into final negotiations over the interim constitution.

It was late February, and by then the document had a name, the Transitional Administrative Law. The Governing Council convened a series of marathon meetings to hash out the remaining issues. The role of Islam in government was finessed with an artful two-step: Islam would be only "a source" of legislation, but no law could contradict "the universally agreed tenets of Islam." A quota for female representation in the national assembly gave way to language stating that the country's new electoral law "shall aim to achieve the goal of having women constitute no less than one-quarter of the members." Members squabbled and even walked out for a time. Several Shiite members refused to sign the finished charter—the ratification ceremony had to be postponed for three days—because they objected to a provision that gave the Kurds effective veto power over the permanent constitution. (The provision would later be used, albeit unsuccessfully, by Sunni Arabs in an attempt to defeat the constitution.) The Shiites eventually agreed to sign the TAL, after consultations with al-Sistani. But through it all, Bremer took a backseat. He and the top British diplomat in Iraq, Sir Jeremy Greenstock, helped work through disagreements, but the ultimate decisions were made by the Iraqis.

CPA staffers joked among themselves that they had never seen
Bremer sit so quietly for so long.

"The TAL was a turning point," said Adel Abdel-Mahdi, the
Shiite politician who helped kill the caucuses. "It's when Bremer
stopped acting like a dictator."

On June 1, United Nations envoy Lakhdar Brahimi announced
the names of the members of the interim government that
would assume power on June 30, when Bremer was scheduled
to leave and the CPA was to be dissolved. Brahimi had consulted with hundreds of Iraqis—with professors, judges, clerics, and members of the Governing Council. He had even met
with Grand Ayatollah al-Sistani. But the selection of the government, the most significant step on Iraq's path to democracy
after Saddam's ouster, was anything but democratic.

Brahimi decided who was in and who was out, in consultation with Jerry Bremer and Bob Blackwill. Allowing Iraqis to
choose would have been more democratic but also more
chaotic, and the last thing Washington wanted was chaos. The
only election that mattered was the one in November—in the
United States.

Brahimi wanted to reduce the role of politicians in the interim government. He believed that an interim government
composed of technocrats instead of politicians would make
things work, and that they would be less likely to use their status to promote one party over another.

Brahimi's strategy was torpedoed from three directions.
Bremer and Blackwill argued for the inclusion of Governing
Council members. Better to go with the devil you know, they
said, than the one you don't.

Al-Sistani also stuck his oar in. Brahimi had sent him a list
of four candidates being considered for prime minister: Ayad
Allawi, a secular Shiite who led a party called the Iraqi
National Accord; Adel Abdel-Mahdi, a religious Shiite, of the
Supreme Council for Islamic Revolution in Iraq; Ibrahim al-
Jafari, another religious Shiite, of the Dawa party; and Hussein
Shahristani, a moderate Shiite who didn't belong to a party.
Shahristani, a nuclear scientist who had been jailed by Saddam
for refusing to work on weapons projects, was Brahimi's

favored candidate. Bremer and Blackwill preferred Allawi, a former Baathist who had spent years on the CIA payroll. They regarded him as someone who wouldn't shirk from fighting the insurgents, but who also would be able to persuade former Baathists who had joined the resistance to lay down their arms. Al-Sistani didn't indicate a favorite. He simply made it clear, through an emissary, that Allawi, Abdel-Mahdi, and al-Jafari were acceptable. There was no mention of Shahristani. Brahimi crossed him off the list and moved Allawi's name up. Allawi was secular and he was America's guy. He'd become the prime minister.

Governing Council members demanded that the top jobs in the interim government be given to political party leaders, and they opposed Brahimi's choice of former foreign minister Adnan Pachachi for president. Pachachi, a secular Sunni, was close to the Americans. He was one of Bremer's allies on the council, and he had been Laura Bush's guest at the State of the Union Address in January. Some of his fellow council members questioned his impartiality and instead backed a rival Sunni, Ghazi al-Yawar, a businessman and tribal sheik who had no government experience beyond his ten-month stint on the council. Pachachi eventually withdrew his candidacy for president, forcing Brahimi to hand the job to al-Yawar.

Pressure from Bremer, Blackwill, and the council guided Brahimi's hand in filling other posts. He named al-Jafari and Rowsch Shaways of the Kurdistan Democratic Party as vice presidents. Another Kurdish politician was made deputy prime minister and yet another was tapped to be foreign minister. Abdel-Mahdi became finance minister. A leader of the Iraqi Islamic Party became the minister of industry. The powerful post of interior minister went to a leader of another party.

At the ceremony announcing the government, held at a clock tower that had been Saddam's personal museum, a rumpled and drawn Brahimi kept a brave face, calling the new government "effective and capable." But offstage, he did little to mask his disappointment. He had wanted to plant the seeds of secular, nonpartisan government, but the CPA and the members of the Governing Council had foiled him. Brahimi felt used. The Americans didn't want his advice, just his imprimatur.

"We missed a great opportunity," one of Brahimi's aides told me later. "But that's the story of the Americans in Iraq: missed opportunities."

The interim government Brahimi selected would remain in power for seven months, until January 2005, when elections would be held for a national assembly. The assembly would form a new government and, more important, it would draft a permanent constitution. After voters approved the constitution in a national referendum, there would be another election, in December 2005, to select leaders of the new government outlined in the constitution.

It was a complicated three-step process, but the most important step was clearly the first. The constitution, and the government it would enshrine, would depend on the composition of the assembly elected in January. Would it be dominated by religious extremists? What role would moderates and secularists have? What about women and minorities? The answer would depend, in large part, on a law setting down rules for the election, a law that was drafted by the CPA.

The Election Law received none of the attention that the interim government did. Key decisions were hashed out by the governance team, in consultation with a group of United Nations elections experts who had come to Iraq with Brahimi. The Iraqis were kept at arm's length, partly because the CPA didn't want to complicate matters, and partly because there was no easy way to get their input. The Governing Council had dissolved itself on June 1, and Allawi's government was in the process of moving in.

The biggest impediment to holding elections was the lack of an up-to-date census—the same obstacle that had bedeviled the governance team in November 2003, when it wanted to organize an election before the handover of sovereignty. Without a census, there was no accurate way of knowing how many people lived in each province and, as a consequence, how to apportion seats in the assembly.

The United Nations team determined that there was no reasonable way to conduct a nationwide census before January 2005, the date by which the interim constitution required the first election to be held. The UN team, which put the goal of holding a perfect election over everything else, told the CPA that the only way to meet the deadline was to consider the entire country a single electoral district. All Iraqis, no matter where they lived, would get to choose from the same list of candidates. The candidates could choose to run on their own, or they could band together with other members of their party and run as a slate. The number of votes a party received would determine how many members of its slate got seats in the assembly.

It was technically sound, if convoluted, but it had major flaws. The system, which required candidates to campaign nationwide, gave large parties a clear advantage over individuals and smaller parties. It would mean that the two dominant Kurdish parties and the two largest Shiite religious parties, SCIRI and Dawa, would likely win a clear majority of seats, marginalizing moderates and secularists. Sunni representation was also a problem: If parts of the country were too dangerous to conduct balloting in, there would be no way to apportion seats for those areas; people there would wind up with nothing. The Sunnis also didn't have large parties, which put them at a further disadvantage.

The single district wasn't the only option on the table. Several CPA staffers maintained that a national database used to dole out monthly food rations could be used to provide a reasonably accurate estimate of how many people lived in each province. It was an approach that al-Sistani himself had suggested to circumvent the problem of a census.

The question of whether to hold a single-district election sparked intense debate within the Bush administration. The Pentagon, the State Department, and Vice President Cheney's office all argued against it on the grounds that it would give religious Shiite parties a head start. Bremer and the White House worried that using the ration database could draw objections from Iraqis—particularly Shiites who believed that they had been undercounted by Saddam's government—resulting in a delay. That was unacceptable to the viceroy and to the president's advisers.

"There were plenty of us who said that a single-district

election would be a disaster and that you could have a proportional-representation system with the ration [database]," a senior CPA official told me. "But Bremer and his keepers at the White House didn't care. The type of election was a secondary issue to them. What mattered more than anything else was holding it on time. It was style over substance."

On June 15, Bremer signed CPA Order 96. It stated that Iraq "will be a single electoral constituency."

THE GREEN ZONE, SCENE XI

About a month before the handover of sovereignty, Joshua Paul, a young CPA staffer, typed up a joke on his computer and sent it to a few friends in the palace. The recipients forwarded it to their friends, who did the same thing. In less than a week, almost everyone in the Green Zone had seen it.

QUESTION: *Why did the Iraqi chicken cross the road?*

CPA: *The fact that the chicken crossed the road shows that decision-making authority has switched to the chicken in advance of the scheduled June 30th transition of power. From now on, the chicken is responsible for its own decisions.*

HALLIBURTON: *We were asked to help the chicken cross the road. Given the inherent risk of road crossing and the rarity of chickens, this operation will only cost $326,004.*

SHIITE CLERIC MOQTADA AL-SADR: *The chicken was a tool of the evil Coalition and will be killed.*

U.S. ARMY MILITARY POLICE: *We were directed to prepare the chicken to cross the road. As part of these preparations, individual soldiers ran over the chicken repeatedly and then plucked the chicken. We deeply regret the occurrence of any chicken-rights violations.*

PESHMERGA: *The chicken crossed the road, and will continue to cross the road, to show its independence and to transport the weapons it needs to defend itself. However, in the future, to avoid problems, the chicken will be called a duck, and will wear a plastic bill.*

AL-JAZEERA: *The chicken was forced to cross the road multiple times at gunpoint by a large group of occupation soldiers, according to witnesses. The chicken was then fired upon intentionally, in yet another example of the abuse of innocent Iraqi chickens.*

CIA: *We cannot confirm or deny any involvement in the chicken-road-crossing incident.*

TRANSLATORS: *Chicken he cross street because bad she tangle regulation. Future chicken table against my request.*

14

Breaking the Rules

BY EARLY 2004, leaders of the CIA-led team searching for weapons of mass destruction had all but concluded that Iraq didn't possess nuclear, biological, or chemical munitions. The laboratories that Dick Cheney and others in the Bush administration claimed were production facilities for biological and chemical agents turned out to be agricultural testing stations and decrepit medical research centers.

But what Iraq did have, and there was no doubt about it, was the knowledge to manufacture anthrax, nerve gas, and, quite possibly, a crude nuclear device. Hundreds of Iraqi scientists had been involved in clandestine weapons projects during the twenty-four years Saddam was in power, and they were still around, many of them living quietly with their families in homes they had received from the government. Some of them had been captured by the CIA and the American military. Many others had been interrogated and released. Scores more had never been questioned.

Of those who were free, most were jobless. The Military Industrial Commission, which employed hundreds of weapons scientists, had been dissolved by Jerry Bremer. Others, who before the war were hired by state-run companies as a cover for their real activities, received the same monthly stipends as rank-and-file government workers, but those handouts were paltry compared with the off-the-books compensation they had gotten from Saddam's government.

With stipends or without, the scientists were an unhappy

lot. They worried that they'd never again find work, that they'd be unable to provide for their families. Some contacted the Iranian government or were approached by Iranian agents. Iran had money, and the desire to increase its stable of weapons scientists. So did other rogue nations, whose agents also began to put out feelers.

Anne Harrington, the deputy director of the State Department's Office of Proliferation Threat Reduction, first warned of the danger posed by disaffected Iraqi scientists soon after the fall of Baghdad. Harrington had worked extensively with former Soviet weapons scientists during the 1990s. She told colleagues at State that the United States needed to reach out to Iraqi scientists, offering them new jobs and additional compensation. The Americans also needed to help them regain their self-worth, she said, by paying for them to join professional associations, receive scholarly journals, and attend international conferences. But her superiors rebuffed her. "Don't even think of it," she recalled being told. "It's off the table. State doesn't have a role."

The Pentagon had claimed the job of dealing with the scientists, and it was in no mood to play nice. Defense Department officials viewed the Iraqi scientists as Saddam's accomplices. Those not in American custody were lucky to be free.

Harrington refused to give up. State had always taken the lead in implementing nonproliferation programs, and she wasn't about to cede ground to the Pentagon, especially when it wasn't willing to reach out to the Iraqis. She began to lobby the National Security Council, which agreed in late June 2003 to allow State to work with Iraqi weapons scientists. By July, a State team was ready to go, but the Pentagon refused to give the go-ahead for its departure. Defense officials kept coming up with new reasons why the State team couldn't deploy. To Harrington, it was "a masterful slow-roll strategy."

Finally, in January 2004, more than six months after Harrington's proposal, the State Department staffer in charge of the redirection program arrived in Baghdad. His name was Alex Dehgan, and he was an unlikely emissary to men who had manufactured deadly weapons for a living.

Dehgan was a mammal man. A beefy thirty-four-year-old with unruly brown hair and rumpled shirts, he had a doctorate in mammalian biology and a law degree. He had lived in Madagascar for three years studying lemurs. He was spending two years as an American Association for the Advancement of Science fellow at State, where he had assumed he would be focusing on conservation issues. Instead, he was assigned to the Bureau of Near East Affairs and was asked to work on subjects ranging from human trafficking to the financing of terrorist organizations. By the time Baghdad was liberated, Dehgan was so frustrated that he began lobbying to go to Iraq, figuring that it would at least be an adventure. One of Harrington's colleagues, also a mammalian biologist, took a shine to Dehgan, recommending that he be sent to Baghdad to open a "science center," a place where Iraqis who had worked on weapons programs could interact with one another and learn about new jobs. "It was all based on the fact that we both study animals that give milk and have a certain number of ear bones," Dehgan said.

Dehgan reminded me of Jim Otwell, the firefighter who became the interim minister of labor and social affairs. Their résumés didn't suggest them for their jobs, but they had plenty of chutzpah and, more important, they weren't political hacks. They believed in pragmatic solutions to accomplish a mission.

For Dehgan, that meant breaking the rules.

The Green Zone turned out to be the most hostile territory he trod in Baghdad. The CIA's weapons hunters and the Pentagon regarded Dehgan as an ignorant do-gooder trampling on their turf. No matter that he had a $2 million budget and a letter from Colin Powell, complete with a ribbon and a wax seal, stating that he was in charge of a United States government program to redirect Iraqi scientists; the CIA team wasn't going to help him. He had a place to stay and an office in the palace, but he was told that he wasn't part of the CPA club.

When Dehgan asked the CPA's accounting office for petty cash, he got the Baghdad equivalent of "Your credit card won't work here." The CPA was a Defense Department entity, the accountants told him. They couldn't give any money to a State guy, even though there were millions of dollars in the palace safe. It's all the same American taxpayer money, Dehgan said. Doesn't matter, they told him.

Desperate for start-up cash, Dehgan hopped a military flight to Kuwait and went to the American embassy there, where his letter from Powell was like a platinum credit card. He withdrew fifty thousand dollars in cash, put it in his backpack, and flew back to Baghdad. Every few weeks, he did another money run, until he came up with a less onerous solution: he had his funds wired from Washington to a Kuwaiti bank, which sent the money to a bank in Baghdad. It worked without a hitch, until one of the CPA's accountants got wind of it and told Dehgan that he was breaking federal law and could wind up in jail. A week later, the same accountant approached Dehgan and said that he needed to arrange to wire funds to the American embassy that would take over from the CPA in June. "Tell me how you did it," the accountant told Dehgan. "We're going to copy it."

Nothing was easy for a State guy in the Emerald City. Halliburton refused to repair his car because he wasn't running a CPA program. So, once again, he had to fly to Kuwait with his backpack. He hauled back two hundred pounds of auto parts.

Dehgan begged American security guards in the Green Zone to help him train the Iraqis he had hired to guard the science center in how to search for car bombs and pat down visitors. One American finally agreed, but on the condition that Dehgan procure a full-length mirror from outside the Green Zone so the guard could look at his Iraqi girlfriend's backside when they had sex in his trailer. Dehgan went to the market that day and had a mirror custom made.

Razor wire was as abundant in the Green Zone as coal is in Newcastle, but when Dehgan asked for a few coils of it to string around the science center, he was told he couldn't have any. Negotiations ensued. The keeper of the razor wire was willing to help Dehgan, but he wanted a set of silverware from one of Saddam's palaces. Dehgan hit the markets again, and after much searching, he found a box of official Iraqi state silver flatware.

All those obstacles were minor, however, compared with the resistance from members of the Iraq Survey Group, the CIA-led team searching for weapons. When Dehgan asked them to suggest Iraqi scientists who should be invited to participate in the center, ISG leaders refused. So Dehgan tracked down the

Iraqis himself. Before long, his list of contacts included dozens of scientists, including a senior microbiologist. When the ISG learned of Dehgan's dealings, he was summoned for a meeting. "Back off!" a senior ISG official yelled at Dehgan. "This is our turf."

A few days later, another ISG member pulled Dehgan aside. "You should be careful," he said. "This is a war zone, and anything can happen."

Dehgan started carrying a nine-millimeter handgun and an AK-47 rifle. He was the only guy in the Emerald City who feared his fellow Americans more than he did Iraqi insurgents.

Because he didn't do business the Green Zone way, Dehgan not only managed to open the science center before the handover of sovereignty, but he also created an institution that was immediately successful. The center, housed in a villa near Baghdad University, was far more lavish than anything the CPA had constructed. He purchased an enormous cherrywood conference table and leather chairs and equipped the building with sophisticated computers and high-speed Internet access. The monthly stipends he offered scientists were several times greater than their government handouts. The scientists were highly educated and successful, and they had been doted upon by Saddam. Dehgan figured they needed a little tender loving care.

He allowed the Iraqis to hold their own meetings in the center to identify ways to help the country, and eventually asked Bremer to send letters to Iraqi cabinet ministers inviting them to tap the center's talent for free. Nobody was foisted upon a ministry; it was voluntary.

"One of the biggest problems of Iraq was that we weren't listening to the Iraqis, and that our presence in the room, just like perhaps Saddam's presence in the room, was preventing people from thinking independently and taking the initiative," Dehgan said later. "The key was not for us to be more involved, but for us to be less involved."

Iraq was rife with militias. The Kurds had the *peshmerga*— "those who face death"—a seventy-thousand-strong force that protected the autonomous Kurdish provinces in the north before the war. The Supreme Council for Islamic Revolution in Iraq had the Badr Corps, which had tens of thousands of members scattered across the south. The other large Shiite party, Dawa, also had a militia. So did the rebellious young cleric Moqtada al-Sadr, whose Mahdi Army fought regular battles with U.S. forces and the Iraqi police. Ahmad Chalabi had his own militia as well, the Free Iraq Forces, which was trained and equipped in Hungary at U.S. taxpayer expense.

Bremer wanted all the militias dismantled before he left. He regarded them as a threat to the development of Iraq's police and military. If parties were allowed to retain their militias— each of the two largest Kurdish parties, for instance, had its own contingent of *peshmerga*—he feared that they could use those forces to intimidate political rivals.

Bremer turned to his director of security policy, David Gompert, the man who ran the office in which Dehgan was based. Gompert was a veteran diplomat who had worked in the National Security Council under President George H. W. Bush and then for the Rand Corporation. He and his aides drew up an ambitious transition-and-reintegration plan to break up the militias. Militia members would be offered a variety of options: they could join the army, the police, or the national guard; they could obtain job training and seek a non-security-related government job; or they could retire and receive a pension. The policy would be applied regardless of which militia a person belonged to. If a militia refused to comply, its members could be subject to prosecution.

SCIRI and the Kurds immediately objected. The Shiites insisted that the Badr Corps was necessary to protect cities in the south from Sunni insurgents. The Kurds argued that the *peshmerga* was necessary to protect the north, where the Americans had deployed only a smattering of soldiers. But Gompert was skeptical. The Badr Corps received weapons and financial support from the Iranian government, and there were reports that the militia was involved in retribution killings of Baath Party members. And if the Kurds were allowed to retain the *peshmerga,* Gompert worried that they would use the militia to evict Arabs from disputed territory in the north.

In Iraq, the ideal solution was rarely possible. But often this wasn't clear from inside the Emerald City.

The Kurds and the Shiites were not going to give up their militias until they could be sure that Iraq was peaceful and stable and their political rights were secure—goals that would take years to accomplish. SCIRI offered to make the Badr Corps a social organization with a security component charged with protecting party offices and Islamic shrines in the cities of Najaf and Karbala. The Kurds offered to put the *peshmerga* under the control of the Kurdish Regional Government instead of the two large political parties. But Bremer and Gompert wanted full demobilization.

Gompert worked up a special plan to deal with the *peshmerga*. Half would be given positions with the National Guard. The other half would be divided into three new units under the control of the Ministry of Defense: a counterterrorism force, a rapid-reaction unit, and a brigade of "mountain rangers" to patrol the hilly terrain of the north. Kurdish leaders told him they would not give up the *peshmerga*. The militiamen had fended off the Iraqi army after the 1991 Persian Gulf War, ensuring that northern Iraq was autonomous from Saddam's rule. They had fought alongside U.S. forces to liberate the northern cities of Kirkuk and Mosul. And they were the only insurance the Kurds had in Iraq's new, chaotic landscape.

But Gompert was insistent. He told the Kurds that Bremer would not compromise on militia demobilization. The Kurds invited Gompert to the north to sign his agreement, which they did after warning him that they could accept the arrangement only "in principle." As Gompert walked to his helicopter, signed agreement in hand, he asked Kurdish leader Massoud Barzani how to translate the term *mountain rangers* into the Kurdish language.

Barzani smiled and said, "We will call them *peshmerga*."

THE GREEN ZONE, SCENE XII

After Uday's menagerie was moved into Baghdad's zoo, most CPA staffers assumed that humans were the only species in the Green Zone, save for the bomb-sniffing dogs and the odd feral cat skittering among the housing trailers. The CPA's senior adviser to the Ministry of Environment pronounced the Emerald City a wasteland, devoid of wildlife.

Alex Dehgan knew better. He was a biologist who had spent three years observing animals in the wild. Every time he walked around the Green Zone, he kept his eyes peeled. He saw bats over the pool at night, barn owls in palm trees, and desert foxes in remote corners of the palace garden. "The Green Zone was filled with life," he said. "It was beautiful, and it seemed like everyone in the Green Zone was unaware of them like they were unaware of many other things."

The other humans did notice the cats—and kittens—scampering in the garden and the trailer parks. Staffers named them and played with them during breaks. They even stole cartons of milk and cheese from the dining hall for their newfound companions.

When Halliburton managers discovered the pets in their midst, they asked the marines guarding the palace to shoot the cats on sight lest they spread illnesses.

Dehgan deemed it bad science. "The danger of disease was probably infinitesimally small," he said. "This wasn't done with any thought to the psychological value that these cats provided."

When the execution orders were announced, CPA staffers saved their favorites, hiding them in trailers, in bathrooms, in the pool house. David Gompert, Bremer's security adviser, kept a cat he named Mickey in his palace office. Mickey was watched over by Gompert's security detail, but he still managed to chew through several sensitive documents.

The Halliburton cat killers finally got wise to the asylum strategy and deployed Filipino contract workers on a hunt-and-kill mission. They opened every trailer while the occupants were at work and rounded up every cat they found.

One night in June, a woman stood wailing outside her trailer. She was due to ship out in two days and had taken her cat to a veterinarian for the necessary shots for entrance to America. When she returned to her room, she found a note from the death squad informing her that her cat had been seized because it was against the rules to house animals in the trailers.

"They killed my pet," she sobbed. "I hate them."

15

Crazy, If Not Suicidal

FIRST SERGEANT JERRY SWOPE groaned as his Humvee pulled out of
the sand-swept base that had been his home for the past four
days. It was 7:30 a.m. and he was in a foul mood. Because there
were no vacant barracks, he had slept on the hood of his vehicle. His platoon had been on patrol until 2:00 a.m. in Sadr City,
a sardine-packed slum in Baghdad, for one of the American
military's regular shows of force. Desperate for every last
minute of shut-eye, Swope skipped the scrambled eggs and
bacon in the chow tent. Breakfast would have to be an MRE,
one of the army's meals-in-a-bag, eaten on the run. Beef stew,
perhaps. Or chili.

The mission that balmy Sunday morning was, quite literally,
crap. Swope's platoon would be escorting three septic tank
trucks through Sadr City as they vacuumed pools of sewage
bubbling from corroded underground pipes. The truck drivers
were hired and paid by Baghdad's city council, but if U.S. soldiers did not accompany them, they would demand bribes
from residents before turning on the suction pumps.

Watching over the trucks was unpleasant work, but it was
just the sort of thing Swope had expected to do in Iraq. He and
other soldiers from the army's First Cavalry Division had
planned to conduct "stability operations" upon their arrival in
the Iraqi capital in late March 2004. By the time they got to
Baghdad, the First Cav's commanders assumed the insurgency
would be waning and they would be working as glorified
policemen and municipal engineers, helping Iraqis to restore

basic services and build the institutions of local government. Before their deployment, officers from the division, which is based at Fort Hood, Texas, had attended seminars conducted by city planners in nearby Austin. Other soldiers had been sent to a British school where police on their way to Northern Ireland are trained to deal with low-grade civil strife.

Nowhere in Baghdad was the challenge of restoring municipal services greater than in Sadr City, a squalid warren of 2.5 million Shiites four miles east of the Green Zone. Residents of the ghetto—known as Saddam City when the dictator was in power—were regarded as a threat by Saddam's government, which was dominated by Sunnis. His regime assiduously suppressed any acts of dissension within the slum's labyrinthine alleys. In a notorious 1999 incident, his elite Republican Guard gunned down as many as a hundred people protesting the government's assassination of a prominent Shiite cleric and his two sons. Precious little had been spent on constructing schools or hospitals in the area. The three-foot-wide sewage pipes that crisscrossed the neighborhood had not been cleaned since 1998. By the time U.S. troops arrived in Iraq, the underground arteries were 60 percent blocked, creating vast swamps of excrement. Seeing the putrid pools, the commander of the First Cav battalion in Sadr City, Lieutenant Colonel Gary Volesky, made sewage cleanup a top priority. Doing so, he assumed, would help promote goodwill toward American troops.

On the morning of April 4, 2004, that goodwill mission fell to Swope and his men. At thirty-three, Swope was the oldest and most experienced soldier in the platoon. He was solid but not stocky, with close-cropped hair and a tattoo of three interlinked skulls on his right wrist. He hung out with the battalion's older noncommissioned officers and smoked Marlboro Reds. Swope had been in the army for fifteen years, serving in the 1991 Persian Gulf War, Bosnia, and Macedonia. A native of Richmond, Missouri, he referred to the septic tankers as a Southerner would, calling them "honeydew trucks."

Swope's boss was twenty-eight-year-old Lieutenant Shane Aguero, a former army brat who had enlisted after graduating from high school in 1994. A lanky father of two who wore wire-rimmed glasses, Aguero had spent eight years taking night classes at a college near Fort Hood to earn a bachelor's degree in international relations and global economics.

As the platoon drove through Sadr City, from one pond of sludge to another, everything appeared normal to Swope and Aguero. There were plenty of scowls and stares, and children even heaved rocks at Swope's Humvee, the last in the column. But he didn't pay much attention to the stones dinging off the armor plating. Back at Fort Hood, at a predeployment briefing on dangers in Baghdad, the soldiers had been shown a map of the city with red splotches denoting recent attacks. There were fewer in Sadr City than almost anywhere else. The improvised explosive devices—what everyone else referred to as roadside bombs—that bedeviled American soldiers in other parts of Baghdad almost never turned up in Sadr City. The only attack there of significance that Swope could remember was on October 9, when a patrol was ambushed and two soldiers were killed. All in all, he calculated, Sadr City was a pretty good place to be a soldier—if you could stand the stench.

The safety of Sadr City made sense to Swope. The Shiites were the people the Americans had come to liberate. Unlike the Sunnis, who had been privileged under Saddam, the downtrodden Shiites were thankful to be free of the dictator. The challenge wasn't going to be winning them over, he thought, it was going to be rebuilding a place that was more disgusting and dysfunctional than anything he'd ever seen.

After dumping the contents of the tankers into a canal on the edge of Sadr City at around 4:30 in the afternoon, the three Iraqi drivers refused to continue working. Through an interpreter, they told Aguero and Swope that residents had warned them earlier in the day against returning with the soldiers. "We'll be killed if we go back," one of the drivers said. Then they drove off.

When Aguero radioed the tactical operations center at the base with news of the defecting drivers, he received new orders. On your way back to the base, drive down Route Delta—the neighborhood's main drag—to see if anything is going on there, one of Volesky's deputies told Aguero. That seemed pretty easy, Aguero thought. They'd be home in less than half an hour.

The platoon—eighteen soldiers and one interpreter—was traveling in a convoy of four Humvees. Aguero was in the lead vehicle because he knew his way around. Unlike the rest of the soldiers, who had arrived in Baghdad only four days earlier, he had been in Sadr City for a month to help the First Cav prepare to assume responsibility for the capital from the army's First Armored Division. Aguero's Humvee and Swope's in the rear had factory-built armoring. The windows were bulletproof, and the sides were made of thick reinforced steel. Atop both those Humvees was a fifty-caliber machine gun that could spit cigar-size bullets powerful enough to disable oncoming vehicles and punch through concrete walls. The two Humvees in the middle had only what soldiers called add-on armor. They were standard models with metal plates welded to the side and 7.62-millimeter machine guns mounted on the roof. They were better protected than regular, soft-skinned Humvees, but their roofs, windshields, and engines had no extra fortification.

The platoon had been driving for only a few minutes when they saw two men with AK-47 assault rifles in the street. Aguero ordered the platoon to stop. The men were in clear defiance of orders issued by the U.S. occupation authority restricting the possession of such weapons to private property. The men insisted to the soldiers that they were guards at a nearby mosque. Aguero wanted to seize the guns, but he didn't want to provoke a confrontation with religious leaders. Eventually, they settled on a compromise: an Iraqi police colonel would take custody of the weapons. An hour after the platoon stopped, the colonel arrived, several black-turbaned clerics emerged, and the weapons were surrendered. As the soldiers remounted the Humvees and drove off, Swope thought, *Two more guns off the street. We're making this place safer.*

The most important building along Route Delta was the local office of Moqtada al-Sadr. In the hierarchical Shiite establishment, al-Sadr was just a portly, low-ranking cleric with angry eyes, rotting teeth, an unkempt beard, and a ten-gallon black turban. But his father, Mohammed Sadiq al-Sadr, was a revered ayatollah who had built up a mass following through control of clerical schools, a network of social services, and a metaphorical message of resistance to Saddam's rule. The senior al-Sadr's assassination in 1999 had unleashed bloody unrest in the slum that would later take his name. In the tumult that followed Saddam's fall, Moqtada emerged on the strength of his father's legacy, commanding the loyalty of rebellious, largely young clerics who bridled at the reticence and conservatism of the mainstream clergy. He was blunt in his criticism of the United States, blaming it for failing to support a Shiite uprising after the 1991 Persian Gulf War and for allowing the looting and lawlessness that erupted after Saddam was toppled. He denounced the American occupation and demanded the withdrawal of U.S. forces, which won him legions of followers, most of them young, unemployed men who had believed that the American invasion would bring them prosperity and political power.

Despite Moqtada's fiery rhetoric, what he really wanted was a seat on the Governing Council. He figured there was no better way to get one than to demonstrate his street credibility to Jerry Bremer by drawing thousands to his Friday sermons. But CPA staffers rarely traveled into Sadr City and didn't know how popular al-Sadr had become. And SCIRI and Dawa, the two largest Shiite parties, didn't want a rival on the council. In August 2003, a month after the Governing Council was established, al-Sadr formed a militia called the Mahdi Army to protect himself and to give him leverage with other Shiite leaders. Six months later, as the First Cav arrived in Baghdad, the militia had an estimated ten thousand fighters across the country.

Members of the Mahdi Army harassed local government officials in Sadr City and in towns across southern Iraq, but other than in a few isolated incidents, the militia hadn't targeted American forces. Within the Republican Palace, however, al-Sadr's army was regarded as a gathering threat to the establishment of democracy that, if left unchecked, could be used to intimidate voters and government workers. By late 2003, members of the CPA's governance team began lobbying Bremer to arrest al-Sadr and dismantle his militia. But when Bremer raised the issue with American military commanders, and even with Rumsfeld, they punted. Al-Sadr isn't shooting at our soldiers, they said, so why should we pick a fight? We've got enough trouble with the radical Sunnis. No need to provoke the radical Shiites.

Bremer backed down. But by late March 2004, al-Sadr's militia once again commanded his attention. The interim constitution was done, and sovereignty would be handed over in three months. He felt there wasn't much time left. If democracy was going to flourish in Iraq, the militias had to go. David Gompert was working up a plan to deal with the *peshmerga* and SCIRI's Badr Corps, but Moqtada al-Sadr was unwilling to demobilize the Mahdi Army. To Bremer and others in the CPA, the time had come for a confrontation.

Exactly a week before Aguero and Swope's septic truck mission, Bremer ordered al-Sadr's newspaper shut down. For weeks, *al-Hawza* had been printing inaccurate and inflammatory articles about the American military and the CPA. The clincher for Bremer was a story in February headlined "Bremer Follows in the Footsteps of Saddam," which accused him of deliberately starving the Iraqi people. On March 28, American troops ushered *al-Hawza*'s staff into the street and snapped a padlock on the office gate.

Bremer had expected that shuttering the paper would pressure not just al-Sadr but also General John Abizaid, the overall American commander in the Middle East, and Lieutenant General Sanchez, the top commander in Iraq. Bremer and his staff assumed that al-Sadr would lash back through protests and small-scale attacks, instigating a manageable fight that would compel Abizaid and Sanchez to put the cleric out of business.

But al-Sadr's response was fiercer than Bremer and his staff had expected. Within hours, the cleric's deputies had ordered a full mobilization. Protesters flooded the traffic circle in front of the newspaper's offices for a noisy rally. They came back the next day. On the third day, hundreds of al-Sadr supporters marched in a tight military formation to the Assassin's Gate. "We are followers of al-Sadr!" they shouted. "All the people know us. We will not be humiliated!" Many of the young men were dressed entirely in black, save for green sashes on their brows. Marshals rushed between the units shouting warnings to keep the ranks sharp. Clerics in white turbans swept down the fringes with a proprietary air. "Just say the word, Moqtada," they screamed, "and we'll resume the 1920 revolution!" Later, the chants became more ominous. "Today is peaceful," they warned. "Tomorrow will be military."

.   .   .

While the protests brought other parts of Baghdad to a stand-still, life in Sadr City appeared to be no different. But on April 4, as the platoon swung a left on Route Delta to drive past al-Sadr's office, the normally bustling road had only a trickle of traffic. The sidewalks were empty.

Unbeknownst to Swope and Aguero, American Special Operations forces had arrested al-Sadr's top deputy the night before. At 4:30 p.m., al-Sadr issued an order to his followers from his headquarters in the town of Kufa, about one hundred miles south of the capital. "Terrorize your enemy," the order read. "God will reward you well for what pleases him. It is not possible to remain silent in front of their violations."

When the platoon neared the Sadr Bureau, a one-story con-crete-and-brick former Baath Party building, Aguero saw more than a hundred young men milling about in front. As soon as they noticed the Humvees, all but about fifteen of them scat-tered. Some jumped into minivans and sped off. Those who remained were gesticulating in the street. Aguero told Special-ist James Fisk, sitting behind him, to make a note of the scene. Fisk opened his standard-issue lime green notebook and began by jotting down the time: *17:36*.

When Swope's Humvee was about two hundred yards beyond the Sadr Bureau, the soldiers inside heard a loud pop-ping sound.

"What the fuck was that?" Specialist Josh Rogers yelled.

"Was that gunfire?" Sergeant Eric Bourquin asked.

"Stop the vehicle!" Swope shouted.

The shooting had come from the driver's side, so the sol-diers jumped out and took up positions on the other side of the Humvee, training their M16A2 rifles at nearby rooftops. Sergeant Shane Coleman, his eyes covered with yellow gog-gles, was in the Humvee's turret, manning the fifty-caliber gun. He couldn't see exactly where the shooting was coming from, but he felt certain it was from a few adjoining buildings to the north. He pointed the barrel of his gun in that direction and squeezed the dual triggers, unleashing a powerful fusillade, which was followed by a deafening echo. The others joined in with their M16s. But as soon as they got off a few rounds, another group of gunmen opened up on the Humvee from the other side of the road.

"Get in the vehicle!" Swope screamed to his men. "Let's get the hell out of here!"

As soon as Bourquin closed his door, a rocket-propelled grenade smacked against it. Normally that would have been enough to kill him and perhaps a few others in the Humvee, but the RPG lacked an armor-piercing tip. It exploded harmlessly against the steel-reinforced exterior. Bourquin wasn't sure what was going on. *Oh, shit,* he thought. *I'm gonna die.*

As Swope's Humvee accelerated and closed in on the three other vehicles ahead of him, he figured they were out of danger. But Route Delta, which had been unobstructed a few hours earlier, now was strewn with tin cans, iron bars, and large rocks. Farther down, refrigerators, car axles, wooden cabinets, and entire sidewalk kiosks had been dragged into the road. Tires and piles of trash had been set alight, cutting down visibility to a few hundred feet.

When they reached the debris, the shooting resumed. But instead of a few snipers, bullets and RPGs were raining down from almost every building along the road. To Swope, it felt as if the whole slum were firing at them. Although they were at opposite ends of the column, he and Aguero came to the same conclusion: There was no way to take these guys on. The platoon had to run the *Mad Max* gauntlet and get out of there.

For almost everyone in the platoon, it was their first time in combat. And it felt, at moments, like a video game. Most of the RPGs missed the vehicles, landing with loud but harmless explosions on the road. The bullets hitting the Humvees clanged against the armor like stones. *Yee-haw,* thought Fisk, who was sitting behind Aguero. *We're finally getting to do what we're paid for.*

His thrill ended a few seconds later. As soon as his lead vehicle crossed the next intersection, Sergeant Yihjyh Chen, the fifty-caliber roof gunner, collapsed in his turret. A bullet had entered his chest from the side, just above the top of his flak vest. Chen, a thirty-one-year-old from the Pacific island of Saipan, lost consciousness almost immediately and began bleeding from his mouth. Fisk tried to see where Chen was hit, but he couldn't find a wound. He tried to check Chen's pulse and felt nothing. Fisk pushed Chen's body onto the lap of the other passenger in the back of the Humvee—an Iraqi interpreter named Salam who had first-aid training—before climbing into the turret to take over the fifty-cal.

"Why the fuck are we still on the road?" Specialist Jonathan Riddell, the driver, shouted to no one in particular as he tried to swerve around the obstacles. "We need to get out of here."

Aguero screamed into the radio. "We have contact! We have contact!"

Because both of the Humvee's rearview mirrors had been shot off, Riddell and Aguero couldn't tell how far behind the other three vehicles were. They tried asking Fisk, but he couldn't hear them over the thunderclaps of the fifty-caliber. Aguero told Riddell to stop. Then they opened their doors for a quick glance. As bullets hit the inside panel of Aguero's door, sending chunks of black foam flying into the air, he looked back and didn't see a single Humvee.

"You gotta turn around," he told Riddell.

Riddell looked at him incredulously. *You want me to go back? That's crazy.* But it was an order. He pulled a wide left turn and began driving down the sidewalk, knocking over wooden stalls used to sell vegetables. After a block, Riddell ran into a clump of razor wire. Unwilling to wait for him to extricate the vehicle, Aguero jumped out and ran to the other three Humvees.

"Let's go," Aguero screamed at Staff Sergeant Trevor Davis, the driver of the second Humvee.

"My Humvee won't move." Davis gunned the engine for emphasis, and a large cloud of dark smoke wafted from under the hood. The vehicle behind Davis had the same problem. Humvees two and three had been shot too many times and had driven over too much debris.

Sitting in Humvee three, Sergeant Justin Bellamy, a twenty-two-year-old from Warsaw, Indiana, prepared for the worst. *This is it,* he thought. *We're gonna die.*

Aguero contemplated packing all nineteen men into the two working Humvees, but there was no way everyone would fit. It would be suicidal, he concluded, to drive down the road with people on the hood and roof. They had to get off the street and take cover somewhere. Swope got on the radio to request guidance from the tactical operations center. Could he ditch the two broken vehicles? Affirmative.

As bullets continued to fly, Aguero told half the platoon to strip off the radios and weapons systems from the two disabled Humvees. The rest of the soldiers and the other two vehicles sped down the nearest alley. About a hundred yards in, they spotted a three-story building poking up from a landscape of two-story ones. *Tactical advantage,* Aguero concluded. He ordered the soldiers to charge inside. Staff Sergeant Darcy Robinson blew open the door with a shotgun and a half dozen men followed him in. They rounded up the occupants and shoved them in one room. Another room turned into a casualty collection point. Chen's lifeless body was dragged in there along with Staff Sergeant Stanley Haubert, who had been hit with shrapnel and was bleeding from his mouth. The machine guns stripped from the disabled Humvees were hauled up to the roof, where half the platoon had set up a defensive position. The others stayed in the alley, where the two working Humvees shielded them as they guarded against a ground assault.

Before long, the attackers converged on both ends of the alley, firing their AK-47s wildly and launching RPGs at the Humvees. The soldiers opened up with their machine guns, mowing down dozens of attackers. *That was a retarded move on their part,* Swope thought. Another wave of gunmen tried to approach from the roofs of neighboring buildings. The machine guns did the trick again.

As the standoff dragged on, the attackers began varying their tactics. Young children were sent into the alley to act as spotters for snipers. Hand grenades were heaved from parallel streets. One bounced off Aguero's Kevlar helmet and hit a wall, sending shrapnel slicing into one side of his body, from his ear to his foot. He limped off to the casualty room.

Through it all, Swope remained in his Humvee, manning the radio, which wasn't portable. When they had left the base that morning, nobody thought they would need one.

Back at the base, Lieutenant Colonel Volesky formally

assumed command of the Sadr City area from the First Armored Division at 6:00 p.m. He had planned to hold a ceremony to unfurl his battalion's flag. By 6:15, as Swope and Aguero were running for cover into the alley, Volesky put the proceedings on hold and scrambled reinforcements. Within twenty minutes, two QRFs—quick-reaction forces—of ten armored Bradley Fighting Vehicles apiece, one of which included Volesky, rumbled out of Forward Operating Base Eagle toward Route Delta.

With the rescue squad on the way, Swope had to explain where the platoon was. But he couldn't pinpoint the alley on a map with any certainty. On the roof, Sergeants Robinson and Bourquin fired off smoke grenades to draw the attention of two OH-58 Kiowa Warrior observation helicopters overhead, but the smoke from the burning tires obscured the signal.

The two QRFs ran into trouble minutes after leaving the base. One of the units was besieged by hundreds of attackers along Route Silver, a street perpendicular to Delta. Four soldiers from that QRF were killed in the fighting and more than a dozen were injured, forcing the unit to turn back. The other QRF, the one with Volesky, also ran into an ambush as it attempted to approach Route Delta, which led them to double back and approach from another route. But once they finally made it onto Delta, where attackers had lined the road for two miles, they had no idea where to find the platoon.

From his Humvee, Swope saw the Bradleys rumble past on Delta. And then he saw them head back in the other direction. He tried to radio them, but the channel was jammed with calls for help from the other QRF. *Hey, we're here,* he wanted to shout toward the road. But they wouldn't have been able to hear him.

Watching the Bradleys drive away, Fisk said wryly, "The guys back at the FOB"—the forward operating base—"would have kicked ass to be here." At Fort Hood, the soldiers had wondered if they would be eligible for the army's combat infantryman badge. Earning one required participating in some bang-bang. After repelling the first wave of attackers, Riddell turned to his platoon mates and announced, "I think we got it."

With the two QRFs unable to rescue the platoon, the army's

heaviest armor was summoned: seven M1A2 Abrams battle tanks from the First Armored's Crusader Company. The sixty-eight-ton tanks, powered by a jet engine and equipped with a 120-millimeter main gun, were impervious to small-arms fire and even RPGs. But they still needed to know where the platoon was.

On the roof, Robinson and Bourquin were getting desperate. It was 9:00 p.m. and dark. They had been under siege for almost three hours. They were out of smoke grenades, and ammunition was running low. The bright orange reflective panel they had placed on the roof was useless now that the sun was down. They had tried lighting some discarded shoes they had found, but the flame wasn't bright enough. Finally, Robinson walked up to Bourquin and ripped off the sleeves of his buddy's desert camouflage uniform. He told Bourquin to do the same to him. Then they torched the fabric. The Kiowas spotted them.

But there still was the problem of getting the information to the tanks. In the alley, Swope saw the first tank roll by. Then the second. *Oh shit,* he thought. *They're going to miss us.* And the third. The fourth. *We're toast.* The fifth. The sixth. *We're here for the night.*

The seventh tank got word from the choppers to stop at the entrance to the alley. The tank crew summoned others in the column. They loaded up everyone from the platoon and brought them back to the base.

Late that night, Volesky tallied up his losses. Eight soldiers were dead, including Casey Sheehan, whose mother, Cindy, would later become a prominent antiwar activist. At least fifty were wounded. He estimated that more than four thousand Iraqi militiamen had been involved in the uprising.

As he sat in the operations center, dipping snuff and spitting into a Styrofoam cup, he wondered what had gone wrong. He was certain that the attackers belonged to al-Sadr's Mahdi Army. But they were far stronger and better armed than his intelligence reports had indicated. *Why,* he asked himself, *was there not better information about these guys? We went into this without a plan,* he concluded, *and now we've got a big problem.*

Over the next few days, the scope of the crisis became even more alarming to the generals commanding military operations in Iraq. Not only had al-Sadr's militiamen seized every police station and government building in Sadr City, they had also unleashed a fierce rebellion across Shiite-dominated central and southern Iraq. The entire cities of Najaf, Kufa, Kut, and Karbala were in their hands. Within hours, the Mahdi Army overran elements of a Polish-led multinational military unit entrusted by the Pentagon to control that region. Black-clad militiamen swaggered in front of a gold-domed Shiite shrine. They set up checkpoints and roadblocks and proclaimed that they were the new sheriffs in town.

The American military had stumbled into the sort of perilous urban combat that top commanders had tried so diligently to avoid since the start of the war. At the same time, the commanders found themselves in the middle of a two-front conflict: the bloody Sunni insurgency to the north and west of the capital, which American troops had tried for months to quell but could not, was compounded by a Shiite revolt to the south and east. Baghdad was more thoroughly cut off than it was during the American invasion a year earlier. Every major road out of the capital was shaded red—meaning it was a no-go route—on the military's daily threat report.

The Mahdi Army didn't limit its attack to American forces. They also set upon Iraqi police stations in Sadr City. When the militiamen converged on the Rafidain police station, officers inside the blue-walled building sprang into action. They grabbed their possessions and ran home.

"To shoot those people would have been wrong," Sergeant Falah Hassan, a lanky veteran whose uniform consisted of rolled-up jeans and a rumpled blue shirt, told me later. "If a man comes with principles and I believe in those principles, I will not shoot him."

The collapse of police and civil-defense units across Iraq in the face of al-Sadr's uprising stunned CPA officials. A few days later, the CPA was surprised again when a battalion of Iraq's new army mutinied rather than obey orders to help the marines fight insurgents in the streets of Fallujah. Both events revealed fundamental problems with the CPA's strategy to build up the Iraqi police force and to create a new army after

Bremer's fateful order to disband the old one. The decision to hire back as many former policemen as possible, even without training, had been meant to reassure Iraqis by putting more officers on the street. But it also put thousands of ill-prepared men, some with ties to the insurgency, into uniform—a problem that the CPA long feared but did not fully grasp until the Mahdi Army rebellion. Of the nearly ninety thousand police on duty at the time of the rebellion, more than sixty-five thousand had not received any training.

Another major mistake, Iraqi and American officials said, was the failure to provide enough equipment to the police and the Civil Defense Corps, a forty-thousand-member paramilitary force. At the Rafidain station, only half of the 140 officers had handguns. There were just ten AK-47 assault rifles in the armory, three pickup trucks in the parking lot, and two radios in the control room. No one had body armor, save for a few guards at the front door who wore American military vests.

In the case of the Iraqi army, the problem wasn't equipment or training but esprit de corps. Bremer and his first security adviser, Walt Slocombe, had outsourced the training of new soldiers to a contractor. Upon graduation from the contractor-run boot camp, the new soldiers were assigned to U.S. Army units, headed by American officers they had never met. When those officers asked the Iraqis to fight, there was no rapport, no bond of trust forged through training, no reason why the Iraqis should put their lives on the line for a foreign army. In other nations, American Special Forces soldiers trained units and then deployed with them, a system that always seemed to work. But in Iraq, there weren't enough American soldiers to do that.

"The Americans misunderstood us," said Major Raed Kadhim, the senior officer at the Rafidain station. "We will fight for Iraq. We will not fight for them."

Bremer's move to close the newspaper was a profound miscalculation. When he ordered the shutdown of *al-Hawza*, there was no comprehensive backup strategy for military action in case al-Sadr and his militia chose to fight back. There was no advance warning provided to soldiers in al-Sadr strongholds such as Sadr City. There was no coordination with senior army commanders. Attempts by the U.S. military to regain control of areas seized by the Mahdi Army resulted in two months of ferocious ground combat that was more intense than anything American troops had encountered during the year-old occupation or even the initial invasion of Iraq.

Bremer chose to pursue al-Sadr at the same time tensions were boiling over in Fallujah, a Sunni-dominated city west of Baghdad. Two days before the newspaper closure, American marines killed fifteen Iraqis during a raid. Later that week, on March 31, four American security contractors were murdered by a mob. The contractors' mutilated bodies were hung from a bridge over the Euphrates River.

Bremer vowed that the deaths of the contractors would "not go unpunished." But there was little agreement among the Americans on the response. The marines wanted to wait until they could identify the culprits and then mount operations to apprehend them. "We felt . . . that we ought to probably let the situation settle before we appeared to be attacking out of revenge," Lieutenant General James Conway, the top marine commander in Iraq, told me later. At the time, he said as much to his boss, Lieutenant General Sanchez, who passed it up the chain of command to General Richard Myers, the chairman of the Joint Chiefs of Staff. Myers conveyed Conway's position to Donald Rumsfeld.

But back in Washington, the desire for revenge was overwhelming. On April 1, the day after the attack, Rumsfeld and General Abizaid went to the White House to plot a response with President Bush and his national security team. Rumsfeld didn't share Conway's position with the president. Instead, the defense secretary presented a plan to mount "a specific and overwhelming attack" to seize Fallujah. Bush approved it on the spot.

Sanchez would later tell Conway and his aides that "the president knows this is going to be bloody. He accepts that." But at the April 1 meeting, according to a White House official involved in the discussions, Rumsfeld said that an attack on Fallujah "was something they could do with a relatively low risk of civilian casualties."

On April 4, the same day Swope's platoon was attacked in Sadr City, two thousand marines converged on Fallujah. The following day, they began attacking—and encountered stiff resistance. Insurgents hiding in homes and mosques unleashed gunfire and rocket-propelled grenades. Five marines died that first day, as did an untold number of insurgents and civilians. The next day, the insurgents employed an anti-aircraft gun to fire on American helicopters. The Americans responded with an escalating barrage of bombs, mortars, and gunfire, killing more insurgents and civilians. It was never clear how many civilians died, but it didn't really matter. Al-Jazeera and other Arab television stations broadcast breathless reports of large-scale civilian deaths in the city.

Rumsfeld and other proponents of a massive attack had believed that the threat of force would lead residents of Fallujah to hand over the contractors' killers. If not, they believed the insurgents could be targeted with "smart bombs" and other munitions in surgical operations. But instead of giving up the insurgents, many residents rallied around them. And it wasn't just in Fallujah. People in other cities, including Shiites who used to regard Fallujah's residents as the hillbillies of Iraq, rushed to donate blood and money. And Sunnis in Fallujah and other Sunni-dominated cities in central Iraq, who had deemed al-Sadr a troublemaker, began to laud him as a hero. Each side was drawing strength from the other.

The Emerald City went into lockdown. Force Protection forbade CPA staffers to travel outside the Green Zone, no matter how important the business. Contractors stopped going to construction projects. Reconstruction work ground to a halt.

CPA staffers moped around the palace. With only three months before the handover of sovereignty, there was no time to spare. They huddled in the dining hall and in the bars. The news from both fronts of the new war was grim. They wondered if they'd ever be able to leave the bubble.

Some of them began to question the management of Iraq outside the walls of the Green Zone. Taking on al-Sadr at the same time the marines were attacking Fallujah seemed ill-conceived. "Did we have to go after him right now?" one senior CPA official told me at the time. "It should have been delayed.

Dealing with both these problems at one time is crazy, if not suicidal."

As news reports focused on the mounting civilian casualties in Fallujah, Bremer and Bush ran into a new front of opposition. British prime minister Tony Blair telephoned President Bush on April 7 to object to the marine offensive. Three influential Sunni members of the Governing Council warned Bremer that they would resign if the military operations did not cease. Lakhdar Brahimi, who was in Baghdad to begin selecting members of the interim Iraqi government, also threatened to quit. At a news conference, Brahimi, a Sunni, lashed out at the way the Americans were dealing with Fallujah, calling it "collective punishment."

Faced with the prospect of the CPA's political transition plan imploding yet again, Bremer urged the White House to consider a cease-fire to allow Sunni politicians to negotiate a peace deal with city leaders. Bob Blackwill, who was back in Washington, also lobbied for a cease-fire. He didn't want Brahimi to quit.

On April 8, the marines were ordered to cease offensive operations by noon the following day. Lieutenant General Conway and his aides seethed. Although they didn't support the all-out offensive attack by Bush, they wanted to finish the mission they had started. Marine units were already near the city center. Conway's deputy, Major General James Mattis, estimated that the marines would have taken Fallujah with two more days of fighting. "When you order elements of a marine division to attack a city, you really need to understand what the consequences of that are going to be and not perhaps vacillate in the middle of something like that," Conway told me later. "Once you commit, you've got to stay committed."

The CPA, the marines, and members of the Governing Council all attempted to strike an agreement with city leaders to hand over the contractors' killers. After two weeks of fruitless talks, Conway turned to former members of Saddam's army. Working with the CIA, Conway met with the head of Iraq's intelligence service, Mohammed Abdullah Shahwani, who introduced the marine commander to a handful of former Iraqi army generals. The generals offered to set up a force of more than a thousand former soldiers from Fallujah who would control the city and combat the insurgents, if the marines pledged to withdraw from the city. Conway agreed.

The Iraqi force, called the Fallujah Brigade, would turn out to be a disaster. Instead of wearing the desert camouflage uniforms the marines had provided, members dressed in their old Iraqi army fatigues. Instead of confronting insurgents, the former soldiers merely manned traffic checkpoints on roads leading into the city. After a few weeks, even that ended. Eventually, the eight hundred AK-47 assault rifles, twenty-seven pickup trucks, and fifty radios the marines had given the brigade wound up in the hands of insurgents.

Although the anger spawned by the marine offensive subsided in other parts of Iraq, insurgents from Fallujah metastasized to Samarra, Ramadi, Bayji, and other Sunni-majority cities, where they enlisted legions of impressionable young men. All of a sudden, it wasn't just Fallujah that was off limits to Americans, but most of the Sunni-dominated center of Iraq. Reconstruction projects and programs to promote democracy in those places were put on hold, and eventually canceled altogether.

After a while, CPA staffers and American contractors were again allowed to leave the Green Zone for day trips, but they couldn't travel outside Baghdad, except in military helicopters. The constraints on travel, and the daily compilation of insurgent attacks, which had ballooned from about a dozen to more than seventy-five, prompted another round of soul-searching in the dining hall and the bars. The CPA had been focused on minutiae: How many foreign banks should be licensed? What needed to be in the new copyright law? Should there be traffic courts?

"We were so busy trying to build a Jeffersonian democracy and a capitalist economy that we neglected the big picture," one of Bremer's aides ruefully told me in late May. "We squandered an enormous opportunity, and we didn't realize it until everything blew up in our faces."

THE GREEN ZONE, SCENE XIII

A few weeks before the handover of sovereignty, CPA staffers gathered by the palace pool for a farewell barbecue. Everyone was there, except the Iraqis working in the palace. Nobody had told them to stay away. They just did.

Halliburton brought out hot dogs, burgers, grilled chicken, and corn on the cob, served by the crisply uniformed Indians and Pakistanis who worked in the dining hall. Blackwater, the private security firm that had the lucrative contract to guard the viceroy, provided the booze.

For the occasion, military officers waived General Order 1, which prohibited soldiers from consuming alcohol. Nineteen-year-old privates got hammered and dove into the pool.

It felt like a college graduation party. It was a last chance to say goodbye, to exchange e-mail addresses, to take a group photo. Some looked back on their time in Baghdad with regret. Others laughed and slapped one another on the back. They had done a great job. They were heroes.

They all talked about their summer, about vacations and family reunions. Some were returning to their old jobs. Others would work for the Bush-Cheney reelection campaign.

After an hour or so, a CPA press officer noticed two journalists in the crowd. She pulled them aside. "Who invited you here?" she barked. "What are you doing here? No press is allowed here."

The journalists said they had been invited by a CPA staffer. The press officer told the journalists to stay put while she consulted with a superior. She returned a few minutes later with a handheld video camera. Kicking them out might cause a scene and would inevitably result in a story. The journalists could stay, but they would have to promise on tape that they wouldn't write about what they saw.

"We never came to a CPA barbecue," one of them said on camera. "These people behind us aren't CPA people drinking beer. We were never here."

"We will not report the fact that everyone here is celebrating the end of the CPA," the other said.

A short while later, Bremer and Lieutenant General Sanchez joined the party. Everyone wanted a picture with the two men. Some even asked for an autograph.

There were plans for a few skits and musical performances. One guitar-playing staffer had even worked up a parody about Bremer to the tune of "The Man Who Never Returned." But senior CPA officials, fearing satire, canceled the show.

As the crowd peaked, Bremer walked onto a small stage. The world would look back on the CPA, he said, and "recognize what we've done."

"We've made Iraq a better place," he said. Everyone applauded. He shed a tear.

The British ambassador read a congratulatory letter from Tony Blair. Then a brief recorded message from President Bush was projected onto a large screen. He, too, heaped hosannas on the CPA.

"Thank you and God bless you," he said. "And enjoy your barbecue!"

16

A Lot Left to Be Done

JOHN AGRESTO HAD BEEN IN BAGHDAD for two weeks, and his ivory-tower plans to overhaul Iraq's university system, crafted back home in New Mexico, had met reality. Promoting academic freedom and opening liberal-arts colleges would remain pipe dreams until he addressed the devastation wrought by postwar looting. His big ideas would have to wait. He needed desks, chairs, books, and blackboards.

Agresto, the CPA's senior adviser for higher education, didn't have a budget. In September 2003, before the Supplemental, America's paltry reconstruction funds were controlled by the U.S. Agency for International Development. So he walked across the palace to the USAID office to ask for help. He'd heard that they had $25 million set aside for Iraqi universities.

A USAID program officer told Agresto that the money was already earmarked for grants to American universities that wanted to establish partnerships with Iraqi institutions. Agresto was dumbstruck. *American universities?* What about rehabilitating looted buildings? Restocking libraries? Reequipping science laboratories? Perhaps the American universities will help with that, the program officer said. It's up to each school to decide how it wants to use the money.

Well, Agresto replied, can I at least see the proposals from the American universities? Sorry, the program officer said. I'm not authorized to show them to you.

When Agresto threatened to file a Freedom of Information Act request with USAID, bureaucrats in Washington relented. He read the documents in near disbelief.

The University of Hawaii's College of Tropical Agriculture had been selected to partner with the University of Mosul's College of Agriculture to provide advice on "academic programs and extension training." Not only was Mosul's near-alpine climate far from tropical, but the college had been burned to the ground by looters. What it needed was a new building.

A consortium led by the University of Oklahoma was tapped to work on "leadership strengthening" with five Iraqi schools, including the University of Anbar, based in Ramadi. Anbar province was the most dangerous area in all of Iraq, a no-go zone for Americans. How, Agresto wondered, would a bunch of Oklahomans ever meet up with their counterparts in Anbar? A team from the State University of New York at Stony Brook won a $4 million grant to "modernize curricula in archaeology" at four of Iraq's largest universities—schools where students were sitting on the floor because they lacked desks and chairs.

"It was like going into a war zone and saying, Oh, let's cure halitosis," Agresto said.

With no money from USAID, Agresto set his sights on the Supplemental. He heard that Bremer was going to ask the White House for $20 billion. Such a large request, he figured, had to have a budget line for Iraq's universities. He assembled what he deemed to be an exceedingly modest proposal, asking for only $37 million to reconstruct the universities.

Bremer's office rejected it without explanation.

Agresto, a stalwart Republican, eventually got a little help from Representative Nita Lowey, a Democrat from New York. During negotiations over the Supplemental in Congress, she insisted that $90 million be devoted to education. Of that, $8 million would go to universities.

It wasn't much, but it was better than nothing. Then Agresto discovered that USAID was claiming that it held the purse strings. He went ballistic and sent a letter to Bremer saying he'd rather not have the money than have it go to USAID. Bremer's secretary called Agresto and told him to rewrite his letter; it was too inflammatory.

A few days later, he confronted a USAID official by the pool. "You folks go on all the time about how we work together. We never work together," he growled. "You never listen to me. You know I put in for this money. You know I put in for thirty-some-odd million dollars, and all I'm getting is eight, and now you want to take my eight away. I'm not gonna let you take my eight away."

USAID relented, but Agresto still had to work with a new bunch of Pentagon bureaucrats whose job was to disburse the billions of Supplemental dollars. He was told that he'd have to deduct $500,000 for administrative fees. He reluctantly agreed and told the bureaucrats what he wanted to do with the remaining $7.5 million: buy basic science lab equipment for every Iraqi university. The bureaucrats told him it would take a while. They needed to write up a request for proposals, solicit bids, select a winner, and then manage procurement and distribution. By the time Agresto left Iraq in June 2004, just before the handover of sovereignty, no lab equipment had yet arrived.

None of the $400 million in international pledges, made months earlier at a donors' conference in Madrid, had come through either. He also couldn't get a cent from the CPA to support the "College of Humanity" at the University of Dohuk—the project that had made Agresto want to stay in Iraq for "the duration." Agresto had asked the palace bean counters for just $3 million to build the college.

With only pocket change for reconstruction, he turned back to the item atop his original to-do list: promoting academic freedom. It didn't cost a thing.

With the help of CPA lawyers, he assembled an eight-point bill of rights that called for universities to be "independent in the managing of their academic affairs" and guaranteed the "freedom of thought, belief, and clothing." It prohibited weapons on campus and the coercion of others "to join a religion, sect, race, or political ideology." It was a direct challenge to Shiite student activists who had been threatening secular-minded professors and hectoring female students to cover their hair. The university presidents unanimously adopted the bill of rights in March and had it printed up as a large poster to hang on the walls of every campus.

Agresto regarded the document as one of his most significant achievements, although it didn't really change anything other than the dynamics of the minister's meetings with the university presidents. Like the traffic code and all of the other CPA edicts, it sounded good on paper but there were no resources to implement it. The colleges couldn't afford to hire guards to confront the Shiite activists, who continued to swagger around the campuses, forcing women to wear head scarves and demanding holidays for religious festivals. When I asked Taki Moussawi, the president of Mustansiriya University, why he didn't enforce the bill of rights, he pointed to the hallway walls, which were plastered with photographs of Shiite ayatollahs. "The bill of rights is a good thing and I agree with it, but I cannot use it," he said. "It would be very dangerous to confront the students."

Two days after the November 15 Agreement, the CPA's Governance Office sent an e-mail to Agresto and his fellow senior advisers asking for their thoughts on the decision to hand over sovereignty by the following June. Agresto typed up a short note, but before hitting Reply, he added one more address on the carbon-copy line: "All Hands"—everyone in the Republican Palace.

> If you're asking how the departure of the CPA will affect all that we have tried to do in our Ministry, the short and sad answer is that there is much that we had hoped to do that we now know we cannot. Serious curricular reform? Beginning an American University? Reorganizing 20 universities into some kind of rational system? Starting Western-style business schools? We can do all the groundwork on these we'd like, but once we're gone the inertia of the system will take over and all will wither. We will concentrate our efforts on those things that have hope of surviving our departure—infrastructure rebuilding, partnerships with some American universities, some scholarship programs, and the like.
>
> If you're asking our view on the transfer of sovereignty, my answer is even more pessimistic. Thirty years of tyranny do terrible things to a people: It breeds a culture of dependency; it breaks the spirit of civic

responsibility; it forces people to fall back upon tight-knit familial, ideological or sectarian groups for safety and support. The professors I work with are still incapable of believing they can do something on their own, freely, and not ask permission. Freedom, democracy and rights are not magic words. The transfer of sovereignty will bring about some form of "democracy." But a liberal democracy, with real notions of liberty and equality and open opportunity—without strongmen, or sectarian or sectional oppression—well, I think that's doubtful.

Agresto's bitterness was bred of experience. Two weeks before he had arrived, the Governing Council appointed twenty-five ministers. Each of the members staked claim to a different ministry—and the right to appoint the minister. Governing Council member Mohsen Abdul Hamid, the leader of the Iraqi Islamic Party, a Sunni organization with ties to the radical Muslim Brotherhood, demanded the Ministry of Higher Education. Hamid appointed Ziead Abdul-Razzaq Aswad, a professor of petroleum engineering and an ardent supporter of Hamid's party, as minister. Aswad's first act was to fire all of the university presidents. He wanted to replace them with his allies, many of whom were Sunnis. Agresto didn't want to meddle in the day-to-day operations of the ministry, but Aswad had gone too far, and Agresto commanded him to rescind the order.

Agresto had never worked in an emerging democracy before, but his bookshelves in New Mexico were filled with volumes by Hobbes, Locke, Mill, Rousseau, and Tocqueville. He had read the Federalist Papers and countless histories of America. Forming a democracy was easy, but forming a liberal, moderate democracy wasn't. He believed that the CPA had committed a catastrophic error by establishing a quota for Sunnis, Shiites, and Kurds on the Governing Council, and then by filling many of those seats with politicians and religious leaders who were more interested in doling out favors to their supporters than in doing what was best for their country.

Agresto believed that Iraqis hadn't focused on ethnic and religious divisions before the war, and that it was the CPA's quota system that had encouraged them to identify themselves by race and sect. He and the few others in the palace who shared this opinion were half right. Iraqis hadn't flaunted their differences under Saddam's Sunni-dominated government. Shiites and Kurds were fearful they would get classified as troublemakers and shipped off to Abu Ghraib. And Sunnis, in order to mask the fact that a minority was ruling the majority, perpetuated the myth that "we're all Iraqis." Liberation finally allowed the Kurds and, to a greater degree, the Shiites to worship openly. They could cover their car windows with paintings of the Imam Ali and make pilgrimages to the holy cities of Najaf and Karbala. Shiite political leaders also demanded a majority of seats on the Governing Council. Even so, many of the Iraqis I met wanted leaders who would overcome divisions of race and sect, not those who pandered to differences.

Bremer and his governance team gave the Shiites the majority they sought, and allowed religious Shiite political leaders, particularly Abdul Aziz al-Hakim of the Supreme Council for Islamic Revolution in Iraq, effective veto power over the selection of other Shiite members. As a result, several more liberal and secular Shiites favored by the CPA were kept off the council, strengthening the position of SCIRI and Dawa. Leaders of the governance team argued that SCIRI and Dawa would have refused to participate in the council had more moderates been selected. Perhaps, but Agresto and others in the palace maintained that Bremer and the governance team hadn't pushed hard enough to get secular, nonpartisan professionals on the council.

Bremer's approach "magnified rather than muted the very divisions that so many Iraqis rejected," Agresto said. "The best Iraqis knew that they could not form one country, one *democratic* country, unless they were somehow able to get these categories behind them and look for leaders who, one way or another, would transcend these divisions. The best Iraqis . . . knew this. We didn't."

On January 18, 2004, a white pickup truck loaded with a thousand pounds of plastic explosive and several 155-millimeter artillery shells exploded at the Assassin's Gate. More than twenty people were killed and at least sixty were wounded, almost all of them Iraqis. Many of them worked for the CPA.

Agresto, who heard the blast from inside the palace, assumed that the attack would rally popular sentiment against the insurgency and in favor of the goals of the occupation. "What I expected was the 'Mothers' March for Peace' or the 'Don't Kill Our Kids Movement' or somebody to come out and say: Stop this. We want democracy," he said. But Iraqis held funerals and went on with life. U.S. troops erected larger concrete blast walls in front of the gate. When Agresto asked Iraqis working for the CPA why there was not more outrage, everyone he talked to was too scared to condemn the insurgents in public. "I saw people still afraid," he said. "I saw how easy it was to speak against the Americans and how dangerous it was to speak for democracy and liberty."

During anguished rumination in the days after the bombing, he concluded that America had been shooting for the moon. It was a profound break with his ideological allies, with Cheney, Rumsfeld, and Wolfowitz. "We should have been less ambitious," Agresto said. "Our goal should have been to build a free, safe, and prosperous Iraq—with the emphasis on *safe*. Democratic institutions could be developed over time. Instead, we keep talking about democratic elections. If you asked an ordinary Iraqi what they want, the first thing they would say wouldn't be democracy or elections, it would be safety. They want to be able to walk outside their homes at night."

Agresto tried to discuss these ideas with members of the governance team, but they pushed him away. He was the guy who worked on universities. He offered to help advise the Iraqis drafting the interim constitution. Perhaps, he said, they'd want to talk to someone who knew a bit about the history of democratic thought. Once again, he was dismissed. With nobody willing to listen, he wrote a note to a friend in the palace who worked for the CIA and had studied at St. John's College:

> The problem with democracy-building is that I think
> we think democracy is easy—get rid of the bad guys, call
> for elections, encourage "power-sharing," and see to it

somebody writes a bill of rights. The truth is exactly the opposite—government by the few, or government by one person is what's easy to build; even putting together good autocratic rule doesn't seem to be that hard. It's good, stable and free democracies that are really the hardest thing.

America's been so successful at being a free and permanent democracy that we think democracy is the natural way to rule—just let people go and there you have it: Democracy. But all the ingredients that make it good and free—limited government, separation of powers, checks and balances, calendared elections, staggered elections, plurality selection, differing terms of office, federalism but with national supremacy, the development of a civic spirit and civic responsibility, and, above all, the breaking and moderation of factions—all this we forget about. We act as if the aim is "democracy" simply and not a mild and moderate democracy. Therefore . . . we seek out the loudest and most virulent factions and empower them. . . .

We, as a country, don't have a clue as to what has made our own country work, and so we spread the gospel of democracy-at-all-costs abroad. Until this country can find a Madison, it would be far better off with just a good ruler.

Before the handover, Bremer said a long goodbye. He flew in one of the army's Black Hawk helicopters, skimming atop the palm trees to avoid shoulder-fired missiles, to visit cities in the Shiite south and the Kurdish north. He threw dinner parties in his villa for Iraqi politicians, and he stopped CPA staffers in the palace halls to thank them for their work.

In his farewell meetings, he insisted that the CPA had set Iraq on the path to a democratic government, a free-market economy, and a modern infrastructure. He ticked off the CPA's accomplishments: nearly 2,500 schools had been repaired; 3 million children had been immunized; billions of dollars had been spent on reconstruction; 8 million new textbooks had been printed. New banknotes had replaced currency with Saddam's visage. Local councils had been formed in every city and province. The most expansive bill of rights in the Arab world had been written into the interim constitution.

But where the CPA saw progress, Iraqis saw broken promises. As Bremer prepared to depart, electricity generation remained stuck at around 4,000 megawatts—resulting in less than nine hours of power a day to most Baghdad homes— instead of the 6,000 megawatts he had pledged to provide. The new army had fewer than 4,000 trained soldiers, a third of what he had promised. Only 15,000 Iraqis had been hired to work on reconstruction projects funded with the Supplemental, rather than the 250,000 that had been touted. Seventy percent of police officers on the street had not received any CPA-funded training. Attacks on American forces and foreign civilians averaged more than forty a day, a threefold increase since January. Assassinations of political leaders and sabotage of the country's oil and electricity infrastructure occurred almost daily. In a CPA-sponsored poll of Iraqis taken a few weeks before the handover of sovereignty, 85 percent of respondents said they lacked confidence in Bremer's occupation administration.

Because of bureaucratic delays, only 2 percent of the $18.4 billion Supplemental had been spent. Nothing had been expended on construction, health care, sanitation, or the provision of clean water, and more money had been devoted to administration than all projects related to education, human rights, democracy, and governance combined. At the same time, the CPA had managed to dole out almost all of a $20 billion development fund fed by Iraq's oil sales, more than $1.6 billion of which had been used to pay Halliburton, primarily for trucking fuel into Iraq.

In early June, I ventured to the Daura Power Plant in southern Baghdad. It was supposed to be a model of the American effort to rebuild Iraq. Bombed in the 1991 Persian Gulf War and neglected by Saddam's government, the station could operate at no more than a quarter of its rated capacity, which had led to prolonged blackouts in the capital. After CPA specialists had toured the decrepit facility in 2003, they'd vowed to bring it back to life. It was placed atop a list of priority projects, and German and Russian firms were hired to make repairs. But the paroxysm of violence that gripped the country in the spring halted reconstruction work at Daura and almost every-where else.

The German contractors fled in April. The Russians departed in late May, after two of their colleagues were shot to death as they approached the plant in a minivan. As I walked through the power station, I saw parts strewn on the floor, awaiting installation. Iraqi technicians in blue coveralls loitered and smoked cigarettes. In the turbine room, graffiti on the wall read LONG LIVE THE RESISTANCE.

Work proceeded at a far more active pace at recruiting facil-ities for Iraq's army and police force. The CPA and the U.S. mil-itary had finally settled upon what it deemed to be a successful training strategy once Bernie Kerik and Walt Slocombe were out of the picture. The CPA's missteps, a senior American gen-eral told me, "cost us one very valuable year."

Within the Green Zone, there was an aching sense of a mission unaccomplished. "Did we really do what we needed to do? What we promised to do?" a senior CPA official asked over drinks at the al-Rasheed bar. "Nobody here believes that."

In an interview before his departure, Bremer insisted to me that Iraq was "fundamentally changed for the better" by the occupation. The CPA, he said, had put Iraq on a path toward a democratic government and an open economy after more than three decades of a brutal socialist dictatorship. Among his biggest accomplishments, he said, were the lowering of Iraq's tax rate, the liberalization of foreign-investment laws, and the reduction of import duties.

As our conversation was drawing to a close, I asked a broad question about unfinished business. "When I step back," he answered, "there's a lot left to be done."

After returning to America, Bremer ruefully complained that the Pentagon had failed to send enough troops to Iraq. His implicit argument was that had there been enough soldiers on the ground, he could have accomplished his grand plans. But Bremer's original political plan hadn't been doomed by attacks; it had been done in by a half-page fatwa written by an old man in Najaf.

The day after my interview with Bremer, I met Adel Abdel-Mahdi for breakfast in the front courtyard of his modest house. As we nibbled from a plate of dates and pastries, I asked him what the CPA's biggest mistake had been. He didn't hesitate. "The biggest mistake of the occupation," he said, "was the occupation itself."

He, of course, had wanted the United States to anoint exiled politicians as Iraq's new rulers in April 2003. But his self-interest aside, what he said was true. Freed from the grip of their dictator, the Iraqis believed that they should have been free to chart their own destiny, to select their own interim government, and to manage the reconstruction of their shattered nation. Their country wasn't Germany or Japan, a thoroughly defeated World War II aggressor to be ruled by the victorious. Iraqis needed help—good advice and ample resources—from a support corps of well-meaning foreigners, not a full-scale occupation with imperial Americans cloistered in a palace of the tyrant, eating bacon and drinking beer, surrounded by Gurkhas and blast walls.

The compromise between their desire for self-rule and the absence of a leader with broad appeal could have taken many forms, as the State Department's Arabists pointed out over the months after the invasion: a temporary governor appointed by the United Nations, an interim ruling council, or even a big-tent meeting—similar to the *loya jirga* convened after the defeat of the Taliban in Afghanistan—to select a crop of national leaders. There certainly was a role for a tireless, charismatic American diplomat to shepherd the process. It could easily have been Bremer, with a different title and a shorter mandate, with a viable political plan and meaningful resources for reconstruction.

Would that have made a difference? We'll never know for sure, but doing a better job of governance and reconstruction almost certainly would have kept many Iraqis from taking up arms against their new leaders and the Americans. There still would have been an insurgency, led by zealots who saw no room for compromise, but perhaps it would have been smaller and more containable.

"If this place succeeds," a CPA friend told me before he left, "it will be in spite of what we did, not because of it."

.   .   .

At 10:00 a.m. on June 28, Bremer's motorcade traveled across the Green Zone to Prime Minister Ayad Allawi's office. The viceroy walked into a nondescript room where Allawi, President Ghazi al-Yawar, Deputy Prime Minister Barham Salih, and Chief Justice Mahdi Mahmoud were waiting. They greeted each other and sat on chairs upholstered in gold fabric.

Bremer began by noting that Allawi's government had taken control of all of Iraq's ministries. The participants stood, and the viceroy opened a blue portfolio. He read from the document inside.

"The task of the Coalition Provisional Authority will end on the twenty-eighth of June, and at this time, the occupation will end and the interim Iraqi government will assume complete sovereignty on behalf of the Iraqi people," he said. "We welcome the steps of Iraq toward assuming its legitimate role among all free countries of the world."

When Bremer had finished, he turned to Allawi and al-Yawar. "You are ready now for sovereignty," he declared.

He handed the portfolio to the chief justice. With that simple act, America ended the occupation.

Allawi uttered a few sentences, as did al-Yawar, who called it "a historic, happy day, a day that all Iraqis have been looking forward to . . . a day we take our country back." There was no pomp or circumstance, no marching band or fireworks, no honor guard or grand speeches, no spectators or live television coverage. The Iraqi people didn't know the handover had occurred until afterward. Everyone had expected it to happen on June 30, but Bremer had moved it up, at President Bush's suggestion, to avoid the risk of an insurgent attack. The ceremony lasted no more than five minutes.

After a round of brief but tearful farewells in the palace, Bremer climbed into a dual-rotor Chinook helicopter idling on the Green Zone's landing strip. Removing his sunglasses, he strapped a camouflage flak vest over his white French cuff shirt. As the chopper rose into a cloudless sky, he remained seated instead of peering out of the portholes for one last glimpse of his domain. But he had seen the Green Zone from the air many times before. From above, the majesty of the palace wasn't apparent. It was only a blue-domed roof sprouting a dozen satellite dishes, surrounded by the PX, the parking lot sowed with Suburbans, hundreds of corrugated-metal housing trailers, and finally, the seventeen-foot-high blast walls that separated the Emerald City from the rest of Iraq. From the air, the Green Zone was shaped like a giant jigsaw puzzle piece cast down in the middle of a dusty, sprawling city.

Epilogue

A YEAR AFTER JERRY BREMER left Iraq, CPA staffers gathered for a reunion in Washington. The party, held at a furniture showroom on the top floor of a downtown office building, featured three kegs of beer, mini artichoke quiches, and a cheese platter. A slide projector displayed a series of high-school-yearbook-like shots of CPA personnel in Iraq—clowning around the palace, posing in front of a Black Hawk chopper, eating in the dining hall, lounging by the pool.

WELCOME TO THE GREEN ZONE, a spray-painted plywood sign proclaimed at the room's entrance. WHO'S YOUR BAGHDADDY? asked another wooden placard, propped up next to the bar. Near a table with hors d'oeuvres was a plastic children's tub filled with bubble wrap, intended to evoke the palace pool. Flak jackets and Kevlar helmets were strewn about on the floor.

More than a hundred people showed up, many coming straight from the jobs they had landed at the Pentagon, the White House, the Heritage Foundation, and elsewhere in the Republican establishment, upon their return from Baghdad. Several men in suits had changed into tan combat boots—the official footwear of the Green Zone—before walking in the door. Others adorned their lapels with pins depicting an American flag crossed with an Iraqi one.

There were handshakes, hugs, and even Iraqi-style kissing on the cheeks—left, right, left. It was the first time most Green Zone alumni had run into one another since the occupation, and they soon slipped back into their old roles, talking up their former bosses, praising one another for a job well done, lauding the Bush administration's foreign policy. They reminisced about their work in Iraq and dismissed media coverage of the war as defeatist. Success was just around the corner.

"Things are not as bad as people think," one man told me. "Oh," I said, "how recently were you there?" He had left a year earlier, he said, as had almost everyone in the room.

Conversations at the party began with an unspoken premise: the CPA was responsible for Iraq's progress, and Iraqi politicians were responsible for the problems. We've set them on the right path, one woman told me. It's up to them to follow it.

Another woman, who worked in Paul Wolfowitz's office at the Pentagon, proclaimed to me that she and her colleagues had become impervious to criticism of the administration's handling of the war. In her office, she said, the phrase "drinking the Kool-Aid" was regarded as a badge of loyalty.

John Agresto wasn't there. It was his old crowd—the neoconservatives, the true believers—but their self-congratulation now made him queasy. He was at home in New Mexico, reading, writing, and making homemade sausage. A month later, he would send me an e-mail telling me he had just returned from a brief trip to Iraq with a few American experts in history and law. They had gone to meet with members of Iraq's constitution-writing committee. "I'm even more pessimistic than before," he wrote. "Or, at least, no less."

Bremer and his wife entered. Everyone wanted to shake his hand, to say hello. He waded through the crowd in his old combat boots. There was a relaxed ease in his bearing that I had rarely seen in Iraq. A few times, he threw his head back and laughed. He had recently finished writing *My Year in Iraq*, a book about his experience as viceroy. Now his only obligations were a series of speaking engagements, and his only worry was the progress of kitchen renovations at his country house in Vermont, which included the installation of a custom-made, $28,000 La Cornue stove.

At nine o'clock, the crowd moved into a glass-walled room with a flat-screen television. President Bush would be addressing the nation from Fort Bragg, North Carolina. The Bremers sat on a sofa. The rest of the group gathered around them.

It was June 28, 2005. The toll of American military personnel killed had reached 1,745. The number of Iraqi dead was estimated in the tens of thousands. Large swaths of the country to the north and west of Baghdad remained under the control of insurgents. Almost every day, death squads assassinated Iraqis working for the transitional government.

Thousands more Iraqi soldiers and policemen had been trained by the Americans, but they still were unready to defend against the insurgents on their own. Only one battalion of the new Iraqi army was deemed by U.S. generals to be prepared enough to fight without American assistance.

In Baghdad and elsewhere, suicide car bombings—of police stations, army recruitment centers, mosques, funerals—had become so frequent that many Iraqis stopped leaving their homes unless they absolutely had to. Wives worried that their husbands wouldn't return from work. Parents worried that their children wouldn't return from school. The fear was worse, several residents told me, than during the three-week war to topple Saddam or the monthlong American blitz in 1991 or even the eight-year conflict with Iran.

Unemployment continued to hover around 40 percent. The private investors who Peter McPherson hoped would avail themselves of the new flat tax and the reduced tariffs stayed away. Oil production was below prewar levels, and hours-long blackouts still pocked the power grid.

Efforts to reconstruct Iraq's infrastructure had resumed after the violence in the spring of 2004, but new security precautions slowed every project. Only a third of the $18.4 billion Supplemental had been spent, and as much as forty cents of every dollar was being used to pay for guards, armored vehicles, and blast walls. The CPA's plan to build grand water, sewage, and power plants—which staffers such as Steve Browning had cautioned against—had become a money pit. The Iraqis didn't have the skills or the resources to maintain such structures.

Defense Department auditors had begun to question the CPA's spending spree with Iraqi oil funds in the waning days of the occupation, noting that as much as $8.8 billion could not be properly accounted for, including $2.4 billion in one-hundred-dollar bills that was flown to Baghdad from the Federal Reserve Bank of New York six days before the handover of sovereignty.

The Green Zone had been renamed the International Zone,

but it was only a semantic change: the Americans continued to run the enclave, and they remained in the Republican Palace, although they did allow Iraqi government leaders to set up homes and offices in unoccupied villas. With the CPA dissolved, the palace was no longer the domain of the Pentagon; it had become the State Department's largest embassy, which instituted its own rules. A new business-casual dress code forbade safari vests, holsters, and cargo pants. Stricter security regulations prevented staffers from traveling outside the palace grounds, even to other parts of the International Zone, without a security escort. The PX, the Chinese restaurants, and the al-Rasheed were all out of bounds—with good reason.

The Emerald City had been breached. On October 14, 2004, a suicide bomber had detonated himself inside the Green Zone Café; another blew himself up at the Green Zone Bazaar. The restaurant and the shops were demolished in the blasts, and five people, including three American civilians, were killed. In an instant, the International Zone became almost as dangerous as the city outside.

Some embassy staffers spent months on end in the palace bubble, working, eating, and exercising there, and then walking a few hundred feet to sleep in trailers in the rear garden. The PX was moved inside the walls of the palace. For those who grew tired of the dining hall, there was a new option: a Burger King in the palace compound.

Although most of the CPA's Republican Party loyalists had been replaced with nonpartisan diplomats, many of whom spoke Arabic and wanted to interact with Iraqis, they were trapped in a fortress. Some Iraqis came to the palace and the Convention Center for meetings, and some of the Americans traveled out in armored convoys, but the opportunities for communication remained limited, and neither side fully understood the other.

Millions of Iraqis had headed to the polls in January 2005 for the country's first democratic elections in decades. In Baghdad, in the Kurdish north, and in the Shiite south, the day was a stunning triumph. Men and women waved ink-stained fingers to show that they had voted. There was far less violence than expected, largely because American and Iraqi troops put most cities under a three-day curfew, preventing vehicular traffic and searching pedestrians at random checkpoints. One Iraqi remarked to me that American soldiers should have done the same thing when they arrived in April 2003.

But in the Sunni-dominated areas to the north and west of the capital, the election was a failure. Local politicians had boycotted the balloting, and insurgents warned residents to stay away from the polls. In Ramadi, only six people voted at one polling station. In Dhuluyah, a town north of Baghdad along the Tigris, the eight polling stations never opened.

The results mirrored turnout. A coalition of Shiite parties endorsed by Grand Ayatollah al-Sistani won 48 percent of the vote. The two major Kurdish parties picked up a combined 26 percent, and a bloc led by interim prime minister Ayad Allawi, a secular Shiite, got almost 14 percent. The few Sunnis who ran fared miserably: a party headed by interim president Ghazi al-Yawar won less than 2 percent, and a coalition formed by former foreign minister Adnan Pachachi didn't get enough votes to pick up a single seat in the 275-member National Assembly. All told, Sunni Arabs, who comprised about 20 percent of Iraq's population, wound up with fewer than 8 percent of the seats in the legislature. Bremer's single-district electoral law had shut the Sunnis out of the new government, depriving the Americans, and the Iraqis, of a valuable opportunity to win over Sunnis and weaken the insurgency.

All the key ministries were claimed by the Kurds and the Shiites, whose militiamen swept up legions of young Sunni men—sometimes torturing and killing them—with the acquiescence of the new government. Sunni insurgents began attacking Shiite and Kurdish civilians with the same ferocity they directed at the Americans. Shiites living in Sunni areas north of Baghdad began to flee south. Sunnis in Shiite communities to the south of the capital left their homes and moved north. A civil war had begun.

The problem would become even more serious a few months later, when it was time to write a permanent constitution. The lack of Sunni participation would result in a charter that most Sunnis opposed. Although they would not be able to muster enough votes to reject the document in a national referendum, it would be yet another opportunity lost to reach out to Sunnis and fracture the insurgency.

The audience at the CPA reunion quieted as Bush's image filled the screen in front of them. America, he said, had made "significant progress in Iraq."

"Our mission in Iraq is clear," he said. "We're hunting down the terrorists. We're helping Iraqis build a free nation that is an ally in the war on terror. We're advancing freedom in the broader Middle East. We are removing a source of violence and instability, and laying the foundation of peace for our children and our grandchildren."

He conceded no errors.

After Bush had finished, Bremer addressed the crowd.

"We will complete the mission, as the president said tonight. When I go around the country, I usually make the point that this is going to be a tough, long struggle. It's going to take a lot of patience. But I also point out that we Americans are not quitters. We didn't quit in the eighteenth century until we turned out the British. We didn't quit in the nineteenth century until we had abolished slavery. We didn't quit in the twentieth century until we chased totalitarianism off the face of Europe, and we're not going to quit in the twenty-first century in the face of these terrorists."

Everyone applauded. Bremer smiled.

"*Mabruk al-Iraq al-Jedeed*," he said before making his way to the door. Congratulations to the new Iraq.

ACKNOWLEDGMENTS

This book would not have been possible without the willingness of so many people who worked for the CPA and ORHA to speak with me, often repeatedly and at length, about life in the Green Zone and the inner workings of the occupation administration. I am deeply grateful for their time and trust. Unfortunately, many of them, including several who served in high-ranking CPA posts, did not want to be identified by name because of fears of retribution from the Bush administration. I am thankful as well for information provided by senior officials at the White House, the State Department, and the Pentagon, most of whom also did not want to be named but did want me to develop a fuller, and more critical, understanding of the CPA.

I also could not have written this book without the generous support and encouragement of the editors and executives of *The Washington Post*. Their commitment to covering events in Iraq has been, I believe, without parallel in American journalism. In June 2003, on my first visit back to Washington after the liberation of Baghdad, Don Graham, the *Post*'s chairman, pulled me aside and told me that the paper would do whatever was necessary to ensure my safety and that of my colleagues. And it did.

Executive Editor Len Downie and his managing editor while I was in Iraq, Steve Coll, are two of the very best in the news business. With the support of the *Post*'s publisher, Bo Jones, they created a climate within the newspaper that encouraged my colleagues to produce excellent journalism about America's involvement in Iraq. Phil Bennett, who was the paper's assistant managing editor for foreign news and is now managing editor, deserves special gratitude. He is a brilliant editor, a mentor, and a friend. When others were focused on the bang-bang of military operations, he encouraged me to keep my sights on Bremer and the CPA.

Reporting from—and living in—Iraq is impossible without the help of Iraqis. The *Post* has been fortunate to have an amazing team of Iraqis working as interpreters, drivers, and guards. They put their lives on the line every day to help me understand what was really happening in their country. For that, and so much else, I am eternally grateful to Dhia Ahmed, Khalid Alsaffar, Omar Assad, Naseer Fadhil, Sabah Fadhil, Omar Fekeiki, Falah Hassan, Moyad Jabbar, Muna Jawad, Mohammed Mahdi,

Rifaat Mohammed, Mohammed Munim, Jawad Munshid, Fawziya Naji, Saif Naseer, Ghazwan Noel, Naseer Nouri, Muhanned Salem, Saad Sarhan, Bassam Sebti, and Ahmed Younis.

I was privileged to work with some of the *Post*'s very best correspondents and photographers in Baghdad, among them Andrea Bruce, Michel du Cille, Pam Constable, Steve Fainaru, Peter Finn, Bart Gellman, Theola Labbé, Molly Moore, Bill O'Leary, Lucian Perkins, Lois Raimondo, Michael Robinson-Chavez, Anthony Shadid, Jackie Spinner, Doug Struck, Kevin Sullivan, Karl Vick, Daniel Williams, and Scott Wilson. There is nobody better at covering the Arab world than Anthony Shadid, who became a wise guide and good friend.

I was also blessed to have many friends, some old, some new, among the pack of journalists in Baghdad. They included Hannah Allam, Jane Arraf, Christina Asquith, Anne Barnard, Rym Brahimi, Thanassis Cambanis, Jill Carroll, Jack Fairweather, Lourdes Garcia-Navarro, Bill Glauber, Dan Harris, Caroline Hawley, James Hider, Larry Kaplow, Birgit Kaspar, Laura King, Jacki Lyden, Evan Osnos, Catherine Philp, Alissa Rubin, Somini Sengupta, Christine Spolar, and Nick Watt.

The conflict in Iraq has claimed the lives of too many good people, among them three friends: United Nations diplomat Sergio Vieira de Mello, *Boston Globe* correspondent Elizabeth Neuffer, and aid worker Marla Ruzicka. I miss them dearly.

In Washington, I was grateful for the wisdom and assistance of several *Post* colleagues, particularly Karen DeYoung, Bradley Graham, Glenn Kessler, Dana Priest, Tom Ricks, Peter Slevin, Josh White, and Robin Wright. Foreign Editor David Hoffman helped me conceptualize stories and then deftly edited them. Others on the Foreign Desk were invaluable, including Nora Boustany, John Burgess, Ed Cody, Peter Eisner, Ginny Hamill, Tiffany Harness, Lou Ann McNeill, Emily Messner, Andy Mosher, Tony Reid, Keith Sinzinger, Dita Smith, and Robert Thomason. Many others at the *Post* have provided good counsel and friendship over the years, among them Glenn Frankel, Tracy Grant, Fred Hiatt, David Ignatius, and Keith Richburg.

Two institutions in Washington granted me fellowships that provided me a place to write the book and, more important, share ideas with smart people. The first was the International Reporting Project at the Johns Hopkins School for Advanced International Studies. Director John Schidlovsky and his staff—Jeff Barrus, Louise Lief, and Denise Melvin— gave me a welcome home upon my return from Baghdad. I also benefited greatly from my interactions with eight smart young journalists who were IRP fellows: Ryan Anson, Aryn Baker, Adam Graham-Silverman, Raffi Khatchadourian, Cathryn Poff, Fernanda Santos, Kelly Whalen, and Mary Wiltenburg.

The second was the Woodrow Wilson International Center for Scholars, where I am grateful to Director Lee Hamilton as well as to Haleh Esfandiari, Steve Lagerfeld, Michael Van Dusen, and Sam Wells. My research assistant there, Tiffany Clarke, provided invaluable help in poring through reams of government documents.

The Wilson Center is where I met Sarah Courteau, a whip-smart editor at the *Wilson Quarterly*. Sarah spent countless hours reading and editing, and rereading and reediting, my manuscript. Without her sagacious suggestions, this book would be far less readable. I am eternally grateful for her help, and for her friendship.

This book would never have been printed had David Ignatius not introduced me to my agent, the indomitable Rafe Sagalyn, who patiently guided me through my first foray into book writing. Rafe's team, including Eben Gilfenbaum, Amy Rosenthal, and Bridget Wagner, provided valuable assistance along the way.

At Knopf, Jonathan Segal and Sonny Mehta helped to shape my sprawling reporting into a defined narrative about the Green Zone. It was a privilege to work with Jon, whose extraordinary intelligence and enthusiasm for a good story is matched only by his skill with an editor's pencil.

My friends provided support, encouragement, and endless good meals to help keep me sane during my months of writing. I am especially indebted to Mike Allen, Peter Baker, Katia Dunn, Susan Glasser, Mike Grunwald, Spencer Hsu, Dafna Linzer, Leef Smith, and Anne Marie Squeo. Nurith Aizenman and Theresa Everline not only helped read sections of the manuscript, but they spent hours on end helping me shape my outline. Elizabeth Terry, another dear friend, provided great advice throughout.

If not for her willingness to help dig out a photo of Michael Battles from *Fortune* magazine's archive, I never would have met the wonderful Julie Schlosser. Getting to know her was even more fun than finishing the book.

Above all else, I am thankful to have such a wonderful family. To my brother, Ravi, his wife, Jennie, and my parents, Uma and Kumar: much love and gratitude.

NOTES

This book is the result of nearly two years of reporting in Iraq for *The Washington Post,* beginning with my first trip to the country in September 2002. I lived in Baghdad almost continuously from November 2002 until the start of the American-led invasion in March 2003. I returned on April 10, 2003, the day after the statue of Saddam was felled in front of the Palestine Hotel, and I resided in Iraq full-time until September 30, 2004. Although I had a few brief holidays, by my count I spent more days in Iraq during the fifteen-month occupation than almost any other American print reporter.

I continued reporting for this book upon my return to the United States, holding additional conversations with people I had first met in Iraq and conducting interviews with dozens of others whom I had been unable to speak with while they were resident in the Green Zone. I have also pored through thousands of pages of internal CPA e-mail messages and documents in an effort to develop a fuller understanding of the occupation.

Although some of the material in my narrative has appeared in different form in the *Post,* much of my account is based on more than one hundred original interviews conducted exclusively for this book. Because of concerns about retribution, several of my sources requested not to be identified by name; in those cases, I have tried to be as specific as possible about their role in the CPA or the U.S. government without compromising their identity.

I have benefited greatly from the reporting of my *Post* colleagues, in particular Thomas E. Ricks, Anthony Shadid, and Robin Wright, as well as from the outstanding research and interpretation services provided by Khalid Alsaffar, Omar Fekeiki, Naseer Nouri, and Bassam Sebti in the *Post*'s Baghdad bureau.

Unless cited below, all statements quoted in the book are from interviews with me or public sources. Where conversation is recounted, it is on the basis of the memory of at least one person who could hear what was said. Although memories do slip, and recollections differ even among eyewitnesses, I have attempted to describe past events as accurately as possible.

2 A Deer in the Headlights

28 *President George W. Bush:* Bob Woodward, *Plan of Attack* (New York: Simon & Schuster, 2004), p. 2.

29 *Feith's office conducted its postwar planning:* In addition to my own reporting, I gleaned insights from James Fallows's article "Blind into Baghdad," *The Atlantic,* January 2004.

33 *As soon as Garner left:* Dan Morgan, "Deciding Who Builds Iraq Is Fraught with Infighting," *The Washington Post,* May 4, 2003.

3 You're in Charge!

54 *Among them was L. Paul Bremer III:* In his book *My Year in Iraq* (New York: Simon & Schuster, 2006), Bremer writes that he was contacted about serving in Iraq by I. Lewis "Scooter" Libby, Dick Cheney's chief of staff, and by Paul Wolfowitz.

4 Control Freak

61 *Bremer would later write:* Bremer, *My Year in Iraq,* p. 10.

63 *Shortly after Bremer arrived:* This meeting was described to me by two people with direct knowledge of the conversation.

65 *In a 2002 article:* L. Paul Bremer III, "Corporate Governance and Crisis Management," *Directors & Boards,* January 1, 2002.

66 *He was fifty then:* Bill Powell, "The CEO of Iraq," *Fortune,* August 11, 2003.

66 *When a visitor noted:* Patrick E. Tyler, "Overseer Adjusts Strategy as Turmoil Grows in Iraq," *The New York Times,* July 13, 2003.

67 *Even in his early years:* James T. Yenkel, "Couples: The Price of Success," *The Washington Post,* May 11, 1982.

68 *In 1994, the couple converted:* Mark Zimmerman, "Iraq Envoy Says Faith Gives Him Strength," *Catholic Standard,* June 19, 2003.

70 *He wrote a memo to Pentagon officials:* Michael R. Gordon, "Debate Lingering on Decision to Dissolve the Iraqi Military," *The New York Times,* October 21, 2004.

73 *When CPA officials complained:* In an op-ed piece in *The New York Times* on January 13, 2006, titled "In Iraq, Wrongs Make a Right," Bremer acknowledged that it was a mistake to leave implementation to Iraqi politicians. "De-Baathification should have been administered by an independent judicial body," he wrote.

5 Who Are These People?

85 *Years earlier, when he was appointed:* Christopher Drew, "A Street Cop's Rise from High School Dropout to Cabinet Nominee," *The New York Times,* December 3, 2004.

86 *Kerik's first order of business:* Hamza Hendawi, "Adviser: Iraq Police Reform to Be Tough," Associated Press, May 26, 2003; and NBC *Today* show transcript, May 27, 2003; and Romesh Ratnesar, "Can a New York Cop Tame Baghdad?," *Time,* June 9, 2003, p. 41.

88 *Steele, who served as Bremer's counselor:* In addition to my own

reporting, I gleaned insights from Jon Lee Anderson, "The Uprising: Shia and Sunnis Put Aside Their Differences," *The New Yorker,*
May 3, 2004, p. 63.

91 *One former CPA employee:* The e-mail was first published in the
Web log of Daniel Drezner, a professor of political science at the
University of Chicago. It has been archived at http://www
.danieldrezner.com/archives/001326.html.

95 *Jay Hallen didn't much like his job:* Unless otherwise cited, all direct
quotes from Hallen are from a transcript of an interview of Hallen
conducted by Susan M. Klingaman of the Association for Diplomatic Studies and Training, on October 1, 2004, for the United
States Institute of Peace's Iraq Experience Project.

96 *It wasn't just Hallen who was:* Yochi J. Dreazen, "How a 24-Year-Old
Got a Job Rebuilding Iraq's Stock Market," *The Wall Street Journal,*
January 28, 2004, p. A1.

96 *At Yale University:* Ann Ritter, "Rediscover Your Inner Child at 'The
Lorax,' " *Yale Herald,* January 23, 1998.

98 *Five days after Hallen arrived:* Jay Hallen, "Greetings from Camp
Arkansas," *TCS Daily,* September 23, 2003. Available on the Web at
http://www.tcsdaily.com/article.aspx?id=092303E.

7 Bring a Duffel Bag

129 *Behind the podium:* Senor made the statement about Iraqis not
wanting Coalition forces to leave at a May 24, 2004, CPA press
briefing. A poll conducted for the CPA by the Independent Institute
for Administration and Civil Security Studies from April 14 to 23,
2004, in six large Iraqi cities, including Baghdad, Basra, and Mosul,
reported that 55 percent of respondents said they would feel "more
safe" if Coalition forces left immediately. Forty-one percent of
respondents said they wanted Coalition forces to "leave immediately," and 45 percent said they wanted Coalition forces to "leave
after a permanent government is elected." Only 7 percent of respondents said they had confidence in Coalition forces. A poll conducted for the CPA by the same organization from May 14 to 23,
2004, reported that 866 of 1,068 respondents wanted Coalition
forces to leave Iraq.

134 *Several days later:* Michael Furlong, SAIC's project manager in
Baghdad, and Ahmed al-Rikaby, a senior Iraqi journalist with the
IMN, said they were present at the meeting where Senor asked
North why IMN didn't broadcast the tape. Both men told me they
recalled North's comment to Senor. They also described Senor's
questioning of Bremer as an interview. Senor insisted to me that he
did not interview Bremer for IMN. Senor claimed that the incident
in question involved one of Bremer's addresses to the Iraqi people,
during which he prompted Bremer while the tape was rolling.

135 *IMN staff worried that running:* Kathleen McCaul, "Troubles at Iraqi
Media Network," *Baghdad Bulletin,* July 21, 2003.

136 *Michael Battles arrived in Baghdad:* Neil King, Jr., and Yochi J.

Dreazen, "Amid Chaos in Iraq, Tiny Security Firm Found Opportunity," *The Wall Street Journal,* August 13, 2004, p. A1.
139 *We got that contract:* Ibid.

8 A Yearning for Old Times

168 *Physical reconstruction was a means:* Most quotations and other material attributed to Agresto come from several interviews I conducted with him in Iraq and in the United States. A few quotes have been taken from an unpublished book manuscript he shared with me.

10 The Plan Unravels

193 *I don't think it would be responsible:* Bremer, *My Year in Iraq,* p. 205.
198 *Bremer landed at Andrews:* Ibid., p. 224.
203 *Frankly, I'm disappointed:* Ibid., p. 231.

11 A Fool's Errand

210 *Despite its selective admission of Iraqis:* "Iraqi Hospitals to Regain First-Class Status Quickly," Agence France Presse, February 27, 2004.

12 We Cannot Continue Like This

229 *A few weeks after he arrived in Baghdad:* As with the earlier section, all direct quotes from Hallen, unless otherwise cited, are from the Association for Diplomatic Studies and Training interview.

15 Crazy, If Not Suicidal

274 *But back in Washington, the desire for revenge:* In addition to my own reporting, I gleaned insights from Alissa J. Rubin and Doyle McManus, "Why America Has Waged a Losing Battle on Fallouja," *Los Angeles Times,* October 24, 2004, p. A1.

INDEX

Carney, Timothy *(continued)*
 Industry Ministry
  reorganization and, 47–51
 ORHA living conditions and,
  49–50
 postwar planning and, 31–2,
  35–6, 40, 45, 51
 vegetable oil company and, 102,
  105, 223
 Wolfowitz's relationship with,
  44–5
Carpenter, Scott, 194–7
 sovereignty and, 194, 197, 199,
  201–3, 205, 207
Central Bank, Iraqi, 41, 45
Central Command, U.S., 41, 74
Central Intelligence Agency (CIA),
  56, 63, 73, 84, 136–7, 192,
  245, 250–1, 276, 286
 de-Baathification and, 69–71
 infrastructure and, 149, 151
 postwar planning and, 29, 31,
  36
 scientists and, 251, 253
 sovereignty and, 164, 198
 and weapons of mass
  destruction, 44, 251, 253–4
Chalabi, Ahmed, 73–4, 194, 241,
  256
 de-Baathification and, 69–70, 73
 interim government and, 51–2,
  77–8
 postwar planning and, 29–30,
  32–3, 37
 sovereignty and, 189, 200–1,
  203
Chalabi, Salem, 241–2
Chen, Yihjyh, 267–9
Cheney, Dick, 5, 37, 69, 81, 115,
  195, 251, 278, 286
 interim government and, 52, 54
 sovereignty and, 198, 200, 247
Civil Defense Corps, Iraqi, 273
Coalition Provisional Authority
  (CPA), 12–19, 55, 56–60,
  62–73, 79–81, 84–6, 108,
  133–41, 146–7, 156–63,
  178–84, 258, 282–91, 293–6

 administration of, 12, 16–17
 Baghdad airport security and,
  137–40
 Bremer's long goodbye and,
  287–8
 Bremer's management style
  and, 63–8, 70–1
 Bremer's political advisers and,
  194, 196
 Bremer's school visits and,
  59–60
 BSE and, 94–6, 98, 230–2
 constitution and, 79–80, 241–4
 criticisms of, 233, 290
 de-Baathification and, 69–73
 economy and, 110, 117–20, 123,
  125, 156–7, 225–8, 230–2
 elections and, 199, 246–8
 employees of, 12, 16–17, 24–5,
  91–7, 114–15, 165–6, 169,
  174–5, 178, 180–2, 184
 entertainment for, 18, 56–7
 farewell barbecue of, 278–9
 Governing Council and, 163,
  196, 284–5
 Green Zone attacks and, 175,
  178, 180, 285–6
 infrastructure and, 149, 152–4,
  156–61, 288, 295
 insurgency and, 272–3, 275–6
 isolation of, 19, 21, 24–5
 living accomodations of, 13–15,
  57, 174, 180–1, 220–1
 media and, 17, 127–30, 134–6
 medical care and, 210, 213–14,
  216–19
 military and, 75–6, 289
 police and, 85–6, 88–90, 288–9
 reunion of, 293–4, 298
 Sadr and, 264–5, 272–3, 275–6
 scientists and, 253–5
 secrecy of, 24–5
 security of, 25, 181–3, 233, 275,
  277
 sovereignty and, 192, 194,
  197–9, 202, 204, 206–7,
  217–18, 226, 241–9, 276, 278,
  283, 288, 291

A NOTE ABOUT THE AUTHOR

Rajiv Chandrasekaran is an assistant managing editor of *The Washington Post*. He was the newspaper's bureau chief in Baghdad from April 2003 to September 2004, and he has reported from more than two dozen countries in Asia and the Middle East. He lives in Washington, D.C.